# The Otherworld in Myth, Folklore, Cinema, and Brain Science

# The Otherworld in Myth, Folklore, Cinema, and Brain Science

By

Jim Kline

Cambridge
Scholars
Publishing

The Otherworld in Myth, Folklore, Cinema, and Brain Science

By Jim Kline

This book first published 2019

Cambridge Scholars Publishing

Lady Stephenson Library, Newcastle upon Tyne, NE6 2PA, UK

British Library Cataloguing in Publication Data
A catalogue record for this book is available from the British Library



ISBN (10): 1-5275-3040-X
ISBN (13): 978-1-5275-3040-9

Dedicated to the students of Northern Marianas College for their inspiring stories about Otherworld experiences.

# TABLE OF CONTENTS

# List of Illustrations

# INTRODUCTION

# WHAT AND WHERE IS THE OTHERWORLD?

The Otherworld is a living reality that complements waking world reality. It is structured out of eternal ideas about life, time, and space, inhabited by eternal beings, and powered by an eternal, inexhaustible life force. It has its own language based upon metaphors, symbols, and motifs which, like any human language, can have different modes and forms of expression but still convey an underlying universal meaning.

The Otherworld usually manifests itself to individuals during times of extreme emotional states: trauma, panic, and near-death experiences. It can also manifest itself through the use of mind-altering, hallucinogenic drugs or other trance-inducing states of ecstasy. Aspects of the Otherworld most commonly appear in certain types of dreams usually associated with REM (rapid eye movement) sleep and triggered by crucial moments in a person's life filled with anticipation, anxiety, and fear. Because of its relationship with emotionally volatile states of being, the Otherworld is a world of extremes. To remain in the Otherworld indefinitely, one must be dead to the mortal realm.

Religious scholar Mircea Eliade underscored how the Otherworld was once thought of as primarily the land of the dead since those who have suffered a mortal death are thought to inhabit this realm: "…although originally the Other World is the world after death, it finally comes to mean any transcendent state, that is, any mode of being inaccessible to fleshy [i.e. mortal] man and reserved for 'spirits,' or for man as a spiritual entity."[1] Eliade emphasizes the importance of accessing the Otherworld through methods that transcend waking world reality since it is the realm of spirit that lies beyond the mortal realm; by shaking off ego consciousness, one can begin to access this nonrational, unconscious realm.

---

[1] Eliade (1958) 2005: 65.

The archetypal substratum of the human unconscious—what C.G. Jung called the collective unconscious or impersonal psyche--is a manifestation of the Otherworld, embodying and expressing characteristics of this realm. The characteristics referred to previously about the Otherworld—its eternal dimension, its inhabitants made up of spirit or post-mortal entities, its language made up of metaphors and symbols—all pertain to the archetypal dimension of the unconscious. This means that an aspect of the Otherworld exists within all of us. And yet, one must also understand that archetypal reality has a type of existence somewhere outside of us. Jung considered archetypes living energies with an autonomous relationship with ego consciousness. This seemingly contradictory location of the Otherworld—both an inner and outer reality--relates to Jung's ideas about how the physical and the psychic realms are two aspects of the same reality:

> Since psyche and matter are contained in one and the same world, and moreover are in continuous contact with one another…it is not only possible but fairly probable, even, that psyche and matter are two different aspects of one and the same thing….[The] nonpsychic [i.e. materialistic representations] can behave like the psychic, and vice versa, without there being any causal connection between them….In archetypal conceptions and instinctual perceptions, spirit and matter confront one another on the psychic plane.[2]

William G. Roll, professor of psychology and psychical research from the University of West Georgia who also served as president of the Oxford University Society for Psychical Research and project director of the Psychical Research Foundation at Duke University, echoed Jung's ideas about the relationship between psyche and matter, emphasizing the emotional factor: how strong emotions can leave an imprint upon a location. As he explained:

> Events that would give us strong memories in our minds—death, accidents, and so forth—are the same kind that are strong outside our bodies. All we need to say is that there is no sharp distinction between mind and matter, and that the processes that go on in the human brain may also go on in the human environment. To me, the main interest of these phenomena is that they suggest body and mind and mind and matter are not as clearly distinguished as we have been led to believe, that mind is enfolded in matter…that the physical environment has mental qualities that come from the people who have lived in that environment.[3]

[2] Jung (1946) 1969: 215-216.

[3] Adams, ed.: 36.

Roll also mentions that psychological imbalance within an individual or a family can evoke a response from the environment that attempts to illustrate or even fill the void necessary to restore psychic equilibrium: "It's like a dream that has become real, a strong need that has somehow created a situation that satisfies it."[4]

When our reliance upon physical reality for security and permanence is threatened during times of stress and the fear of death, the eternal elements of the Otherworld, linked with the archetypal reality of the human psyche, become more of a living reality. A potent example of how archetypal reality can permeate waking world reality during times when death becomes a real threat, and "a strong need" creates "a situation that satisfies it," is illustrated in the autobiographical narrative, "You Can Count on Miracles." Its young author Aphonetip Vasavong relates how, at the age of eight, he was attempting to flee with his family from their home country of Laos to Thailand in order to escape political persecution. The family left on foot in the middle of the night and struggled through jungle terrain as they made their way to a large river where a boat was waiting to take them to Thailand. Along the way, Vasavong became separated from his family and hopelessly lost. Terrified of being left behind, Vasavong wept to himself as he frantically looked around for any sign that would help him find his family. Suddenly, a glowing object appeared out of the darkness:

> I could see that it was a rabbit. It was beautiful and bright like a light. It came back toward me and stood in front of me. I reached out to pet it, but it ran toward the same path that it had come from a moment ago. I decided to follow the rabbit along the path. As I did, I was able to see my way through the woods because the rabbit and the path were bright....I continued to follow the rabbit along the path until it disappeared into the darkness. I looked around for the rabbit, and what I saw instead was my family getting into the canoes. I turned back once more to look for the rabbit, but it was gone.[5]

Vasavong concludes by emphasizing the importance of recognizing "unusual coincidences" fraught with meaning that "could not have happened by chance alone:"

> Unusual experiences such as mine occur to people everywhere, but most people do not take the time to think about their meaning. Some critics argue that these occurrences are merely coincidental. My experience leads me to

---

[4] Adams, ed.: 36.

[5] Vasavong: 221-222.

> believe otherwise. Being lost in the woods and having a brightly lit rabbit lead me safely to my family cannot be attributed to chance alone.[6]

Vasavong's experience is a classic example of what Jung called synchronicity, unusual but meaningful coincidences that occur during times of great emotional turmoil when archetypal reality becomes more active and can express itself through projection. In this case, it could be said that Vasavong's inherent survival instincts manifested themselves as a glowing rabbit that led him out of a life and death situation to safety. Jung referred to archetypal reality as linked with instinctual patterns of thought and behavior, essentially calling archetypal images pictorial representations of instincts. In Vasavong's narrative, the survival instinct appears as a projected archetypal image: the figure of the helpful animal featured in numerous myths and folk tales from around the world.

Marie-Louise von Franz, a close colleague of Jung's, explained the universal significance of this archetypal image in folklore and its link with human instinctual patterns. After reading countless examples of world folklore, von Franz came to the conclusion that there was only one universal rule inherent in folk and fairy tales:

> ...one must never hurt the helpful animal in fairy tales.... [You] may temporarily disobey the advice of the helpful fox or wolf or cat. But if basically you go against it, if you do not listen to the helpful animal or bird, or whatever it is, if any animal gives you advice and you don't follow it, then you are finished....This would mean that obedience to one's most basic inner being, one's instinctual inner being, is the one thing which is more essential than anything else. In all nations and all fairy tale material, I have never found a different statement.[7]

Von Franz underscores how inner, instinctual energies that keep us alert to danger are personified by the figure of the helpful animal in folk tales. Von Franz also explains how experiences such as the one reported by Vasavong are the inspiration for most folk tales:

> Personally, I think it likely that the most frequent way in which archetypal stories [i.e. folk tales and myths] originate is through individual experiences of an invasion by some unconscious content, either in a dream or in a waking hallucination...whereby an archetypal content breaks into an individual life....Such invasions of the collective unconscious into the field of

---

[6] Vasavong: 222

[7] Von Franz (1974) 1995: 145-146

> experience of a single individual probably, from time to time, create new nuclei of stories and also keep alive the already existing material.[8]

In other words, similar experiences reported by Vasavong are the original source materials for tales featuring helpful animals. Such stories are ignited by an experience perceived as life threatening; in these situations, unconscious energies are activated and sometimes overwhelm ego consciousness, resulting in a type of "waking hallucination" in which the projection of unconscious contents into the physical environment occurs, resulting in a supernatural experience filled with numinous energy. A person who has had such an experience might share it with others; if it's compelling enough, it could inspire similarly-themed stories.

It is interesting to note that Vasavong never questioned the reality of his vision despite its dreamlike qualities: a friendly rabbit appearing out of nowhere as a glowing object of light encouraging him to follow it, a phenomenon straight out of *Alice in Wonderland*. Vasavong's youthful age was a major factor. The sudden appearance of a lit-up bunny might have sent someone older with a less open attitude toward the supernatural running in panic deeper into the jungle. As fantastic as the creature might have seemed, he accepted it as real, behaved accordingly, saved his life, and ultimately fashioned a tale presented as autobiographical but could also substitute as a folk tale about encountering a helpful animal.

The figure of the black dog in certain legends and folk tales, most notably in the United Kingdom and other parts of Europe, as well as in India, could be variations of the type of experience reported by Vasavong. Although reports of the black dog usually connect the figure to the devil—such as the black dog that appears in Goethe's *Faust*—other reports of people seeing the black dog have described it as helpful. The majority of the sightings take place on the edge of forests or in deep woods, indicating that the black dog could be a personification of an individual's dread over being surrounded by the unknown. Two reports, one from Somerset, England, and another from a former resident of Somerset but living in Toronto, Canada, feature the black dog in the role of helpful animal:

> "When I was a young girl I was living outside of Toronto in Canada and I had to go to a farm some miles away one evening. There were woods on the way and I was greatly afraid, but a large black dog came with me and saw

[8] Von Franz (1970)1996: 24.

> me safely to the door. When I had to return he again appeared, and walked with me till I was nearly home. Then he vanished."
>
> [A cottager from Somerset] once had occasion to climb the Quantocks late one winter afternoon. When he had climbed up Weacombe to the top, the sea-mist came down, and he felt he might be frozen to death before he got home. But as he was groping along he suddenly touched shaggy fur and thought that old Shep, his sheep-dog, had come out to look for him….The dog turned and led him right to his cottage door, where he heard his own dog barking inside. He turned to look at the dog who had guided him, which grew gradually larger and then faded away. "It was the Black Dog, God blest it" he would always say.[9]

In these examples, legends of the black dog with which the individuals might have been familiar as residents of Somerset could have inspired their reported encounters with this spectral figure. In each report, the fear factor is significant; the results are nearly identical examples of projection of instinctual energies as reported by Vasavong, with the helpful animal figure materializing and leading each person to safety before vanishing.

A helpful entity that appears out of nowhere in a time of crisis can take other forms, as the following example illustrates, reported by a woman climbing in the Bavarian Alps who had become hopelessly lost:

> Having started a little late for the return, with light beginning to fade, I found myself in a really dangerous… [and] hopeless position. All of a sudden, I noticed a sort of a big ball of light, and this condensed to a shape of a tall, rather Chinese-looking gentleman. Extraordinarily, I was not a bit frightened, and not astonished; it all seemed quite natural to me. The gentleman bowed, spoke a few words, led me a small path to the tourists' way, and disappeared as a ball of light.[10]

It is interesting that the woman reports having no fear of this "Chinese gentleman" who appears to her first as a ball of light, similar to how the white rabbit appeared to young Vasavong who also demonstrated no fear of his glowing animal specter. Commenting on this report, paranormal investigator Hilary Evans provides an insightful explanation: "Various scenarios suggest themselves, but the simplest one is that her subconscious mind sent out a mayday call, to which the BOL [ball of light]/Chinese gentleman responded."[11] Evans' explanation complements Willian G.

---

[9] Briggs, ed. (1971) 2011: 95
[10] Evans: 86-87.
[11] Evans: 87.

Roll's comment about how a strong desire triggers "a situation" that "satisfies" the desire. The woman's survival instincts responded to her life and death situation by manifesting an unconscious, archetypal entity, what Jung would call an animus or male soul guide, also known as a Wise Old Man figure, who could lead her to safety. Unless, of course, Chinese gentlemen disguised as balls of light regularly patrol the Alps to assist those in need. I will explore this projection phenomenon further in Chapter Four when examining the Otherworld/waking world overlap.

Perhaps those most familiar with the Otherworld are shamans, indigenous healers from various traditional cultures whose main task is to journey through ecstatic trance states to the Otherworld as a way to assist a member of the community by gaining knowledge from this realm that can benefit the individual or community as a whole. An example of the long association that shamanism has with the Otherworld can be found in the ancient Lascaux Caves in France. The Lascaux Caves are dominated by paintings, approximately 20,000 years old, depicting huge animals—bison, horses, stags, and bulls--galloping en mass along the walls and ceilings of these caves. One painting, located in the deepest recesses of the caves, depicts a stick-figure human lying naked and sporting an erection; the figure has the head of a bird as he lies with arms extended as if in flight. Near the figure is a staff with a bird emblem perched on top. Looming over the human figure is a giant bison drawn with more significant details in shades of brown, gold, and black. The bison faces the man, its huge body dwarfing him. Although the animal appears alive with piercing eyes and cocked head, the underbelly of the beast is pierced with a lance and the animal's entrails are spilling out (Fig. I-1).[12]

This intriguing image has been studied by experts in art, anthropology, and archeology and earned numerous interpretations. One of the most often-repeated interpretations is that the image depicts a shaman dressed as a bird as he flies in ecstatic trance—indicated by his erect penis--to commune with a bison spirit in the land of the dead. Numerous other images associated with shamanism feature the shaman depicted with bird-like attributes or riding upon the back of a long-necked water bird. As Joseph Campbell explained:

> I have tried to suggest…the rich context of associations linking the figure of the bird to the spiritual flight of the shaman… [and] to the Paleolithic context of shamanism. Let me now add that the Hindu master yogis, who in

[12] Creative Commons

their trance states go beyond all the pales of thought, are known as…"wild ganders," and "supreme wild ganders." In the imagery of traditional Hinduism, the wild gander is symbolic of the *braham-atman*, the ultimate transcendent yet immanent ground of all being, with which the yogi succeeds in identifying his consciousness, thus passing from the sphere of waking consciousness…passing even beyond dream, where all things shine of their own light, to the nonconditioned, nondual state "between two thoughts," where subject-object polarity is completely transcended and the distinction between life and death dissolved.[13]

Figure I-1: Lascaux cave painting, circa 20,000 B.C. (Creative Commons)

Campbell's description of the visionary trance-flight of the shaman and its relationship with the flight of the Hindu yogi emphasizes the symbolism of the bird as not only illustrating the trance state but also the Otherworld itself as a "nondual state" where "the distinction between life and death" has dissolved. Campbell also hints in his comments that the Otherworld is the true reality, the origin of both the material and the spirit realm, "the ultimate transcendent yet immanent ground of all being." Campbell's comments relate to the Aboriginal Australian concept of dreamtime—explored in more detail in Chapter Six--and Jung's ideas about the dual nature of the psyche

[13] Campbell: 134-135.

with ego consciousness having its origins in the archetypal reality of the unconscious.

Joan Halifax echoes Campbell's association with shamanism and bird symbolism with the Otherworld in her description of the Lascaux image, stating that the shaman featured in the painting has journeyed to this life-in-death realm to commune with his deity—the fatally wounded bison who appears alive in this realm. As Halifax states: "The spirit of the shaman and the bison are both liberated—one through death, the other through trance. Thus communication is established....The spirit of the shaman is self-fertilized in the experience of ecstasy."[14]

Because shamans are known to be experts at effecting and immersing themselves in otherworldly visionary experiences, shamanic descriptions of their journeys to the Otherworld have had a major impact on the content of folklore and myth. As it will become apparent in subsequent chapters, many common motifs found in folklore and myth, such as the motif of the journey to the underworld--one of the most universal of all mythic themes--are based upon shamanic visionary experiences. Other shamanic elements such as experiencing flight, encountering spirits of the dead and other fabulous creatures, and being subjected to torturous extremes including death and dismemberment followed by resurrection, show up frequently in folklore and myth.

Two nineteenth century tales from the Grimm brothers, for example, have obvious shamanic elements, both featuring fabulous bird-like creatures. The first tale, "The Fitcher's Bird," is a unique variation of the famous "Bluebeard" folk tale in which a mysterious aristocrat marries, kills, and dismembers a succession of wives and keeps their bodies stored in a bloody chamber. In the Grimm's version, the aristocrat is a magician or wizard who kidnaps girls and takes them to his mansion in a deep forest. Each potential bride is given the keys to all the rooms of his palace and has the run of the castle except for one room that remains off limits. When the magician leaves the palace to take care of business, he tests the loyalty of each bride by giving her an egg to protect from harm. After he leaves, each bride gives into temptation and unlocks the forbidden room which contains the dismembered corpses of the magician's previous brides. Each bride is so shocked by the sight of the bloody corpses that she drops her egg which then becomes permanently stained with blood. After the magician returns

[14] Halifax: 11.

from his business trip and inspects the egg, he notices the bloodstains and ends up killing and dismembering his latest bride.

The cycle of destruction is disrupted when the magician captures three sisters in succession, two of whom end up dismembered. The third sister, however, protects her egg from harm before opening the bloody chamber. When she sees the dismembered bodies of her two sisters among the other corpses, her reaction is not fright and panic but pity. She ends up arranging the body parts in their correct positions, and in doing so brings her sisters back to life. When the magician returns from his business venture and inspects the girl's egg, finding it unblemished, he bows down before her and proclaims her his superior in magic. He tells her they will be wedded in a spectacular wedding ceremony. While he prepares for the ceremony, the girl has her sisters secretly return home and warn family and friends of the evil wizard. She then strips down and covers her body in honey, then rips open some pillows and lets their feathery contents stick to her body until she is completely covered in bird feathers. The girl then places the skeletal remains of one of the wizard's previous victims in the upper window of the mansion and begins to walk through the countryside. Whenever she comes across someone, she squawks like a bird and invites the person to the wedding (Fig. I-2).[15] After the wizard returns and spies the skeletal corpse in the window, he runs to his so-called bride. The girl's family and friends then show up and set the mansion on fire, killing the wizard and his wedding guests.[16]

One of the key motifs that mark the tale's influence by shamanic practices is the theme of initiation which includes ritual dismemberment. When a young shaman hopeful is being tested for his or her potential status as a community healer, the candidate is put through rituals that simulate dismemberment by ancestor spirits. Dismemberment can also occur in a potential shaman's dreams; if such a dream occurs, the individual is considered a superior candidate since it's believed that the spirits themselves have visited the individual and conducted the initiation in the dreaming state--the realm of the Otherworld.

[15] Creative Commons.

[16] Tatar, ed.: 148-151.

Figure I-2: Dressed as a fabulous bird, the young girl/shaman wanders through the countryside inviting friends of the evil wizard to a fateful wedding. Illustration for "The Fitcher's Bird," by Maurice Sendak. (Creative Commons)

Bird symbolism is predominant in the tale as it is in numerous shamanic traditions. Certain traditional shamanic belief systems speak of potential shamans born in the cosmic tree of life, hatched out of eggs laid by a great mother bird. After the shaman candidates are born, the great mother bird nurses them before turning them over to demons who dismember them, after which the mother bird reassembles the body parts and brings them back to life with new attributes beneficial to their new shamanic profession.[17] This tradition featuring the great mother bird appears in the tale, with the girl taking on the role of the mother bird who has the power to resurrect dismembered individuals and restore them to life. The girl ultimately dresses as a mother bird figure as she wanders through the countryside inviting people to her wedding. Ultimately, the tale as a whole illustrates the

[17] Eliade (1951) 2004: 36-37.

making of a shaman through the performance of certain rituals that test the candidate's expertise. The rites involve simulated death, dismemberment, and resurrection. Note that death in this tale, as it is in shamanic initiation rites, is followed by resurrection or transformation of some sort. Death is never a finality in the Otherworld.

The other Grimm's tale with strong shamanic themes is "The Juniper Tree." The tale begins with a woman giving birth to a boy, then dying soon afterwards and being buried next to a juniper tree. Several years after the mother's death, the father remarries. His new wife has a young daughter, Marlene, who befriends the boy, causing the wife to become jealous of the boy's favorable status with his new sister and with his father. She plots to kill the boy, and ultimately succeeds, after which she chops up his body and makes a stew out of his body parts which she later feeds to his father. Her own daughter Marlene is horrified by her mother's actions and ends up burying the boy's bones underneath the juniper tree. Not long afterwards, the tree splits apart and in a blast of lightning, a fabulous bird appears out of the trees' trunk (Fig I-3).[18]

The bird begins flying through the village singing this song:

My mother, she slew me
My father, he ate me
My sister, little Marlene,
Gathered up my bones,
Tied them up in silk,
And put them under the juniper tree.
Tweet, tweet, what a fine bird I am![19]

Those in the village who hear the bird's song are enchanted by it. Some throw up gifts to the bird: a golden chain, a pair of new shoes, and a miller's stone. The bird flies back with its presents to the boy's home and throws down the golden chain to the father, the new shoes to little Marlene, and then drops the miller's stone on the stepmother's head who is crushed by the weight and dies in an explosion of lightning and thunder. After the smoke clears, the bird is nowhere to be found. Instead, the boy emerges in its place from the rubble. He takes the hand of his father and sister, and they walk back inside the cottage to finish their supper.[20]

---

[18] Creative Commons.
[19] Tatar, ed.: 193.
[20] Tatar, ed.: 190-197.

Figure I-3: Little Marlene lays the bones of her dismembered brother under the juniper tree, resulting in an amazing transformation of the boy's spirit into a fabulous bird. Illustration from "The Juniper Tree," by Louis Rhead, 1917. (Creative Commons)

Like "The Fitcher's Bird," "The Juniper Tree" has initiatory themes of dismemberment, transformation, and resurrection. There is also the appearance of another fabulous bird, this one born out of the juniper tree, a type of cosmic tree of life. The bird flies through the village and restores harmony and joy with its appearance and with the song it sings. The bird is the boy in spirit form, experiencing an initiatory flight. His initiation is conducted by an ancestor spirit—his stepmother. He passes her brutal tests and emerges resurrected from the dead. Once again, the idea that death is not the end of life becomes a major motif, one of the distinguishing aspects of the Otherworld.

Most traditional initiation rites, whether they are puberty rites, shamanic preparatory rites, or hero-in-training rites, involve a simulated death followed by resurrection. This indicates that, like folklore and myth, certain ceremonial rites were influenced by shamanic visionary experiences in which the Otherworld is evoked to help keep a community and its members healthy and in harmony with the spirit realm, the source of all life. This harmonious balance between the spirit realm and the material realm mirrors the balance between ego consciousness and the unconscious. Outer and inner harmony must be maintained; otherwise, the spirit realm will become more active, as it attempts to reestablish a healing balance between the two realms.

The following chapters explore the Otherworld while also exploring the relationship between consciousness and the unconscious, noting how the characteristics of the human psyche and the Otherworld relate to one another and reflect their interrelationship. Each chapter emphasizes an aspect of the Otherworld, how this reality is linked with the inner reality of the human psyche, and how this link has been expressed in folklore, myth, shamanistic practices, traditional rites, and contemporary examples found in cinema as well as in contemporary experiences of individuals reporting various types of supernatural encounters.

Since aspects of the Otherworld live inside of us, we all seem to know of its existence on an instinctual level, yet we let our big, rational-thinking brains convince us of something different. According to the brain's reasoning center--the cerebral cortex--the Otherworld is like Santa Claus. After children reach a certain age, they are informed by big-brain adult caregivers that Santa doesn't exist, that he is just a fantasy, a symbol of the spirit of Christmas, so they should stop believing in him. Up until that point, most children probably had little problem believing in such a fantastic figure. But now, continuing to do so would mark them as childish: capable of believing in the wildest fantasies.

Ironically, some scholars believe that the original Santa Claus was based upon shamanic practices. Note that Santa flies throughout the world on his annual wintertime journey, helped by his spirit animals, in this case reindeer rather than birds, since the influential shamanic elements associated with Santa Claus are thought to have originated by the indigenous peoples of Lapland--located not all that far from the North Pole—where reindeer play an important role in their culture. Like the boy in "The Juniper Tree," Santa distributes gifts to both the good and the bad. Also, Santa is somehow able to perform his journey by flying over the entire world in one night, another attribute of the Otherworld where time doesn't follow the usual 24-hour cycle but can be extended indefinitely. And Santa's mission is the same as the shaman: to create harmony among his community, in this case, the people of the material world.[21]

Although the reasoning centers of the brain insist that the Otherworld doesn't exist, other parts of the brain actually encourage us to believe in this reality, just as many of us believed at one time in such otherworldly spirits as Santa Claus. Every night, certain parts of the brain remind us: the Otherworld is real.

---

[21] Dalton: n.p.

# CHAPTER ONE

# THE PSYCHOLOGICAL BASIS OF THE OTHERWORLD

In 1912, C.G. Jung published the first book-length presentation of his psychological views: *Transformations and Symbols of the Libido*, also known as *Psychology of the Unconscious*. The book's first section was devoted to Jung's exploration of what he called two kinds of thinking: directed thinking and fantasy thinking. Directed thinking, also known as logical or reality thinking, deals with solving problems affecting the person at any given moment: it is "a thinking that adjusts itself to actual conditions, where we…imitate the succession of objectively real things, so that the images in our mind follow after each other in the same strictly causal succession as the historical events outside of our mind."[1] The highest form of directed thinking is scientific thinking. Jung, therefore, considered directed thinking an evolutionarily advanced mode of cognitive functioning superior to fantasy thinking: "…the directed thinking of our time is a more or less modern acquisition, which was lacking in earlier times."[2] Fantasy thinking "…leads us away from reality into phantasies of the past and future. Here, thinking in the form of speech ceases, image crowds upon image, feeling upon feeling; more and more clearly one sees a tendency which creates and makes believe, not truly as it is but as one indeed might wish it to be….The customary speech calls this kind of thinking 'dreaming.'"[3]

Further defining the differences between these two modes of thinking, Jung stated that:

> Thus, we have two forms of thinking—directed thinking and dream or phantasy thinking. The first, working for communication with speech elements, is troublesome and exhausting; the latter, on the contrary, goes on

[1] Jung (1912) 2001: 13.
[2] Jung (1912) 2001: 18.
[3] Jung (1912) 2001: 19-20.

> without trouble, working spontaneously, so to speak, with reminiscences. The first creates innovations, adaptations, imitates reality and seeks to act upon it. The latter, on the contrary, turns away from reality, sets free subjective wishes, and is, in regard to adaptation, wholly unproductive.[4]

It would appear from these comments that Jung had a prejudicial attitude toward these two kinds of thinking, with fantasy thinking considered an inferior and more primitive form of thinking than the more logical and productive directed thinking. However, what Jung was attempting to do in his first major work was to distinguish his psychological views from Sigmund Freud's and noting how all thinking is fueled by libido or psychic energy. According to Freud's dogmatic attitude, libido is driven primarily by sex and aggressive tendencies, while Jung considered libido to be a much more creatively expressive drive within the psyche. Although Jung referred to fantasy thinking as infantile and primitive, he also called it the source of the mythopoetic or myth-making source of the psyche; since certain mythic themes and motifs can be found universally in the cultures of the world from various points in historical time, Jung insisted that the fantasy mode of thinking responsible for the creation of myths must have an objective or impersonal dimension:

> …the products arising from the unconscious are related to the mythical. From all these signs it may be concluded that the soul possesses in some degree historical strata, the oldest stratum of which would correspond to the unconscious….[There] come to light pronounced traits of an archaic mental kind which under certain circumstances, might go as far as the re-echo of a once manifest, archaic mental product.[5]

The "archaic mental product" of the unconscious expresses itself most often with symbolic images and motifs appearing in dreams. In many cases, dream symbolism does not appear to have relevance to waking world concerns; it appears to be irrelevant, nonsensical, and "wholly unproductive." Yet, as Jung goes on to investigate in great detail, these strange, seemingly irrelevant images and motifs, are made up of a type of archaic language expressing concerns and concepts universal to humanity.

Jung rightly raises the question: what is the source of this symbolic language? "How are phantasies created?"[6] Because of the tremendous influence that Freud still had upon Jung's psychological views at this stage

[4] Jung (1912) 2001: 20.
[5] Jung (1912) 2001: 32-33.
[6] Jung (1912) 2001: 28.

of his professional career, Jung concluded that repression of id-driven wish fulfillment urges was the source of dream fantasies which consisted of unfulfilled desires: "We imagine that which we lack."[7] In other words, the source of dreams is the conscious human imagination desiring taboo wishes and dreaming up scenarios of fulfillment. This early view of the source of dream content reflects the more commonly accepted view of dreams which emphasizes how dreams reflect waking concerns and are made up of symbolic content reflective of the dreamer's personality and daily subjective experiences; also, according to this view, imagery and scenes that appear to have nothing to do with the person's waking life concerns are considered meaningless, random spurts of neural activity.

Jung also originally considered the concept of God based upon the Freudian view of God deriving from parental figures who appear omnipotent and all-powerful to a child. Classical scholar Jane Harrison eloquently expressed the Freudian concept of God in her examination of Greek religion. Although a superb interpreter of Greek art depicting references to religious and mythological scenarios, Harrison herself was an atheist and considered Greek religion based upon barbarous, "wholly unproductive" rituals derived from delusions and fantasy thinking with the primary intent of encouraging fertility and procreation. Writing in the early twentieth century, Harrison was influenced by both Freud and Jung and quoted extensively from their works—the former primarily from *Totem and Taboo*, the latter from *Psychology of the Unconscious*—as she explained the human origin of the God concept derived from fantasy thinking:

> Finding himself helpless in the face of natural powers, man tries to pull the strings of higher powers and so obtain control. He imagines gods and tries to influence them by prayer and sacrifice....Man utterly forgets that his gods are man-begotten....Man hungers to be one again with the [fantasy] image he has himself made....[Phantasy] thinking...is typified by the mental operation of children and savages and by those adults in their dreams, reveries, and mental disorders. It is from this early infantile type of dream or phantasy thinking engendered by the fertility rite that primitive theology and mythology spring....The older mind, still buried in all of us, is and always has been, incessantly weaving dream-images of imaginary wish fulfillment.[8]

---

[7] Jung (1912) 2001: 28.
[8] Harrison (1921) 2001: 34-36.

Harrison emphasizes the human-begotten idea of God, one embraced by Freud and other atheists. According to this view, every human civilization has invented the concept of God and then somehow repressed the creation of this supremely sophisticated manifestation of the human imagination; then, due to some type of mass amnesia, all human civilizations have forgotten that God is an invention of humanity, envisioned as the ultimate parent figure rather than the revelation and experience of an otherworldly, supernatural power.

As previously mentioned, Jung also seemed to accept this man-begotten view of God based upon the Freudian view. However, in *Symbols of Transformation*, the revised version of *Psychology of the Unconscious* written decades later after he had more firmly established his distinctive psychological philosophy, Jung makes his view of the concept of God much clearer. He also retracts the unsympathetic statements he made about fantasy thinking as a less evolutionarily developed stratum of the psyche:

> …one must certainly put a large question-mark after the assertion that myths spring from an "infantile" psychic life of the race. They are on the contrary the most mature product of that young humanity….[Myth-making] and myth-inhabiting man was a grown reality and not a four year-old child….In reality, we are concerned with primitive, archaic thought-forms, based on instinct, which naturally emerge more clearly in childhood than they do later. But, they are not in themselves infantile, much less pathological…. The instinctive, archaic basis of the mind is a matter of plain objective fact and is not more dependent upon the individual experience or personal choice than is the inherited structure and functioning of the brain or any other organ. Just as the body has its evolutionary history and shows clear traces of the various evolutionary stages, so too does the psyche.[9]

After struggling in his first major published work to distinguish his psychological views from Freud, Jung eventually emphasized how, within every human being, there is an "instinctive, archaic basis of the mind." It is this archaic substratum that produces fantasies with universal tendencies and forms. One of these tendencies is the concept of God. As Jung later stated, God and other supernatural beings of omnipotent power are pre-existing psychic energy patterns filled with tremendous numinous power. Man, therefore, does not invent God but projects this internal concept on to figures that reflect and embody this power, the way a child, for example, projects the God image upon parental figures. As Jung explained:

---

[9] Jung (1952) 1967: 24-25.

> …archetypes…are found in every individual, and their effect is always the strongest…where consciousness is weakest and most restricted, and where fantasy can overrun the facts of the outer world. This condition is undoubtedly present in the child during the first years of its life. It therefore seems to me more probable that the archetypal form of the divine [parental couple] first covers up and assimilates, the image of the real parents until, with increasing consciousness, the real figures of the parents are perceived.[10]

As Jung states, the effects of archetypes are strongest when "consciousness is weakest and most restricted," which is not only in the early stages of development but during other occasions when one's directed thinking is less of a factor, such as it is when one is daydreaming. For the longest time, daydreaming has been considered idle and "wholly unproductive" thinking. However, now it is considered the brain's default mode network (DMN), necessary for consolidating memories and for creative imaginings that benefit self-concept and conscious awareness. The brain is actually more active during daydreaming than it is with directed thinking.[11] Fantasy thinking, therefore, is hardly evolutionarily inferior to directed thinking; it complements and influences such thinking, having a similar relationship that consciousness has with the unconscious. It is because consciousness is more aligned with waking reality, where logic and rational methods of problem solving are valued, that fantasy, daydreaming, and other unconscious processes are deemed less important by the developing ego.

Jung raises the question of the origins of the archetypal dimension of the psyche, ultimately stating that its origins are unknown. Why the archetypal substratum expresses itself in symbols is also a mystery. These unfathomable dimensions of archetypal reality could relate to Jung's ideas about the compensatory function of the psyche, that the unconscious compensates for what consciousness lacks in order to maintain a homeostatic balance between these two dimensions of the human psyche. For example, when our lives are threatened, the psyche reacts with images and motifs symbolizing life enduring mortal death. And yet, where did the concept of immortality originate? Is it a wish fulfillment fantasy, something we all crave due to the survival instinct and the fear of death? Or, is immortality a concept inborn within us because it exits in an Otherworld reality?

---

[10] Jung (1936) 1980: 67.

[11] Davanger: n.p.

An example of a universal symbol illustrating the immortal dimension of life seems to indicate that the origins of this concept are archetypal. I refer to this particular symbolic image as an example of the concept of immortality because it is, frankly, bizarre; and yet, despite its irrational nature, it has a long, influential history. Most significantly, the image appeared in a personal dream. It remained an incomprehensible dream image for over two decades until I stumbled upon other examples from mythology and ancient religious practices. The image, therefore, is a potent illustration of how archetypes are not conscious inventions but pre-existing thought patterns hard wired in the brain and activated by outside influences that disturb, confound, and fascinate us.

The image from my dream was at one time so commonly recognized and understood as illustrating life enduring after mortal death that there was a well-known concept expressing an aspect of its universal intent: *bugonia*. The term refers to the ancient idea that bees were born spontaneously from the rotting carcasses of bulls and cows, a type of belief associated with the concept of spontaneous generation. Before spontaneous generation was discredited by scientists of the 18th and 19th centuries, many ancient peoples apparently believed that certain living creatures could be born from inorganic materials. Various formulas existed for creating certain creatures. One could create mice and rats, for example, from discarded pieces of food or piles of dirty laundry. And one could create bees if a person took a dead bull, buried it neck deep so that its horns jutted up from the earth, then waited several months before sawing off the horns; after the horns were sawed off, newly born bees would fly out of them.[12] A variation of this motif can be found in the Bible, in Judges 14:5-9, when the mighty hero Samson kills a lion and leaves its carcass by the road, then returns weeks later to find bees swarming out of the lion's decaying body (Figs. 1-1 & 1-2).[13]

Another reference to bees being born out of dead bodies appears in a myth with a religious undertone. It involves a woman named Melissa, whose name in Greek means "bee." Melissa was a favorite of the Greek's earth and grain goddess Demeter who was associated with a secretive religious initiation ceremony—the Eleusinian Mysteries--in which participants experienced a symbolic descent and death within the underworld, followed by a resurrection from the land of the dead. In the myth, Melissa was personally initiated by Demeter into the goddess' secretive

---

[12] Ransome (1937) 2004: 117.
[13] Creative Commons.

Figures. 1-1 & 1-2 The bugonia motif featuring dead bulls and lions spontaneously giving birth to bees, a belief that inspired ideas about spontaneous generation and life enduring death. (Creative Commons)

rites. Afterwards, Melissa was killed by jealous townspeople, and her dismembered body left in the open air. When Demeter saw Melissa's mutilated body, she commanded that bees emerge from the body parts.

Afterwards, the conductors of Demeter's secret rites were called the Melissae, "the bees," while the goddess herself was known as the Queen Bee.[14]

In all these examples, bees are associated with the birth of new life from dead matter, a vital life force essence enduring death. Because of this association, bees were considered manifestations of *zoe*: the inexhaustible life force that transcends physical death.[15] Why bees were associated with this concept remains a mystery, especially since bees are not normally attracted to dead animal carcasses. Flies, yes, bees, no.

Russian-born entomologist Carl Robert Osten-Sacken attempted to explain the association between bees and dead bulls from a scientific perspective. Osten-Sacken explained the erroneous bugonia belief by claiming that a fly—the *eristalis tenax*—which has a striking resemblance to a bee, was mistakenly identified as such for thousands of years by our less sophisticated and ill-informed ancient ancestors. Osten-Sacken claimed that: "…it is to the *E. Tenax* alone, that the origin of the belief in Bugonia is due; in other words, that if this particular fly had not existed, the belief probably never would have arisen."[16] Osten-Sacken's claim underscores how certain beliefs are considered to have arisen from erroneous observations and faulty cause-effect relationships between natural phenomena. However, my dream discredits Osten-Sacken's more scientifically-grounded explanation, proving that the bugonia motif is an archetype of the collective unconscious.

My dream occurred during an emotionally overwhelming period of my life when I was recovering from the effects of a turbulent personal relationship with a former girlfriend and establishing a new relationship with another woman. During this time, I had an elaborate dream that contained a scene in which my new girlfriend and I were attempting to clean up the common grounds of the apartment complex where we were living at the time. The common grounds were littered with bags of dismembered human and animal body parts covered by swarms of bees—a variation of the bugonia motif. Although I had no idea about the significance of this dream image and its relationship to bugonia at the time I had the dream, I intuitively recognized its connection with the current relationship I had with my new girlfriend, since her nickname was "Be." After gradually becoming

[14] Ransome (1937) 2004: 96-97.
[15] Kerenyi, C. (1976) 1996: xxxiv-xxxvii.
[16] Osten-Sacken: 9

more familiar with Jungian dream interpretation, as well as with mythic themes and religious rites, I finally recognized the reference to the bugonia motif in my dream and how it symbolized the death of my old relationship, signified by the bags of dismembered body parts, and the enduring vitality of the new relationship, symbolized by the swarms of bees, the latter also connected to the name of my new girlfriend.[17]

The archetypal image from my dream has relevance to the famous dream image reported by the 19th century German chemist Friedrich August Kekule von Stradonitz who was attempting to work out the structure of the benzene molecule and one night dreamed of a serpent biting its tail. Upon awakening from the dream, von Stradonitz was struck by the emotionally charged vividness of the image and realized its relevance to the benzene molecule as a self-contained circular structure. Because von Stradonitz was open to accepting such esoteric imagery as relevant to his scientific inquiries, he was able to solve his problem.[18]The dream image of the tail-biting serpent, also known as the uroboros, can be found in numerous cultures and in certain esoteric philosophies, most notably alchemy, with a meaning similar to my bugonia image: as a symbol of an inexhaustible, perpetually self-generating force of life.

The dream examples illustrate something radical about the human psyche: at one time, humans were intimately associated with a language of images and motifs made up of obscure, nonrational references to natural phenomena, a language inherent within all of us, but one with an origin that remains a mystery. In my example, the bugonia motif inspired fantastic ideas about spontaneous generation as well as ancient religious beliefs, celebrated for nearly two thousand years, about life enduring after death, while in von Stradonitz's example, the archaic image of the uroboros serpent inspired ideas about the structure and workings of the universe. I will investigate the uroboros image further in Chapter Six when discussing the concept of dreamtime and the myth of the eternal return.

These two examples and countless others--some of which will be explored in subsequent chapters--raise the question: how many other so-called irrational beliefs have originated within the psyche, influenced by spontaneous experiences with archetypal imagery rather than from anything observed and intimated about the natural world?

---

[17] Kline 2018a: 194-205.

[18] Delano and duMond: 116-117.

What becomes obvious after examining some of the peculiarities of brain functioning is that the brain is trying to convince the individual that fantasy thinking is just as relevant and important for determining aspects of reality as directed thinking. As Jung mentioned, fantasy thinking is tolerated more with children since everyone knows children are unsophisticated and undeveloped thinkers and come up with wild ideas about how the world works. For example, in an early developmental stage, children believe that certain inanimate objects contain a secret power, an enduring life force such as *zoe*--a belief known as animism. According to developmental psychologist Jean Piaget, all of us embrace this so-called nonrational or precausal belief until we gain more sophisticated knowledge about the difference between what is alive and what is dead. However, such a belief is hardly a childish indulgence. In many cases, animism persists well beyond childhood. It is the basis for numerous religious and spiritual belief systems.

As a professor of psychology, I sometimes ask my college-level students to provide examples of their belief in animism. The following are responses from students living in the Northern Mariana Islands:

> I was born on [the island of] Saipan but for my whole life I was raised on its sister island, Tinian [where] there is a place called "Taga Park" and it contains a few of the many [ancient] "Latte Stones," in the CNMI [Commonwealth of the Northern Mariana Islands]. This place is believed to be the home of "Taga," the chief of all the [native] Chamorros [see Figure 1-3].[19] Our elders have always told us to respect the area and to never make loud noises there for the spirit of Taga will come, as well as the "White Lady." The White Lady is said to be a spirit who dwells at the House of Taga at night and will haunt us if we make noises or [show] disrespect around the latte stone areas. Not too far from Taga Park, we have the "Taga Well." I'm not too sure if it's a real well because I was too afraid to go near it because that area too is where the spirits of Taga and the White Lady dwell at night. (Cing, written correspondence to author, 2017)

> Coming from a Catholic background, it is common to give sacred attributes to statues, crosses, and places. What I think I give most to in a Catholic perspective is the cross. I've always believed that disrespecting the cross was a blasphemous thing to commit. I believed that we should always respect the cross. People who are Catholic with cars often put the Rosemary cross in it because it is believed that it should protect you from any accidents. Also, putting these statues and holy figures were considered a must in our house because it was believed to protect us from evil spirits. Another thing

[19] Creative Commons

about the Catholic religion is that we give the animism attribute to scared places such as Mt. Tapochau here on Saipan. Every year during Lent season we walk up Mt. Tapochau to give tribute to Christ. It is common to give respect to this mountain. (Agulto, written correspondence to author, 2018)

Figure 1-3: House of Taga on the island of Tinian featuring latte stones constructed by the ancient native Chamorros. (Creative Commons)

Special stone structures and wells situated in special locales inhabited by ancestor spirits and supernatural specters, and a major world religion embraced by millions that pays homage to iconic statues, objects, and places endowed with supernatural energies, all express a belief in an enduring life force permeating the material world. Animism, therefore, is hardly a belief that dies with childhood.

The above student example that mentions a yearly pilgrimage up a sacred mountain—a common object of reverence found all over the world—has relevance to a modern incident involving tourists who betrayed the respect of the mountain spirits and suffered the consequences. The following description is from a newspaper article with the provocative title, "Malaysian Minister Blames Naked Tourists for Earthquake:"

*June 7, 2015*: A group of western tourists who stripped naked at the peak of Mount Kinabalu last month will be prohibited from leaving Malaysia, as their act of "disrespecting the mountain" could have caused the devastating earthquake that killed at least 13 people. The earthquake, measuring 5.9 on

> the Richter scale, struck Sabah's west coast on Friday, causing landslides on Mount Kinabalu, where at least thirteen climbers so far have been confirmed dead. The earthquake comes a week after a group of foreigners, which included two Canadians, two Dutch and one German national, broke away from their entourage and stripped naked before taking photos at the mountain peak. Sabahans railed against the images, as they consider the mountain sacred and that act of tourists made "mountain spirits mad." Deputy Chief Minister of Sabah, Tan Sri Joseph Pairin Kitingan, said that the tourists showed disrespect to the sacred mountain and will face appropriate action according to native laws. "Whether other people believe this or not, it's what we Sabahans believe," Kitingan said. "When the earthquake happened, it's like a confirmation of our beliefs. There is almost certainly a connection. We have to take this as a reminder that local beliefs are not to be disrespected."[20]

This example illustrates one of the worst acts a person can commit upon a community with a belief system that acknowledges the reality of animism and the spirit world: disrespect for this belief system. According to the community that honors Mount Kinabalu as a sacred site, there was a direct cause-effect relationship between the disrespect shown by the tourists to the spirits dwelling upon the mountain and the resulting earthquake that led to loss of life. Numerous other cultures with a strong connection to certain locations and characteristics of their natural environment would no doubt agree with this nonrational—archetypal--causal relationship, emphasizing how many people believe the Otherworld can manifest itself in the physical world and can effect dramatic changes upon the world. I will explore the concept of animism in more detail in Chapter Three.

Perhaps the most dramatic example of how our psychological make-up encourages fantasy thinking to reveal other dimensions of reality is the relationship between the REM (rapid eye movement) stage of sleep and waking consciousness. The relationship was discovered when brain waves were studied via electroencephalograph (EEG) scans, revealing that REM brain waves are nearly identical to the brain waves of someone awake. The similar features of these types of brain scans contributed to REM sleep being referred to as "paradoxical sleep."[21]

Additional features about REM sleep have added to its paradoxical nature. During REM, certain regions of the brain are as active as when awake: the amygdala which is one of the brain's most important centers for

---

[20] Unnikrishnan: n.p.

[21] Monaghan: n.p.

emotional regulation; the hippocampus, responsible for memory formation and consolidation; the occipital lobe, the brain's key visual center; and the brain stem which regulates crucial physical responses such as breathing, swallowing, and heart rate. One brain region that is nearly nonfunctional is the prefrontal cortex where reasoning and directed thinking take place. In addition, during REM, a person is in a state of sexual arousal, a physical condition mirroring the trance state of a shaman illustrated in the Lascaux cave painting referred to in the Introduction (Fig. I-1). Also, a person's muscle tension is nearly nonexistent, meaning that a person in REM is in a state of physical paralysis.

Most significantly, REM is the stage of sleep when dreaming is most active, vivid, and bizarre. In a sense, a person in REM sleep is forced by body paralysis to experience these bizarre scenarios and accept whatever occurs as real since the reasoning center of the brain is nonfunctional and the only reality is the dream itself.

J. Allan Hobson, one of the most accomplished modern dream researchers, refers to the dreaming state as one of delirium due to the brain's inability to reason adequately. Hobson and colleagues subscribe to the activation-synthesis theory of dreams: because the reasoning centers of the brain are inactive during REM, the content of dreams has little meaning since dreams are the product of organic changes in brain activity with the brain randomly discharging chemical signals that combine with memory signals from the hippocampus and emotional signals from the amygdala.[22] In other words, Hobson embraces the belief of scholars like Jane Harrison who view fantasy thinking as inferior to directed thinking.

Hobson attempted to underscore his view of dreams in *13 Dreams Freud Never Had*, presenting a series of personal dreams and then attempting to interpret them from primarily a Freudian perspective. However, Hobson's real intent was to discredit Freud's view about dreams having meaningful symbolic content while championing the superiority of the activation-synthesis theory. Hobson's attempts to interpret his dreams are, in many instances, infused with sarcasm as he ridicules Freud's view even when Hobson admits that the dream he is investigating has obvious references to his waking concerns. For example, in one dream, which he calls "Italian Romance," he dreams of an elaborate wedding with an Italian woman. The wedding is attended by his family members, all dressed in white, and prior

---

[22] See Hobson, Pace-Schott, and Stickgold.

to the wedding ceremony, men of the family perform an elaborate ritual among themselves involving the carrying of a large glass bowl full of white liquid which Hobson struggles to keep from spilling. Upon awakening from this dream, he told it to his wife who immediately accused him of having an affair during his last visit to Italy. Apparently, she was able to interpret the dream's underlying intent more accurately than Hobson, that their marriage was in trouble. In order to maintain his attitude that dreams have little relationship to waking concerns, as well as little—if any—symbolic meaning, Hobson had to discredit his wife's response as "unscientific:"

> If I were not a scientist, I might even think that this dream was prophetic. While it was true that I had not yet had an affair in Italy, I was trying hard to have one. More important is the fact that after the breakup of my marriage in 1992, it was to Italy that I went, and it was in Italy where I met Lia Silvestri, the woman who became my second wife.[23]

Holding on to his view of dreams as delusional products of an irrational state of mind, Hobson cannot consider the dream as having relevance to his current marital relationship or to a future outcome, since to consider such a possibility defies his empirical evidence about dreams. He has to reject the possibility that fantasy thinking is a legitimate type of cognitive processing like scientific or directed thinking, especially since legitimizing such thinking would discredit his own dream theory. However, according to Jung, such dreams are in many cases based upon habitual actions and thought patterns which can then form a dream scenario that appears to predict future behavior. Jung called such a phenomenon the prospective function of dreams:

> The prospective function…is an anticipation in the unconscious of future conscious achievements, something like a preliminary exercise or sketch, or a plan roughed out in advance….It would be wrong to call them prophetic, because at bottom they are no more prophetic than a medical diagnosis or a weather forecast. They are merely an anticipatory combination of probabilities which may coincide with the actual behavior of things but need not necessarily agree in every detail.[24]

Hobson's reluctance to view his dream as anything except nonsensical illustrates how prevalent the prejudice is about fantasy thinking--even among dream researchers--when compared to the so-called superiority of directed thinking. According to scientists such as Hobson, the nonrational

---

[23] Hobson: 73.

[24] Jung (1948) 1969: 255

dimension of the psyche must be inferior to the rational dimension; otherwise, we would all be in danger of taking too seriously phenomena that do not exist physically, making faulty cause-effect relationships, and finding relevance in dream scenarios that, according to his dream theory, have little relevance to our waking lives. And yet, according to the REM stage of sleep, this stage presents to us a reality we consider legitimate when we are experiencing it, and appears on brain wave scans as equivalent to the waking stage. Why is the brain insisting that this delusion called a dream is presenting a legitimate dimension of reality?

A film that provides a dramatic illustration of the conflict between fantasy and scientific thinking is *Contact* (1997), based upon the novel by scientist Carl Sagan. The film features an astronomer, Ellie Arroway (played by Jodi Foster), researching the possible existence of life forms on other planets. Ellie is depicted as having no tolerance for belief in God and other phenomena that cannot be proven through the scientific method; she remains proud of her atheist scientist status and ridicules those who think otherwise. When she eventually makes contact with an alien civilization, the inhabitants of the planet transmit information that turns out to be plans for building a space ship for travel to their planet. World powers then decide to build the space ship and Ellie ends up chosen to make the journey. However, after she takes the trip and returns safely, Earth-based technicians monitoring her flight tell her she never left the launch area. And yet, Ellie claims that she flew over hundreds of millions of miles to this alien planet by traversing a series of galactic wormholes, then floated down out of her space ship to the planet's surface that had the look of a Florida beach resort, and conversed with one of the alien beings who appeared to her as her dead father. With her scientific reputation, along with her sanity, now in doubt, she appears before a congressional investigation committee and makes this statement:

> I had an experience. I can't prove it, I can't even explain it, but everything that I know as a human being, everything that I am, tells me that it was real. I was given something wonderful, something that changed me forever, a vision of the universe that tells us, undeniably, how tiny and insignificant and how rare and precious we all are. A vision that tells us that we belong to something greater than ourselves…that none of us are alone. I wish I could share that, I wish that everyone, if only for one moment, could feel that awe, and humility, and hope.[25]

---

[25] Zemeckis, dir. 1997: Warner Bros.

Although this film example does not involve a dream experience, it does dramatically illustrate what happens when the ego reality of a rational and intelligent individual with no religious belief system is called into question by a nonrational experience. In fact, what is being described here is the equivalent of a religious experience, emphasizing awe and humility and rapture after encountering a supernatural power. Despite the fact that her experience challenges every notion she has embraced as a scientist about the nature of reality, along with her inability to describe it in scientific—or any rational—terms, Ellie claims that what she experienced was real. Her experience with the nonrational provides a dramatic contrast with Hobson's, who fiercely clings to his scientific view of dreams as delusional despite the possibility that his dreams might actually be saying something insightful and relevant about his present and future life.

The sense of having lived within an otherworldly dream realm, of having experienced a reality transcending all boundaries of ordinary reality, is similar to the dream and visionary reports of shamans who also insist that what they experience is an Otherworld just as real as the waking realm. The confusion and disorientation that results from modern-day dreamers waking from an intensely bizarre dream and struggling to convince themselves that what they experienced was not as real or as relevant to their lives as their waking reality is a significant characteristic of a REM dream inspired in many cases by an emotionally volatile conscious experience. In these instances, the brain is presenting an alternate view of the individual's life that must be taken seriously.

As hard as it is to admit, we must take certain overpowering REM stage dreams as a view of a dimension of reality with its own rules and modes of expression. We must strive to understand this "archaic basis of the mind" that speaks to us in symbolic images expressing our intimate connection with an Otherworld.

# CHAPTER TWO

# THE OTHERWORLD, TRAUMA, AND THE FEAR OF DEATH

An intriguing folk tale from Romania expresses humanity's greatest fear--the fear of death--in a unique way that sheds light on how trauma and the fear of death can trigger an experience of the Otherworld.

The tale, called "The Voice of Death," features a man obsessed with becoming wealthy. After he achieves his goal and amasses a fortune in material goods, he becomes obsessed with finding some place in the world where death doesn't exist so he can live forever in luxury and comfort. He then goes on an epic journey attempting to find a country where no one dies. After much searching, he finally comes upon a place where the people have no conception of death. However, he is told by one of the inhabitants that sometimes a person hears a voice insisting that the person must follow it. Whenever a person hears this voice, he or she wanders out of town and is never seen again. The man is overjoyed to hear of this amazing phenomenon, realizing that, if he wants to live forever, all he has to do is move to this country and ignore the voice if he hears it. So, he moves all of his belongings, along with his wife and children, to this location, confident that he will live until the end of time. After he relocates, he tells his family members about this voice and instructs them to pay no attention to it if they hear it. Unfortunately, one day, while he is enjoying his opulent surroundings, his wife suddenly gets up out of her chair and exclaims, "I'm coming!" and heads for the front door. The man immediately realizes what is happening and tries to restrain his wife, telling her that she must ignore the voice. The wife finally calms down, but then she suddenly sprints to the door, crying "I'm coming!" and runs out of the house and out of town, disappearing forever. The man is crushed over the loss of his wife, but ultimately curses her, calling her foolish for obeying the voice's command. Years later, while he is sitting in a barber's chair having a shave, he too suddenly rises up and then exclaims, "I won't come, do you hear? I won't come!" When the voice beckons him again, he grabs the barber's razor and yells, "I'll teach him to let people alone for the future," and runs off headed for the outskirts of town. The barber chases after him demanding that the man give him back his razor. As the two leave town, a huge pit suddenly materializes in the open countryside and the man tumbles in. The barber sees the massive pit and realizes that this is where all the townspeople who have heard the voice have been led to. He returns to town with his news, and everyone races out of town to see the pit. The pit, however, has vanished, and all they see is the open countryside. After everyone returns to town, the story ends with this final observation: "And from that time the people of the country began to die like ordinary mortals all the world over."[1]

The story could be interpreted as an example of a common folktale motif found in numerous traditions that expresses how people became aware of mortal death. Interpreted from a Freudian perspective, it could illustrate the death drive, which Freud considered the desire to return to the original state of inorganic matter from which life emerged billions of years ago. According to Freud, the death drive, or Thanatos, is the opposite of the life drive, or Eros, the latter expressed as the sexual drive for reproduction which ensures the survival of the species. Thanatos becomes the dominating force for all living creatures in the later stages of life, compelling the living to answer this "voice of death," which cannot be ignored. As Freud stated, "The aim of all life is death."[2]

The way the Romanian story ends indicates that those who were answering the voice of death were following the inherent death drive that cannot be dismissed by ego consciousness in the manner that the man featured in the tale hoped to do. However, in order to appreciate the story's underlying implications, it is important to keep in mind that no one living in that area of the world had any conscious conception of what death is; the people who instinctively followed the compelling voice and disappeared into the pit obviously had no fear of death since death did not exist for them. It was only after the barber saw the man fall into an otherworldly pit that he came to the conclusion that all the other people who had disappeared had been swallowed up into oblivion. It is also crucial to note that, after the townspeople assumed they understood the voice's intent, they no longer heard it, and the miraculous pit never appeared again. People began to die just like everyone else in the world after the finality of death became something other than an instinctual drive that led to an otherworldly pit.

[1] Lang, ed. (1890) 1966: 182-185
[2] Freud (1920) 1989: 46

In numerous traditions with religious implications, people willingly participate in rituals that simulate a descent into the earth, the traditional land of the dead. One such religious ceremony was referred to in Chapter One: the Eleusinian Mysteries. Participants in these mystery rites symbolically descended into the earth and experienced a symbolic death, followed by a resurrection from the dead. The central god figures of these rites were the earth goddess Demeter and her daughter Persephone, the queen of the land of the dead. During the culmination of the rites, participants somehow confronted a representation of Persephone, after which they received her blessing and rose from the dead. Although participants were forbidden to reveal any specific details about the rites of Eleusis to those who had not gone through the ceremony, from the comments made by some of those who were initiated into these secretive rites, it can be assumed that the ceremony was designed to prepare participants about what to expect after their physical deaths. For example, after the Roman statesman Cicero was initiated, he said, "We have been given a reason [by these rites] not only to live in joy, but to die with better hope;"[3] in this context, "hope" refers to a more hopeful fate in the afterlife.

Does the pit featured in the Romanian tale have a similar significance?

An early 20th century folk tale from Hawaii sheds further light upon the significance of the pit. Although the tale appears in a collection of Hawaiian folklore, it is evident that the tale is something other than folklore. It begins with a family gathered around a woman who has recently passed away. As they mourn her passing and prepare her for burial, suddenly the woman takes a deep breath and rises up from her death bed. She then shares with them a story with many similarities to others who have been pronounced dead but suddenly recover:

> I died, as you know. I seemed to leave my body and stand beside it, looking down on what was me. The me that was standing there looked like the form I was looking at, only, I was alive and the other was dead. I gazed at my body for a few minutes, then turned and walked away.[4]

The woman goes on to describe a journey through an area that resembles Kona, emphasizing the beauty of the surroundings and the thousands of happy people populating the expansive countryside. She recognizes some she encounters, while others are strangers, and all of them are like her:

---

[3] Kerenyi (1960) 1991: 14.

[4] Haley: 59.

happy and content with their fate in the land of the dead. The woman feels compelled to walk in a certain direction: "I seemed to be on my way to the volcano,--to Pele's pit,--and could not stop, much as I wanted to do so."[5] The woman walks for many miles until she reaches the area of the volcano. As she begins to approach Pele's pit, the people of this region look at her and tell her that she can't continue: she is not dead yet, and must return to her body. The woman objects. "I cried and tried to stay, but they drove me back, even beating me when I stopped and would not go on. So I was driven over the road I had come, back through all those happy people."[6] As much as she objects, the people in this realm force her to return to her body:

> …I reached my home and stood by my body again. I looked at it and hated it. Was that my body? What a horrid, loathsome thing it was to me now, since I had seen so many beautiful, happy creatures![7]

After the woman finally returns to her body, she ends her tale by stating: "It was cruel to make me come back. My other body was so beautiful, and I was so happy, so happy!"[8]

As it becomes quite obvious, this is not a traditional folk tale but a vivid description of a near-death experience. Such experiences have been reported for millennia from all parts of the world, sharing many of the same characteristics as this Hawaiian example: floating outside one's lifeless form and observing it from an elevated position; wandering away from the body and encountering people known to have passed away; experiencing an exhilarating sense of ecstasy while in this realm; feeling compelled to travel in a certain direction, and in the case of the Hawaiian tale, pulled toward a volcanic pit, while in other cases pulled toward a blinding tunnel of light, with the light producing a sense of exhilaration with each advancing step; and finally, forced to return to one's lifeless body and breathe once again.

This Hawaiian tale emphasizes how the woman is compelled to seek out the volcano, "Pele's pit," a reference to the Hawaiian volcano goddess. Pele shares many characteristics with the underworld goddess Persephone who is sometimes referred to as Brimo, a word from which brimstone is derived; brimstone is a crucial component of volcanic fire.[9] In this regard, the

---

[5] Haley: 60.
[6] Haley: 61.
[7] Haley: 61
[8] Haley: 62
[9] Walker: 118.

Hawaiian tale has similarities not only with the Romanian tale but with the rites of the Eleusinian Mysteries: in all of these examples, people are called to willingly enter a black, all-consuming pit in the earth.

Before I propose an answer to the significance of the pit in the two folk tales, it is helpful to understand what is happening in the brains of individuals who have reported near-death experiences. Neurologist Kevin Nelson has studied dozens of such cases and presented intriguing insights into the workings of the brain during such experiences. First of all, Nelson rightly reports that people reporting near-death experiences are doing just that: they are near death, but not dead. Although the brain might not show activity on any devices to record brain patterns, the brain is still active.

Nelson theorizes that the brain has switched into a mode he refers to as "REM intrusion:" the REM state overpowers a person in a state of near-death crisis. Nelson describes this state as a blending of the REM state of consciousness with a type of lucid dreaming in which a person becomes aware of being in an altered state of consciousness similar to the unconscious dreaming state; this type of awareness increases the intensity of the experience.

As mentioned previously about what happens during the REM state of consciousness, the REM state is when people are most likely to have vivid dreams. Certain parts of the brain are highly active, including the amygdala (one of the brain's key emotional centers), and the hippocampus (the brain's memory center); both of these brain areas are part of the limbic system. The brain stem which regulates basic survival functions is also highly active. Nelson emphasizes that these areas of the brain are less evolutionarily advanced than the human brain's cerebral cortex, responsible for reasoning and problem solving. As he explains, what triggers a near-death experience is the activation of the body's survival instincts, essentially the body's reaction to the most primal of all physical crises: physical death. A person close to death has reduced blood flow to certain parts of the brain which alerts the body to a life-threatening crisis; the brain responds by switching into a REM-type state of consciousness, triggering an emotionally charged and vividly visual experience that the dreamer interprets as real. As Nelson states:

> If dreaming [sometimes] helps prepare waking consciousness for life-and-death struggles, then we should not be astonished if the dream mechanism is activated by a hardwired trigger to REM consciousness in crisis. So it may not be accidental that brain imaging finds that regions activated in

> danger and REM consciousness share the same ancient limbic system. That dreams and danger share this limbic system explains so much about spiritual experience. These amazing moments in our lives are part of and in concert with our survival instincts; they are deeply embedded within us—contained in our existential core.[10]

Nelson refers to the experience of near-death triggering vivid dream images that express the near-death crisis, which relates to a dream theory about nightmares, that such intensely disturbing dreams are actually rehearsal scenarios that help prepare an individual for similar death-threatening situations. Finnish dream researcher Antti Revonsuo, an expert on the study of vividly assaultive nightmares, has theorized that these types of disturbing REM state dreams are the ones most likely to contain scenarios that simulate threats to one's life as rehearsals for dealing with life-and-death situations.[11]

The findings of Nelson and Revonsuo, therefore, imply that near-death experiences in which the body is reacting to a real death crisis, could be preparing the individual for what actually happens after physical death: people are seeing a glimpse of a type of afterlife, an Otherworld that calls to them, compelling them to enter this realm as their bodies experience actual physical death. However, because the body begins to revive after this crisis, the experience ends with images of their returning to their bodies. But, before they revive, they experience images that are the antithesis of a terrifying, assaultive nightmare expressing a physically dangerous threat to their existence. Unlike a nightmare, there is no sense that they should fear and recoil from death: they are not entering a state of oblivion, a return to inorganic lifelessness as Freud's Thanatos theory emphasizes. Instead, they experience ecstasy and revitalization, a sense of wonder and awe within the presence of either a brilliant light, or a dark pit. They are instinctively drawn to it before their bodies begin to revive and they return to waking consciousness.

As the folklore examples from Romania and Hawaii illustrate, along with numerous other examples from those reporting near-death experiences from all over the world, the images from such experiences have similar narrative features. Nelson also refers to this aspect of the experience:

---

[10] Nelson: 216.
[11] Dixit: n.p.

> One characteristic particularly impressed me in our…research subjects' accounts of their near-death experiences. At its very core and center the near-death experience is a *story*….It is often a story with a beginning, middle, and end. Most often, its narrative is about a journey and a return, an old story that…stretches back at least as far as the ancient civilizations in Mesopotamia, Egypt, and Greece, where corpses were ritualistically prepared for their journey into an afterlife.[12]

To a certain degree, the physiological dimension of the near-death experience can explain why people who report such experiences do so in a narrative form: their memory center is active and, coupled with their emotional center, the memories they experience are supercharged with numinous energy. And yet, the stories they relate are more than just personal memories; although they do contain personal and cultural references, they are dominated by archetypal patterns. They follow certain universal motifs emphasizing the archetypal journey to the Otherworld. Because the individuals recover from their brush with death, the journey scenario ends with a return from the Otherworld and revival of the body from the death crisis. In many cases, such as the example of the Hawaiian tale, the return is regrettable after having experienced the bliss and exuberant ecstasy of the Otherworld realm.

Nelson refers to Jung's own near-death experience which Jung included in his autobiography *Memories Dreams Reflections*; Jung's experience occurred after he had a heart attack at the age of sixty-eight. Nelson emphasizes the ecstasy Jung felt and the regret following his return to consciousness, the same reaction reported by the woman protagonist in the Hawaiian tale:

> Jung found himself in space, surveying the earth below—which was "bathed in a gloriously blue light…." He saw oceans, continents, snow-covered mountains, and a temple floating in space. He approached the temple with the certain knowledge that he would encounter a room full of people he knew and meet others who would tell him the meaning of his life. Then his journey took an unexpected turn. His physician, Dr. H….floated up from Europe, where Jung's physical body lay, to deliver a message—he must return. "The moment I heard that," wrote Jung, "the vision ceased." Jung was profoundly disappointed to find himself back on earth and in his body. Yet the experience transformed him….He found it easier to accept "the conditions of existence as I see them and understand them."[13]

---

[12] Nelson: 112-113.

[13] Nelson: 109-110.

Jung's example not only emphasizes the ecstasy of such experiences and the disappointment that follows when the person returns to waking consciousness, but the archetypal narrative triggered by the experience and how this narrative acts to prepare the individual for death, "to accept 'the conditions of existence….'"

As Nelson also mentions, such Otherworld journeys have been recorded by the oldest of our human civilizations. In fact, a story from the Sumerian and Babylonian civilizations, sometimes referred to as the oldest work of literature, features a protagonist who, like the man in the Romanian tale, wants to cheat physical death and live forever. The reason is not because he wants to live in luxury surrounded by material possessions, but because he has watched his best friend die a terrible death and has become traumatized over the reality of mortal death. His terror compels him to wander into uncharted territory in search of the secret to eternal life.

The story, actually an epic poem, is popularly known as *The Epic of Gilgamesh*, named after the poem's protagonist, whom many scholars specializing in ancient Mesopotamian culture believe was an actual Sumerian king. Stories about Gilgamesh were first fashioned by the Sumerians and later embellished and expanded upon for over a thousand years by various Sumerian, Assyrian, and Babylonian scribes. The most well-known version of the epic is credited to a Babylonian poet, described as an exorcist-priest, whose name was Sin-leqi-unninni. His version is referred to by the first line of the epic poem: "The One Who Saw the Abyss,"[14] also translated as "He Who Saw the Deep,"[15] or "He Who Has Seen Everything."[16]

The poem's first line and its references to Gilgamesh having seen the abyss, the deep, or everything, gives a crucial clue to the epic's main intent: it is an elaborate, embellished description of a near-death or trance experience comparable to a religious or mystical experience. Kevin Nelson underscores the relationship the poem's first line has when he refers to key words that people have used to describe their own otherworldly near-death experiences: "The mystical epiphany…varies from culture to culture. Words used to describe it include: boundless, ceaseless, bottomless,

[14] Gardner and Maier: 1.
[15] George: 1.
[16] Kovacs: 3.

nothingness, fathomless, infinite, empty, void, barren, abyss, abysmal, and absolute."[17]

The interpretation of the poem as an elaborate description of a near-death or mystical experience is actually not a popular one.[18] Many consider the poem to be about the exploits of a vainglorious king who went on a futile epic journey to find the secret of eternal life and failed to do so. However, what many scholars fail to take into consideration is that the historical Sumerian king known as Gilgamesh was the central figure of a religious cult that flourished throughout ancient Mesopotamia for nearly two thousand years before the ancient Babylonian civilization fell into dismay and disorder in sixth century B.C.[19] In other words, the religious cult inspired the poem.

With the destruction of Babylon, the cult of Gilgamesh apparently died with it. The poem became lost as well, until amateur British archeologists digging around Nineveh in the mid-19th century unearthed fragments of it and pieced it together again. After it was translated, the misinterpretation of the poem began in earnest. Few translators took into account the influence of the religious cult upon the poem, even though scholars were aware that King Gilgamesh became the god of the underworld after he died, responsible for judging the dead in the Otherworld. The poet Sin-leqi-unninni was probably a priest devoted to the cult of Gilgamesh since he allegedly lived in the same city over which King Gilgamesh ruled, the city of Uruk, the ancient name for Iraq.[20]

Like numerous other accounts of a near-death or mystical experience, Gilgamesh's own experience is presented as an epic journey to the Otherworld as the realm of death, rebirth and immortality. And like all near-death experiences, Gilgamesh is allowed a glimpse of the realm that exists after mortal death before returning to the ordinary realm of consciousness. As mentioned previously, his journey begins when he sees his best friend die and then becomes terrified of mortal death. Gilgamesh panics over the thought that he will die too and end up like his friend, a rotting corpse. In other words, Gilgamesh assumes that death is the finality of all life, essentially echoing Freud's conception of Thanatos: after death, we return to an inorganic state of lifeless oblivion.

---

[17] Nelson: 227.
[18] Kline 2016: 24-36.
[19] Moran: ix.
[20] Kovacs: xxi.

Gilgamesh journeys away from the city he rules into uncharted territory and, at one point, encounters an imposing tunnel carved through a mountain and guarded by creatures who appear half-human, half-scorpion. The scorpion men allow Gilgamesh to enter the tunnel and he walks for league upon league in total darkness, crying out in terror as he is consumed by the terrible void. But, then:

> After nine leagues, he felt the north wind on his face, but the darkness was [still] thick and there was no light, he could see nothing ahead and nothing behind him. After ten leagues the end was near. After eleven leagues the dawn light appeared. After twelve leagues the sun streamed out. There was the garden of the gods; all round him stood bushes bearing gems…beautiful to look at; lapis lazuli leaves hung thick with fruit, sweet to see…hematite and rare stones, agate, and pearls from out of the sea.[21]

The description of Gilgamesh traveling through a dark tunnel and encountering a brilliant light that leads to a fabulous "garden of the gods" has similarities to those who have had near-death experiences and reported being drawn to a splendid light that infuses them with an exhilarating sense of having encountered a god-like power.

Later on, Gilgamesh finally reaches the land of immortality where a man and his wife live forever after having been given the gift of immortality by the gods. Gilgamesh is anxious to know how this couple achieved immortality so he too can experience it. The man, whose name is Utnapishtim, at first ridicules Gilgamesh for believing that he too could achieve immortality. He tests Gilgamesh's potential by commanding him to stay awake for a week. Gilgamesh fails the test, but the test itself reflects a technique that has been used by members of traditional cultures and by shamans to encourage otherworldly hallucinations and visions: through sleep deprivation and fasting. After Gilgamesh fails the sleep deprivation test, Utnapishtim gives him another way to experience a sense of immortality within the mortal realm, telling him to dive into the deepest part of the ocean—the abyss—and pick a branch from a prickly plant that, if eaten, will return him to a youthful state. Gilgamesh follows the immortal man's orders by attaching stones to his feet so he can sink down into the abyss where he plucks a branch from this prickly plant, then ascends again to dry land.

[21] Sandars: 99-100.

It is this scene that gives the epic its original name: "The One Who Saw the Abyss" or "the Deep," or "Everything." Gilgamesh has experienced the terror of near death and returned with a symbol representing rejuvenation and rebirth since the branch he returns with is a sprig from the Tree of Life which, according to Mesopotamian religion, grows in the abyss. The abyss was also the source of fresh waters—essentially the source of life--as well as the home of the god Enki or Ea, known as the god of wisdom.[22] The Mesopotamian concept of the abyss as the source of life where the god of wisdom resides is a potent symbol of the wisdom inherent in the archetypal dimension of the collective unconscious.

After Gilgamesh retrieves a branch of the plant, he gives the plant the name, "The Old Man Will Be Made Young."[23] According to scholars familiar with Mesopotamian culture and language, the plant's name corresponds to Gilgamesh's own name.[24] The implication is that the name "Gilgamesh" was probably not the real name of the Sumerian king who ruled ancient Uruk. It was one given to him after he became a religious cult figure: the underworld judge of the dead with the power to bestow eternal youth and vitality to those he deemed worthy to live forever in an Otherworld paradise, referred to as Dilmun, the realm of the divine couple Utnapishtim and his wife.[25]

Gilgamesh ultimately loses his plant before he returns to Uruk; like other symbols representing the Tree of Life, this one is guarded by a serpent. The serpent appears while Gilgamesh is resting; it eats the plant, after which it sloughs its skin and rejuvenates itself, illustrating the plant's symbolic significance and connection to Gilgamesh's name: the old will be made young. Although it appears that Gilgamesh's own journey to the Otherworld has ended in failure, his exploits illustrate features of the Otherworld and, perhaps, some of the rituals and techniques used by cult members devoted to him to experience an altered state of reality with strong similarities to the near-death experience.

The epic also helps clarify the significance of the dark pits featured in the Hawaiian and Romanian tales. The protagonists in these tales are instinctively drawn to the pit after experiencing near death or hearing the voice of death, compelling them to fall into this pit in order to experience a

---

[22] Sandars: 120.
[23] Gardner and Maier: 249.
[24] Kovacs: xxvii.
[25] Sandars: 97.

rebirth in the Otherworld, the same intent associated with such religious practices as the Eleusinian Mysteries. Although there is not much known about what rituals or practices were associated with the cult of Gilgamesh, the epic is infused with clues pertaining to its main intent: to give participants an experience of immortality within the mortal realm, an experience that prepared them for a better fate in the Otherworld, the same intent of the Eleusinian Mysteries.

What all of these stories indicate—and what the research of neurologist Kevin Nelson affirms--is that trauma and the fear of death trigger an instinctual reaction within us that results in the experience of an archetypal pattern illustrating a journey to, and encounter with, a powerful, life-affirming, god-like energy: the source of life. This encounter infuses the individual not only with new life but a profound view of the continuance of life after death.

As previously stated, other tales with similar Otherworld journey themes associated with trauma and death are found in cultures throughout the world. A potent example is a Native American tale called "In the Land of Souls." The tale begins with the marriage between a young chief and a beautiful maiden who, on their wedding day, falls ill and dies soon afterwards. The chief is devastated by her death and becomes obsessed with journeying to the land of souls to be with her. One can easily recognize the connection the beginning of this tale has with *The Epic of Gilgamesh*: seeing a loved one die throws a person who has a consuming love for the deceased into a state of panic and despair over the loss; the result is activation of the unconscious, triggering the experience of an archetypal journey to the Otherworld.

The chief in this tale is eager to begin his journey, but is first confused over which way to go since the way to the spirit world is shrouded in mystery. After consulting with the elders of his tribe, he is encouraged to proceed south, so on this advice he starts walking, accompanied by his faithful dog. After several days, he finds a wigwam situated on the top of a mountain. An old man stands at the wigwam's entrance and welcomes the chief, saying he was expecting the chief's arrival since the soul of his recently deceased wife had just passed this way. The old man tells the chief to rest a while, but the chief is too eager to see his wife again. So the old man points toward an open plain and tells him:

> "Look…at the water which lies far out yonder, and the plains which stretch beyond. That is the Land of Souls, but no man enters it without leaving his body behind him. So, lay down your body here; your bow and arrows, your

> skin and your dog. They shall be kept for you safely." Then he turned away, and the young chief, light as air, seemed hardly to touch the ground; and as he flew along the scents grew sweeter and the flowers more beautiful, while the animals rubbed their noses against him, instead of hiding as he approached, and birds circled round him, and fishes lifted up their heads and looked as he went by. Very soon he noticed with wonder, that neither rocks nor trees barred his path. He passed through them without knowing it, for indeed, they were not rocks and trees at all, but only the souls of them; for this was the Land of Shadows.[26]

The description of the chief leaving his physical body and floating effortlessly toward the "land of shadows" mirrors accounts of those who have reported out-of-body experiences while in a near-death crisis. The description also has strong parallels with the shamanic visionary trance-flight to the Otherworld.

The chief then floats across the wide plain to the shores of a lake where he finds a canoe. He sets down in the canoe and begins paddling toward an island in the middle of the lake. As he paddles, another canoe appears, and in it is his wife. Both of them head for the island, dodging the remains of corpses floating all around them in the turbulent water. In many tales of a journey to the land of the dead, visitors must cross a body of water to reach their destination. Gilgamesh, for example, also had to cross a body of water that was lethal to the touch before he could reach the land of Dilmun and Utnapishtim.

The chief and his bride are successful in their crossing of this lethal body of water, and reach the island where they wander together in splendor, marveling at all the beauty and vibrancy of this realm. While he is there, the chief feels no hunger or thirst and has no thoughts of hunting, war, or strife. The chief is content to stay forever in this land, but then hears a voice calling to him which he realizes is the "Master of Life." The voice tells him:

> "Return whither you came, for I have work for you to do, and your people need you, and for many years you shall rule over them. At the gate my messenger awaits you, and you shall take again your body which you left behind, and he will show you what you are to do. Listen to him, and have patience, and in time to come you shall rejoin her whom you must now leave, for she is accepted, and will remain ever young and beautiful, as when I called her hence…."[27]

---

[26] Lang, ed. (1894) 1966: 158.
[27] Lang, ed. (1894) 1966: 154.

The story ends with the description of the chief returning to his physical body after having his out-of-body journey to the land of souls, echoing the culmination of the archetypal pattern associated with such experiences.

The story not only has similarities with the Hawaiian tale and the *Epic of Gilgamesh*, but also the Greek myth of Orpheus and Eurydice. In that myth, the great poet/musician Orpheus falls in love and marries the beautiful maiden Eurydice. After an elaborate wedding ceremony followed by an exuberant wedding celebration, Eurydice's beauty inflames the desires of a beekeeper called Aristaeus who pursues her through a meadow until she steps on a serpent, is fatally bitten, and dies. Orpheus is overcome with grief and seeks out an entrance to the land of the dead so he can descend and return his bride to the land of the living. As he descends, he plays upon his lyre and charms all of the inhabitants of the dead, including Hades, lord of the underworld, and his wife Persephone. They agree to allow Orpheus to return to the upper realm with Eurydice but on the condition that he must not look at her until they are out of the land of the dead. Orpheus agrees to the condition, but upon reaching the exit from the underworld, he looks back to see if Eurydice is really following him. At that moment, she turns back into the dark underworld realm, never to return.

Although this version of the Orpheus/Eurydice myth is the most well-known, there are other versions in which Orpheus is successful in rescuing his bride from the underworld.[28] In any case, the motif of descending into the underworld to rescue a recently deceased loved one is widespread. A Native American tale from the Zuni tribe, called "The Spirit-Bride,"[29] for example, blends details found in the Orpheus myth and the "Land of Souls" Native American tale; all of these types of underworld journeys begin as a result of grief and turmoil over the loss of a loved one, compelling the survivor to seek out his lost love in the land of the dead.

The shamanic connection with these tales is extreme, especially when one takes into consideration the tradition of the *ayami* figure, the shaman's spirit bride or lover from whom he learns the secrets about the Otherworld while in a trance state.[30] Orpheus' relationship with Eurydice can be interpreted as a shaman's relationship with a spirit bride since Orpheus was not only considered a poet and musician but a priest who learned secrets of the Otherworld and founded a religious organization based upon his

---

[28] Kerenyi (1959) 1977: 281-284.
[29] Yolen, ed.: 423-427.
[30] Eliade (1951) 2004: 72.

otherworldly experiences; the Orphic tradition was similar to the mystery religion tradition of which the Eleusinian Mysteries were the most well-known.

A personal dream experience illustrates how the fear of death can influence a nightmare infused with the underworld journey motif featuring a spirit bride figure. Since the dream was quite elaborate, I present it here in an abbreviated form:

> My wife and I are driving around as if we are on vacation and end up at what appears to be an amusement park. After parking our car in a multi-level parking structure, we wander through the expansive amusement park area, finding elaborately constructed rides and attractions with satanic themes. It doesn't take long for us to realize that the park is run by Satanists who practice human sacrifice. They use unsuspecting people they've lured into the park as their sacrificial victims. We then attempt to leave the park but can't find the parking structure. As we wander around looking for our car, I tell my wife that we must not let anyone know we aren't Satanists to avoid becoming victims of human sacrifice. The tension and anxiety caused over this concern becomes nearly unbearable as we continue to progress through the labyrinthine park.
>
> At one point, we come upon a huge, roller coaster-type structure decorated with demons and Satan in the middle seated on a throne. Continuing to progress through the park, we're forced at one point to swim across a bubbling, hot swimming pool with glowing, bluish, chunk-like water. After we swim across, we have to shed some of our clothes because they've been damaged by the hot pool water, so we end up half naked in the encroaching darkness. Throughout the park are cabins, and when I decide to investigate one of them, I find a naked woman eating one of the captured visitors, while a man stands over a bed and strangles a young boy. I also notice bloody body parts in other areas of the cabin. As we continue to search for a way out of the park, we end up treading through what we believe is a parking structure but turns out to be a torture chamber filled with nooks devoted to various torture methods. The most gruesome scene features a Satanist fitting a bear claw-looking device over a victim's head, then clamping it down so the victim's face is shredded, after which the Satanist twists the trap so the victim is decapitated.
>
> We ultimately find ourselves in the park's gift shop and I'm surprised to find Christian icons for sale, one of which features a large image of the face of Christ. My wife also finds an annex to the shop with a bubbling hot tub-type pool. Unlike the other pool we had to swim across, this one is filled with dark water and infused with fragrant perfumes and soapy bubbles and surrounded by flickering candles. My wife decides to enter the tub and

> disrobes completely. I'm stunned by her appearance: although both of us are actually well advanced in middle-age, she appears as a youthful, nubile, honey-blonde pin up girl. She enters the pool briefly and frolics in thigh-deep water. I get aroused, undress, and we begin to make love by the pool, even though I'm still worried over being found out that we aren't Satanists and could end up being dismembered and eaten.

This dream was so nightmarish, I awoke from it twice and tried clearing my head of the horrific images of torture and dismemberment before attempting to return to sleep; however, each time I drifted off, the dream picked up from where it left off. It was as if I were being forced to progress through this terrifying journey through a hellish theme park until my wife and I reached the secluded pool where her transformation into a nubile nymph occurred and we made love.

It was only after making a great effort to understand why I would have such a terrifying dream that I realized its true intent. For months before having the dream, I had been receiving steady reports from my two sisters about the failing health of our ninety year-old mother. Since I lived thousands of miles away from my sisters and mother, I struggled to keep from falling into complete despair over my mother's fate. I was terrified of the thought of her dying before I could see her once more and tell her how much I loved her. The fear over losing my mother triggered this horrific dream of a visit to the underworld inhabited by cannibalistic Satanists. As I mentioned, the dream's overwhelming sense of terror was so real, it woke me up twice. However, the dream's ending revealed its true intent.

In numerous traditions, tales, and myths—for example *The Epic of Gilgamesh,* Virgil's *Aeneid*, and Dante's *Divine Comedy* (Fig. 2-1)[31]--one must journey through the land of the dead in order to reach Dilmun, the Elysian Fields, Heavenly Paradise: the realm of rebirth, rejuvenation, and resurrection. Also, scenes of torture, cannibalism and dismemberment are found in the initiatory dreams of potential shamans before they experience a rebirth, and my dream had these same shamanic motifs: I was a witness to numerous scenes of cannibalistic torture and dismemberment before experiencing an exhilarating sense of rejuvenation by making love beside a fragrant pool with my wife who now appeared to me as a youthful and vibrant spirit bride; the old had become young again.

[31] Creative Commons.

Figure 2-1: A scene from Dante's *Divine Comedy* by artist Gustav Dore in which Dante reaches the Heavenly sphere, accompanied by his "spirit bride" Beatrice, after traversing through Hell. The Heavenly sphere resembles a tunnel of light, mirroring reports of near-death experiences. (Creative Commons)

Our rejuvenating experience occurred next to a gift shop featuring Christian icons, most significantly an image of Christ who, according to his legions of followers, went through torturous extremes that led to a resurrection from the dead, an experience that inspired a religious organization that has thrived for over two thousand years and has continued to inspire many to believe in the reality of an Otherworld existence.

Although the dream was truly nightmarish, its message finally became clear: the journey through the underworld leads to the realm of rebirth, a message that I had to experience in all its terrifying, ecstatic intensity in order to better deal with the trauma that comes from the fear of losing a loved one. This nightmarish experience underscores not only the intensity and power of dreams with strong archetypal content, but the connection that nightmares have with preparing one for potential threats and crises in one's life, underscoring the findings of dream researcher Antti Revonsuo in his studies of these types of intensely assaultive dreams.

A film that recreates the nightmarish fear of death leading to an Otherworld journey filled with terror, horror, and finally redemption and peace is *Jacob's Ladder*, released in 1990. The film begins in Vietnam in the early 1970s. Jacob Singer (Tim Robbins) is a U.S. soldier relaxing with the members of his division when it appears that they are being attacked by Viet Cong troops. However, the behavior of his comrades is bizarre: with no enemy in sight, many begin screaming and raging about as they fire randomly into the surrounding jungle while others appear to be having seizures as they lie on the ground in a drooling stupor. Jacob panics and runs into the jungle where he ends up face to face with a fellow soldier who stabs him in the belly with his bayonet.

The scene then abruptly shifts to Jacob waking up on a New York subway train. Apparently, the Vietnam scene was a nightmarish flashback to an incident that happened to him years ago. Jacob is dressed as a postman with an open book of Camus' *The Stranger* on his lap. He gazes around and notices two unusual-looking passengers, one of whom is a homeless man asleep in a corner. Before Jacob exists the train, he catches a glimpse of a thick, reptilian appendage peeking out of the folds of the homeless man's pants.

The opening scenes give the viewer a clue to what is happening to Jacob. The Vietnam incident actually presents his impending death. During the frenzy that erupted among his fellow soldiers, he was fatally stabbed by one of them, and is now in a death crisis. Other subsequent scenes taking place in Vietnam show him being loaded on a helicopter and transported to a military hospital where doctors frantically operate on him to save his life. As Jacob dies, he has visions of his past life as a literature professor with his wife and three children, one of whom dies in a tragic bicycling accident. In other scenes that are influenced by his struggles to stay alive, he is divorced from his wife, working as a postman and living with Jezzie (Elizabeth Pena), a sexy temptress who also works at the post office. The scenes with Jezzie become increasingly horrific as Jacob slowly dies. At a party scene with her, he sees many guests with reptilian features, including Jezzie. During this scene, a woman who playfully gives palm readings looks at Jacob's hand and says he has no lifeline, telling him he's already dead.

Jacob suffers a panic attack at the party, then collapses and suddenly comes down with a raging fever, reflective of the fever he is experiencing as military doctors struggle to save his life. The operating scenes morph into nightmares with strong associations of being tortured by demons from Hell. In the film's most horrific scene, Jacob is rolled on a gurney through a filthy hospital strewn with dismembered body parts to an operating room populated by demon surgeons who tell him to give up and die. The surgeons perform torturous procedures on him as he screams in agony. Jacob is rescued from this nightmarish hospital by Louis (Danny Aielo), a chiropractor friend of his. Louis is actually an angel, who, in an earlier scene, tells Jacob what is happening to him. Referring to the 13th century German theologian/mystic Meister Eckhart, he tells Jacob:

> The only thing that burns in hell is the part of you that won't let go of life, your memories, your attachments. They burn them all away. They're freeing your soul. So…if you're frightened of dying and you're holding on, you'll see devils tearing your life away. But, if you've made your peace, then the devils are really angels freeing you from the Earth. It's just a matter of how you look at it, that's all.[32]

The reason why Jacob is holding on to life is because he wants to understand why his fellow soldiers suddenly went berserk and committed acts of self-destruction. His visions of journeying through a hellish New York landscape populated by demons trying to kill him ultimately give him an answer. In his delirium, he finds out from a sympathetic fellow soldier that he and his comrades were given an experimental drug called the Ladder, designed to make them more aggressive in combat. Instead, the drug made them raging monsters. After Jacob hears this, he returns to the residence where he lived with his wife and children. When he arrives, he finds his youngest son, the one who died in the bicycle accident, sitting at the base of a stairway. The son takes him by the hand and leads him upstairs into a bright light. The film's final scene is of Jacob lying dead on a military operating table with a beatific smile on his face. One of the surgeons who operated on him comments, "Looks kind of peaceful. Put up a hell of a fight though."

Like my dream of a journey through a hellish amusement park that leads to an ecstatic realm of rebirth, the film successfully captures the terrors involved when a person is faced with death but ultimately finds peace and guidance from a youthful figure symbolizing new vitality and life within

[32] Lyne, dir. and Rubin, screenwriter: Carolco/Tristar Pictures.

this otherworldly realm that lies beyond physical death. It also has relevance to people who have experienced a near-death crisis and had visions of meeting dead friends and relatives as they are pulled to a brilliant light. The film's scenes of Jacob apparently envisioning a future life with Jezzie in a hellish landscape and encountering someone who can tell him the truth about what happened to him and his fellow soldiers has a relationship with Jung's ideas about prospective dreams: in his agonized state, Jacob's psyche fashions an answer based upon his near-death condition and the demonic acts of his comrades.

Jacob's psyche gives the experimental drug a name that reflects the film's title and also relates to his own name, both of which refer to one of the most astonishing examples of an Otherworld experience ever recorded, a visionary experience that led to the establishment of a religious shrine. In Genesis 27-28, Jacob, the son of the Jewish patriarch Isaac, runs away from his father after he betrays him and his older brother Esau, believing his brother will kill him if he stays home. Stopping to rest, he lies down, places a stone under his head for a pillow, and has a dream:

> …he saw a stairway resting on the earth, with its top reaching to heaven, and the angels of God were ascending and descending on it. There above it stood the Lord, and he said: "I am the Lord, the God of your father Abraham and the God of Isaac. I will give you and your descendants the land on which you are lying….All peoples on earth will be blessed through you and your offspring. I am with you and will watch over you wherever you go, and I will bring you back to this land. I will not leave you until I have done what I have promised you." When Jacob awoke from his sleep, he thought, "Surely the Lord is in this place, and I was not aware of it." He was afraid and said, "How awesome is this place! This is none other than the house of God; this is the gate of heaven." Early the next morning Jacob took the stone he had placed under his head and set it up as a pillar and poured oil on top of it. He called that place Bethel ["house of God"] though the city used to be called Luz. Then Jacob made a vow, saying, "If God will be with me and will watch over me on this journey I am taking and will give me food to eat and clothes to wear so that I return safely to my father's household, then the Lord will be my God and this stone that I have set up as a pillar will be God's house…." (Genesis 28: 12-22, NIV version)

The Bible is filled with visionary experiences, and the dream of Jacob experiencing the vision of a stairway or ladder reaching up to heaven with angels traversing it and God seated on a throne at the ladder's pinnacle is one of the most astounding examples of a vivid dream triggered by trauma and the fear of death. The image of Jacob's ladder (Fig. 2-2)[33] has relevance to the tunnel of light image found in so many accounts of a near-death experience. The example also has relevance to dreams and visions that inspire religious awe, a blending of terror, astonishment, and humbleness which in many cases leads to a firmer belief in an Otherworld afterlife and sometimes the establishment of a religious organization based upon the experience.

Figure 2-2: Artist Gustav Dore's rendition of Jacob's dream of a ladder or stairway traversed by angels with God seated at the ladder's pinnacle. (Creative Commons)

Perhaps the best film featuring a near-death experience that ultimately inspires a following tinged with religious awe, is *Resurrection*, released in 1980. The protagonist is Edna Mae McCauley (Ellen Burstyn) who, at the beginning of the film, buys a new car for her husband Joe (Jeffrey DeMunn) for a birthday present. As the two of them enjoy the new gift by driving around the Southern California coastline, Edna Mae suddenly alerts Joe to

[33] Creative Commons.

a young boy on a skateboard zooming across the highway in front of them. Joe swerves to miss the boy and the car careens off the road and over a cliff, crashing on the rocky coastline below. In that instant, Edna Mae experiences a vision of being surrounded by an exuberant crowd of people urging her on to an intense tunnel of light (Fig. 2-3).[34] As she approaches the light, she is suddenly pulled back and wakes up in a hospital severely bandaged and hooked up to machines monitoring her vital functions. She eventually learns that Joe was killed in the car crash and she has suffered irreparable damage to her spinal cord leaving her paralyzed from the waist down. She will be confined to a wheelchair for the rest of her life. Edna Mae is devastated by the news and sinks into a depression.

Figure 2-3: The tunnel of light in *Resurrection*, 1980. (Creative Commons)

Not long afterwards, she is visited by her father (Roberts Blossom) with whom she has been estranged for years. He invites her to come back to their home in rural Kansas where she can stay in a modest bungalow in the back of the house and recover. Even though she still seethes with animosity over her father's cold, unloving attitude toward her when she was growing up, she agrees to return home. At one point as they travel back to Kansas, they stop at the "Last Chance" gas station in the middle of the Southwestern desert run by Esco Brown (Richard Farnsworth), a crusty old eccentric eager to show them some of the curiosities he has collected over the years. Edna

[34] Creative Commons.

Mae is charmed, but her father calls him a crazy old coot, and after filling up with gas, they continue their drive to Kansas.

Upon reaching their home town, Edna Mae is welcomed by a crowd of friends and relatives, one of whom is her grandmother Pearl (Eva LeGallienne) whose compassionate demeanor is the antithesis of her father's. Pearl shows Edna Mae some old photos of family and friends, and Edna Mae is shocked to see people from the vision she experienced after the accident, all of whom have passed away. Later, at a family gathering in her honor, a young girl who suffers from hemophilia suddenly begins bleeding profusely from her nose. As others panic and call for the local doctor, Edna Mae takes the girl into her lap, insisting it's just a little nosebleed. She touches the girl's nose and wipes up the blood. The bleeding suddenly stops. The crowd is amazed. Grandma Pearl touches Edna Mae's hands and finds them burning with heat. She then tells Edna Mae of a woman who lived a while ago; the woman suffered from pneumonia and was pronounced dead, but then suddenly came back to life. Like Edna Mae, she spoke of being pulled toward a brilliant light before she recovered. After that brush with death, she began to heal people by laying her hands upon them.

Intrigued by this story, Edna Mae decides to try to heal herself by massaging her paralyzed legs with her hands. Over the next several weeks, she continues to massage her legs until finally she begins to feel circulation returning to them. More weeks pass, and one day Edna Mae invites some of her relatives to watch her rise up out of her wheel chair and walk. Word begins to spread across the town and surrounding areas that Edna Mae has the power to heal those inflicted with severe physical illnesses. Crowds begin to assemble with many coming forward to have Edna Mae lay her hands upon them.

During one of these meetings, a local fundamentalist preacher (Richard Hamilton) denounces her as the antichrist since she doesn't consider her healing powers to come from a Christian God. The reverend has a son, Cal Carpenter (Sam Shepard), a rebellious hell raiser and womanizer. One evening, Cal is brought to Edna Mae in the back of a truck, drunk to the point of unconsciousness and bleeding profusely from a knife wound suffered in a bar brawl. Edna Mae presses down upon his wound and stops the bleeding. After Cal heals from the wound, he visits Edna Mae with the intention of not only thanking her for saving his life, but also to seduce her. Edna Mae at first resists his aggressive seduction attempts, but ultimately succumbs to his rebellious charms, an act that enrages her father who calls her a whore and tells her to leave her bungalow.

Edna Mae leaves with Cal, and journeys to a research center where she has been invited to be tested by a couple that has witnessed her healing powers. One of the tasks they give her is to attempt to heal a woman suffering from a severe degenerative disorder that has deformed her legs and arms and resulted in uncontrollable spasmodic twitches. Edna Mae envelopes the woman in her arms and, to the shock of Cal and the rest of the observers, takes on the deformities and twitches exhibited by the woman until the woman is completely cured (Fig. 2.4).[35] Afterwards, Edna Mae's body assumes her normal physical condition, but she falls into a coma. While in her comatose state, she has a vision of her father being engulfed by the bright tunnel of light, and when she finally comes out of her coma, she learns that her father has suffered a stroke and is on the verge of dying. Returning home, she first rails against her father's heartlessness, but then she tells him of her own experiences with dying, trying to comfort and reassure him that death does not mean the end of life. Days later, in Edna Mae's presence, he begins to cry out in wonder over a brilliant light overtaking him, then passes away.

Edna Mae then continues to invite people to come to her for healing, telling them she has no idea what the source of her power is, only that she shares it with them in the name of love. Cal has been visibly shaken by her amazing powers. Although he says he has rejected his father's hellfire and brimstone fundamentalist Christian teachings, because Edna Mae refuses to name the source of her power as coming from a Christian conception of God, he too begins to view her as the antichrist. He refuses to sleep with her anymore, then falls into a state of delusion, at one point quoting passages from the Book of Revelation as he methodically loads a rifle. During one of Edna Mae's healing sessions, he rides a motorcycle into the crowd gathered around her, screaming out Biblical passages and wielding his rifle. Before losing control of the motorcycle, he shoots Edna Mae. Fortunately, Edna Mae has only been wounded. While she recovers from her wound, she decides to leave her hometown once again. With no destination in mind, she drives off, accompanied by a stray dog that has befriended her.

---

[35] Creative Commons.

Figure 2-4: Edna Mae (Ellen Burstyn) cures a severely disabled woman with her healing touch in *Resurrection*, 1980. (Creative Commons)

The film concludes with a scene taking place at the "Last Chance" gas station once owned by the crazy old coot Esco Brown, but now run by Edna Mae who appears much older, her wildly flowing hair streaked with gray. When a motorhome pulls up, she mumbles incoherently to herself as she services a man and woman and their young son who appears emaciated and sickly. She asks about the boy and finds out he has cancer and only a few months to live; his parents decided to take this road trip and show him parts of the country before he dies. In the movie's final scene, Edna Mae asks for a hug from the boy. She takes him into his arms and presses him close to her body, gently massaging his back, then stares knowingly at the boy and his parents as they prepare to drive off[36] (Fig. 2.5).[37]

[36] Petrie, dir.: Universal Pictures.

[37] Creative Commons.

Figure 2-5: Edna Mae (Ellen Burstyn) cures a boy dying from cancer by embracing him with her healing hands in the final scenes from *Resurrection*, 1980. (Creative Commons)

*Resurrection* is essentially a celebration of a power that comes from the Otherworld and infuses someone who has been exposed to this power during a near-death experience. Edna Mae is like a shaman: she has journeyed to the Otherworld and absorbed its power. Shamans are sometimes called wounded healers since they have healed themselves from the trauma they experienced from early visions of being dismembered and eaten by demons; these horrible visions of death are followed by the experience of being reformulated, reanimated, and brought back to life, endowed with new curative powers and insights into the realm of death. Edna Mae illustrates the self-healing power she has been endowed with by first healing her body from the effects of the car crash that killed her husband, then using this power to heal others in the name of love. In this regard, she embodies the true message of Christ who also healed in the name of a god who loves and forgives as opposed to a god who torments sinners in an everlasting pit of hellfire.

As so many other stories about journeys to the Otherworld illustrate, most significantly *The Epic of Gilgamesh, Resurrection* dramatically underscores the idea that the Otherworld is the source of life. People who have been exposed to this life source--which appears to some as a brilliant light, to others as a dark pit in the Earth, and to others as the deepest part of a watery abyss--sometimes bring back with them elements of this power.

Their journey to, and return from, death's doorstep transforms them, heals them from their trauma, and inspires them to see death as not the end of life but a return to life's primeval source. They are like Gilgamesh: they have seen the source of everything. And with this experience, they more readily accept the "conditions of existence:" they are prepared to die with a better hope for some type of a continuance of life in an Otherworld that lies beyond physical death.

# CHAPTER THREE

# THE OTHERWORLD AND ANIMISM

When she was in her mid-teens, acclaimed journalist Barbara Ehrenreich began keeping a personal journal chronicling her quest to find out the meaning of existence or the "search for the truth about everything."[1] Writing about the contents of the journal as an adult, Ehrenreich admits that many entries are unsophisticated and solipsistic observations about the workings of the universe from an adolescent's nebulous grasp of scientific and religious viewpoints and how her growing up in a household full of hardcore atheists colored her views. The reason Ehrenreich held onto the journal all of her life was because it contained references to an inexplicable incident that occurred when she was a teenager, one that haunted her for decades and compelled her to reexamine the incident from a more informed adult perspective.

The incident occurred in 1959 when she was seventeen and on a road trip with friends in Northern California's Lone Pine area. Just prior to the incident, Ehrenreich had a disturbing dream:

> The dream consisted of a single image: the human brain, my brain in fact, projected onto a screen in what appeared to be a classroom. There it was—the whole thing—a densely corrugated bulb attached to a stem. And this is what I expected to contain the universe in? Just in case the message wasn't clear enough, there was a caption or maybe a voice-over saying: This is what you are—a sac of tissue enclosed in membrane, a *thing* like anything else.[2]

The dream brain appeared pink instead of a gray mass, which further unnerved her since it reminded her of her vagina: "So this is what I was—not just a thing, an object, an intersection of particles in motion—but a big, dumb, multilobed reproductive apparatus, destined to have babies and die,

---

[1] Ehrenreich. This phrase is part of the subtitle of the book that examines her teenage experiences.
[2] Ehrenreich: 109.

exactly like everyone else."[3] The dream was essentially presenting to her a fundamental atheistic view of life, that life is a cosmic accident with no purpose other than to reproduce and ensure the survival of the species, reducing sexuality to a biological drive that provides no inherent answer to the meaning of existence.

After having the dream, Ehrenreich continued to enjoy her road trip, stopping in the Mammoth Mountain area to ski and explore the surrounding environs. After an exhausting day, the group started to drive home to Los Angeles, but after making it to Lone Pine in the middle of the night, they decided to park by the side of the road and sleep in the car before continuing home. Just before dawn, after a fitful night's sleep, still exhausted from the previous day's events and having not eaten anything of substance for nearly two days, Ehrenreich awoke, crept out of the car, and went for a walk headed for the downtown Lone Pine area. Upon reaching the small town and finding it nearly deserted, Ehrenreich began feeling symptoms of dissociation, estranged from her surroundings and her sense of self-identity. At that moment, from out of nowhere, "I found whatever I had been looking for…or perhaps, given my mental passivity at the moment, whatever had been looking for me."[4]

Ehrenreich admits that what happened to her remained inexplicable, impossible to fully describe, which is why she attempted to dismiss the event for years as some sort of mental breakdown. Attempting to describe it decades later, she compared it to:

> …one image, handed down over the centuries…and that is the image of fire, as in the "burning bush." At some point in my predawn walk…the world flamed into life….It was a furious encounter with a living substance that was coming at me through all things at once, and one reason for the terrible wordlessness of the experience is that you cannot observe fire really closely without becoming part of it. Whether you start as a twig or a gorgeous tapestry, you will be recruited into the flame and made indistinguishable from the rest of the blaze….I knew that the heavens had opened and poured into me, and I into them, but there was no way to describe it, even to myself. As for trying to tell anyone else…what would I have said? That I had been savaged by a flock of invisible angels—lifted up in a glorious flutter of

[3] Ehrenreich: 110

[4] Ehrenreich: 115.

> iridescent feathers, then mauled, emptied of all intense and purposes, and pretty much left for dead?[5]

Ehrenreich's experience left her questioning her sanity. Her teenage quest to find a meaning to existence had resulted in what could be described as a violation, a rape of the senses that left her feeling savaged, penetrated and left for dead by an otherworldly power: a violent, living entity, a "wild god."[6]

In her account, Ehrenreich compares her experience with Moses' frightening encounter with the Old Testament God. Moses' encounter occurred upon a sacred mountain, Mt. Horeb, known as the mountain of God: "There the angel of the Lord appeared to him in a blazing fire within a bush. Moses saw the bush ablaze with fire but it was not consumed" (Exodus 3:1-2, NIV Version). Later, after Moses had accepted God's command to rescue the enslaved descendants of Abraham, Isaac, and Jacob from the Egyptians and lead them to the Promised Land, "By day the Lord went ahead of them in a pillar of cloud to guide them on their way, and by night in a pillar of fire to give them light so they could travel by day or night" (Exodus 13:21, NIV). The wild, fiery god of the ancient Israelites does have much in common with Ehrenreich's experience (see Fig. 3-1).[7]

The Old Testament God is untamed and wrathful, willing to wipe out all life on Earth save for a chosen few with a great flood in order cleanse the Earth of sin, or destroy entire cities with fire and brimstone for similar reasons. He also at one point tries to kill Moses until Moses' wife performs a circumcision on their son and offers the foreskin to this wild god as a sign of appeasement and obedience.

Ehrenreich's experience also has relevance to what is described in the opening passages of the ancient Greek *Homeric Hymn to Demeter*,[8] which is sometimes referred to as the "Rape of the Kore by Hades." The hymn was inspired by the secretive practices of the Eleusinian Mysteries. Because it was forbidden by Greek law to reveal any of the secret Eleusinian rites to those who had not participated in them, the hymn uses metaphors, symbols, and references to gods acting like humans to describe what cannot be readily revealed to the uninitiated. In the opening passages, the Kore, or the Maiden,

---

[5] Ehrenreich: 115-116.

[6] This phrase is part of the book's main title, *Living with a Wild God.*

[7] Creative Commons.

[8] See Foley, ed.

Figure 3-1: Yahweh appears to the Israelites as a pillar of fire. Illustration by Paul Hardy, 1896. (Creative Commons)

who is the daughter of the Earth and grain goddess Demeter, is out frolicking with nymphs in a field of wildflowers in a region referred to as the Nysian Plain. At one point, the Kore becomes mesmerized by a particular flower, referred to as a narcissus, but described in fantastic terms, having a hundred heads and an overwhelming fragrance that filled her with a sense of awe and wonder. As she reached out to pluck it, suddenly the earth opened up and Hades, the lord of the underworld, appeared riding a horse-drawn chariot. Hades grabbed her, then rode down into the underworld where he raped her and made her his queen. Afterwards, the Kore was known as Persephone, goddess of the land of the dead.

Because the hymn was inspired by the Eleusinian Mysteries, scholars have attempted to decipher its narrative elements hoping to find references to the secret rites in order to better understand what actually occurred during the initiation ceremony. Some have interpreted the narcissus flower and the Kore's reaction to it as a reference to a narcotic of some sort; the word "narcotic" is derived from narcissus. The drug was possibly made from poppies since Demeter was closely associated with this flower;[9] or it could have been ergot, the latter a fungus that grows upon grain and is a key ingredient from which LSD is made.[10] In other words, along with performing secret rites in honor of the gods associated with the rites—primarily Demeter and Persephone--initiates might have ingested a hallucinogenic substance that resulted in a rape of the senses leading to an otherworldly sense of descending into the land of the dead and experiencing an ecstatic rebirth.

Another clue about the rites is found in the reference to the region in which the rape occurred: the Nysian Plain, sacred to the "god of Nysa:" Dionysus, perhaps the wildest of all the Greek gods (see Fig. 3-2).[11] Dionysus was associated with the ingestion of strong wine laced with other narcotic substances, as well as unbridled dancing or raging, and the eating of raw flesh from animals torn apart by his female followers, the Maenads, from which the words, "mania" and "maniac" are derived. Dionysus is closely related to the underworld god Hades; the ancient Greek philosopher Heraclitus famously claimed that Hades and Dionysus were different aspects of the same god entity.[12] Many, therefore, believe that it was Dionysus who ravished the Maiden on the Nysian Plain after she ingested powerful mind-altering substances that led to manic raging, infusing the Kore with the god's wild essence, an orgiastic state of ecstasy.

An even more relevant comparison between Ehrenreich's experience and the Eleusinian Mysteries is what might have occurred at the culmination of the rites. As I mentioned previously in Chapter Two, the initiates made a symbolic descent into the underworld to experience a rebirth, and they achieved this after some sort of encounter with Persephone who, during the

[9] Kerenyi (1960) 1991: 55.
[10] See Wasson, Ruck, and Hoffman.
[11] Creative Commons.
[12] Hillman 1979: 44.

final moments of the rites, was referred to as Brimo, a fire goddess. Ehrenreich's description of being ravished by a fiery source of power relates to what the initiates encountered during the culmination of the rites: they came face to face with a mighty, all-consuming fire. They were able to endure this confrontation because they were protected by a veil they wore made from asbestos fibers, a fire retardant. Classical scholar Jane Harrison explores the use of asbestos in the rites, mentioning that the initiates at some point were covered in a layer of clay infused with asbestos.[13] Although she does not connect the veiling of initiates with this special clay as a prelude to encountering a mighty fire, the implication is that initiates had a terrifying close encounter with this holy fire and in doing so, were reborn as Brimos, the divine child of the fire goddess Brimo, whose father was considered to be the "wild god" Dionysus.

Figure 3-2: A Greek mosaic image of Dionysus, the wildest of the Greek gods, riding a leopard. (Creative Commons)

[13] Harrison (1903)1955: 492-493.

Hungarian mythologist Carl Kerenyi described the final moments of the rites. Referring to a description given by the ancient Christian scholar Hippolytus, he states:

> We hear from…Hippolytus that the Hierophant [the chief priest of the rites] officiated at night "under a great fire." His throne was protected by a roof of its own [within the sacred temple where the secret rites were performed]. "Celebrating the great and ineffable secrets," Hippolytus writes, "[the Hierophant] proclaims in a loud voice: 'The Mistress has given birth to a holy boy, Brimo has given birth to Brimos!...'" She then gave birth in fire: the goddess of death gave birth. What a message!...And now, it was proclaimed—in the chanting voice of the Hierophant—that the queen of the dead had given birth in fire….[14]

This encounter with a sacred fire was an encounter with the primeval source of life, resulting in a rebirth and resurrection from the land of the dead.

Ehrenreich probes her experience from various points of view, mentioning that it could have been triggered by sleep deprivation combined with a lack of food; she notes that Native Americans participating in a vision quest do something similar to encourage visionary experiences. This method is also one referred to previously in the context of discussing *The Epic of Gilgamesh*. It was also a method used by shamans to induce otherworldly trance states. Because of her strong atheistic beliefs, Ehrenreich was hesitant to consider what had happened to her as having anything to do with a religious experience: "The impasse was this: If I let myself speculate even tentatively about that *something*, if I acknowledged the possibility of a nonhuman agent or agents, some mysterious Other, intervening in my life, could I still call myself an atheist?"[15] Ultimately, she concluded that, yes, she could. Referencing American psychologist William James' classic *The Varieties of Religious Experience*, she mentions that James chronicles:

> …more than a dozen personal accounts of "cosmic consciousness, "the ineffable," even a consuming "fire," and James judges none of them insane or unreliable. In fact, he seems to respect his informants, who include philosophers and psychiatrists, women and men, atheists and believers, and, it has been suggested, possibly James himself, disguised as an anonymous source.[16]

---

[14] Kerenyi (1960) 1991: 92-93.
[15] Ehrenreich: 203.
[16] Ehrenreich: 218.

Attempting to better define this "mysterious Other," she rejects the concept of the monotheistic gods of such organized religions as Judaism, Christianity, and Islam: "Mysticism often reveals a wild, amoral Other, while religion insists on conventional codes of ethics enforced by an ethical supernatural being."[17] Ehrenreich finally concludes that her experience is more closely associated with the concept of animism:

> …which anthropologists found almost universally among indigenous tribal peoples…in which divine life permeates every single object, animal, breeze, and ray of light….[Nonbelievers] have mystical experiences too, and mine seemed to locate me squarely in the realm of animism. That was more or less the state of things as I encountered them in May 1959—a world that glowed and pulsed with life through all its countless manifestations, where God or gods or at least a living Presence flamed out from every object. For most of my adult life I had denied or repressed what I had seen in the mountains…as unverifiable and possibly psychotic. But thanks to my years of research into history, prehistory, and theology, I was intellectually prepared…to acknowledge the possible existence of conscious beings—"gods," spirits, extraterrestrials—that normally elude our senses, making themselves known to us only on their own whims and schedules, in the service of their own agendas. In fact, I began to think, edging to this conclusion bit by bit and with great trepidation, that I had seen one.[18]

As Ehrenreich's experience vividly illustrates, mystical experiences involving encounters with a supernatural force are not exclusive to mystics. Anyone—and indeed everyone—has had these types of experiences. In Chapter One, I gave examples of animistic beliefs held by young adults. According to developmental psychologist Jean Piaget, all human beings, most especially during the early developmental stage, experience what he refers to as a precausal stage in which relationships between living and nonliving things are indistinguishable; this relationship also applies between the psychical and the physical: our minds are inextricably linked with all aspects of the natural world.[19] As Piaget states, in early developmental stages:

[17] Ehrenreich: 226.

[18] Ehrenreich: 214-215.

[19] Piaget: 359.

> Since the child does not distinguish the psychical from the physical world, since in the early stages of his development he does not even recognize any definite limits between his self and the external world, it is to be expected that he will regard as living and conscious a large number of objects which are for us inert. This is the phenomenon we propose to study and we shall describe it by the current word "animism."[20]

Ehrenreich gave a basic definition of animism, but an even clearer definition comes from traditional Native American belief systems:

> According to traditional Indian thinking, there is nothing that can be seen or touched, living or inanimate, that does not have a spirit. Spirituality and ordinary life are as interconnected as the strands of a tightly woven rug….Mysterious powers abide in all things found in the natural world—the flora, the fauna, the very earth itself. Everything that exists possess a soul, and all of these souls are mutually dependent. Or, as one Sioux man explained, "All living things are tied together with a common navel cord."[21]

For Native Americans, the common navel cord that ties all living things together is called by many names: the "Big Holy," the "Great Mystery," "Sila," "Manitou," "Wakan Tanka."[22] I have referred to it as *zoe*, the force of life that endures physical death, essentially the source of life itself, the force responsible for the creation of the universe and everything in it.

Modern scientists continue to struggle with the question of the origins of the universe; they can theorize with impressive accuracy when the universe came into creation—The Big Bang theory--but they cannot as yet determine the source from which the material world originated. Experiments have been conducted to create life from inorganic substances, what is called biogenesis. In a sense, these experiments are attempting to create the life force responsible for the formation of basic organic substances.

In early psychological history, a great debate centered around the question of the origins of the life force. Like the various names given to this force by Native Americans, psychologists and physiologists also gave it different names, one of which was *vitalism*. Nineteenth century physiologist Karl Frederich Burdach described the vitalist force as:

> …an eternal, ideal principle throughout the world which has created every individual thing and harmonized them, in such a manner that nature as a

[20] Piaget: 169.

[21] Debelius: 9-10

[22] Debelius: 7, 11, 14.

> whole is a living thing....It is also the same force which has created the whole world and produced every living thing.[23]

Burdach was objecting to scientists who were attempting to reduce life to a mechanistic view of life's formation, echoing Darwin's theory of evolution and modern biogenic ideas about how the interaction of chemical substances triggered organic life from inorganic substances. Psychology historian Sonu Shamdasani explained Burdach's objection: "No mechanical or chemical theory could fully explain organic formation, so one had to evoke the existence of a vital principle...a natural creative force."[24]

Nineteenth century philosopher Henri Bergson referred to the primal life force as *elan vital.*[25] Bergson's ideas had a major influence upon Jung's own theories regarding libido or psychic energy, which could be considered additional terms for this concept. Jung was also influenced by nineteenth century German gynecologist C.G. Carus who posited a relationship between the psyche and the natural world. Carus considered the human soul residing in the unconscious, which was "the primordial source of life,"[26] responsible for directing human development. A primordial image of this life source existed in the unconscious, essentially a god image, reflecting Jung's ideas about archetypes, specifically the archetypal image of the Self, the central organizing power of the psyche. Shamdasani explained Carus' view by first quoting from Carus' book, *Psyche*:

> "...something in our soul unconsciously produces a copy of the primordial image." The primordial image was responsible for maintaining and expanding the species, as well as the life of the individual. The unconscious was characterized by the fact that it knew neither fatigue, nor disease. The healing power of nature worked through the unconscious. It possessed "promethean" and "epimethean" properties, in that it was oriented towards the future and the past. It was through the unconscious that individuals were connected with the rest of the universe.[27]

What becomes apparent in all of these psychological and philosophical references to a vital force, as well as to the traditional names given to the animistic spirit, is that this force has been recognized by humanity since the beginning of human history. As Carus, Jung and others indicate, this

---

[23] Shamdasani: 179.
[24] Shamdasani: 180.
[25] Shamdasani: 227.
[26] Shamdasani: 175.
[27] Shamdasani: 175.

concept is archetypal. Its origin in the human psyche is the unconscious, which in turn is linked with the force that enlivens and directs the natural world.

In his conception of archetypal reality, Jung emphasized the importance of the central organizing power of the psyche inherent in the collective unconscious, the archetype of the Self, calling it the god image within all of us. In one of his more memorable references to the unconscious, he described the Self as a "collective human being:"

> ...combining the characteristics of both sexes, transcending youth and age, birth and death, and, from having at its command a human experience of one or two million years, practically immortal….[It] would be a dreamer of age-old dreams and, owing to its limitless experience, an incomparable prognosticator. It would have lived countless times over again the life of the individual, the family, the tribe, and the nation, and it would possess a living sense of the rhythm of growth, flowering, and decay….This was the standpoint of past ages which, knowing the untold treasures of experience lying hidden beneath the threshold of the ephemeral individual consciousness, held the individual soul to be dependent upon a spiritual world system….[They] assumed without question that this system was a being with a will and consciousness—was even a person—and they called this being God, the quintessence of reality.[28]

Jung's description of the Self has many similarities with the Native American's conception of the "common navel cord," that binds all living things together, the Big Holy, Great Mystery, Wakan Tanka, etc. In addition, it is interesting to note C.G. Carus' references to this archetypal concept, that this unconscious force "…knew neither fatigue, nor disease" and that "The healing power of nature worked through the unconscious." The implication is that this force permeates not only the unconscious and the natural world, but it is indestructible, immortal, and has the power to heal.

Countless myths, folk tales and esoteric philosophies speak of forces, substances, and objects with the power to heal, raise the dead, and extend one's life. In *The Epic of Gilgamesh*, for example, there was the plant that grew in the abyss that could make the old young again, a reference to the Tree of Life which can be found in numerous other traditions including Greek, Mesoamerican, and Judeo-Christian belief systems. The Sumerian concept of the abyss has a relationship with the collective unconscious, and

---

[28] Jung (1931) 1969: 349-351.

the Sumerian god of wisdom who dwells in the abyss is the equivalent of the Self.

One of the most well-known objects associated with healing and immortality is the Holy Grail, a symbol of Christ's healing power. Other substances with similar powers include the philosopher's stone and *aqua vitae* from alchemical philosophy which Jung investigated in great detail. More recently, references to a substance called red mercury seem to be linked to the alchemical tradition since the god figure Mercurius was the god of the alchemists. Red mercury is sought after by contemporary peoples from the Middle East which has a rich alchemical tradition dating back to ancient Egypt. Red mercury--and its derivatives green and silver mercury--is a legendary substance that has a power equivalent to a nuclear bomb. It can also raise the dead, restore sexual vitality, and summon the jinn from Middle Eastern folklore.[29]

Numerous folk tales illustrate the search for *aqua vitae* or the "water of life" which, like the Holy Grail and philosopher's stone, can restore a person's health and cure any disease. One of the best tales featuring a quest to discover the water of life comes from Ecuador, called "The Search for the Magic Lake." In this tale, the son of an Incan emperor is on the verge of death. The emperor himself is old and worries that his son will die before he does, leaving no one to rule over the kingdom. One evening, the emperor enters a holy temple where there is an altar with a fire that burns constantly. The emperor kneels before the fire and asks for guidance. Just like Moses when he encountered the burning bush, the emperor hears a voice emanating from the flames: "Let the prince drink water from the magic lake at the end of the world, and he will be well."[30] Suddenly, the eternal flame dies, and in its place is a golden flask, a type of Holy Grail.

The emperor then calls to his people, asking for volunteers to search for the magic lake, promising to reward the person who finds this lake and brings back water from it to cure his son. Two brothers from an impoverished family of farmers come forward and assure the emperor that they will find the magic lake. However, after searching for many months, they give up and decide to bring back water from an ordinary lake they came across during their journey, believing the emperor will give them some reward for their efforts. Instead, when the water is poured into the golden

[29] Chivers: n.p.

[30] Cole, ed.: 768.

flask, it immediately disappears. Realizing the brothers have attempted to deceive him, the enraged emperor throws them into a dungeon.

The brothers have a younger sister, Sumac. Even though she is quite young, she is determined to find the lake, hoping that if she finds it and brings back the healing water, the emperor will reward her by releasing her brothers from prison. Early in her journey, she is stalked by a puma. Taking refuge in a tree, she befriends three sparrows and shares food with them. In return, these helpful animals give her three magic feathers with the ability to transport her anywhere she wishes and also protect her from wild creatures. Sumac thanks the sparrows and then wishes she were beside the magic lake. In an instant, she finds herself at the end of the world where the sky meets the lake's waters. When she approaches the lake, she comes face to face with three monstrous creatures: a giant crab, a massive crocodile, and a hideous flying serpent spitting fire. Using her feathers for protection, she conquers the monsters. Then she gathers water from the lake and wishes herself back to the emperor's palace. When she appears before the emperor, she pours the water into the golden flask and watches it fill up to the brim, then gives it to the emperor's son to drink. Moments after he swallows the water, his health is restored. The emperor praises Sumac and asks her for anything she desires. She tells him she desires nothing except to have her family members united again with no worries about their own health and well-being. The emperor releases her brothers and they return home with treasures that will ensure their comfort for the rest of their lives.

The tale ends with these final observations:

> At the palace, the golden flask was never empty. Each time it was used, it was [magically] refilled. The prince's royal descendants never suffered ill health and the kingdom remained strong. But it is said that when the Spanish conqueror of the ancient Incas demanded a room filled with golden gifts, the precious flask was among them. Whatever happened to this golden treasure is unknown, for the conqueror was killed and the Indians wandered over the mainland in search of a new leader. Some say the precious gifts—including the flask—are buried at the bottom of the lake at the end of the world, but no one besides Sumac has ever ventured to go there.[31]

This beautiful South American tale has obvious parallels with medieval European legends about the quest for the Holy Grail. In the grail stories, it is Parzival, an innocent peasant, who finds the mysterious, otherworldly castle where the grail resides. He uses the grail to heal the king who has

[31] Cole, ed.: 773.

been lying sick in the castle for eternity, waiting for a pure-of-heart innocent to give him a drink from the grail. After doing so, the king is restored to health as is the land surrounding his kingdom, which became a waste land during his sickness.

Sumac performs the same feat. Like Parzival, she is a nature child, linked with the land and its animals for whom she cares and befriends and who aid her with supernatural powers from an Otherworld source that permeates the natural world. Her selfless act restores health and vitality to the emperor's son, the son's royal descendants, and the kingdom itself. That is, until everything is destroyed by greed and exploitation, resulting in disharmony and death among the people. The *aqua vitae*, the water of life—the source of life itself--that bound them together and ensured their link with each other and with their environment, returns to its mysterious source at the end of the world, waiting for another pure of heart to seek it out and once more revitalize and harmonize the people and the land with this primeval power whose source is the Otherworld.

Although the Holy Grail became a symbol of Christ's healing power, its origins lie in ancient lore; the golden flask featured in the Ecuadorian tale is just one such example. Jesse Weston, author of the influential *From Ritual to Romance* which explores the medieval grail legends and traditions, traces the origins of the grail as a symbol of the source of life back to the early civilizations of ancient Mesopotamia. Like the Sumerian king Gilgamesh whose epic poem speaks of him journeying to the abyss where he saw the source of life, Weston illuminates another, even more ancient Sumerian king figure who also became associated with this life source. This king figure's original Sumerian name was Dumuzi; later, during the height of the Babylonian civilization, he became known as Tammuz.

As I mentioned during my exploration of the *Epic of Gilgamesh*, King Gilgamesh became a central cult figure, an underworld judge of the dead. Dumuzi/Tammuz also had a religious cult devoted to him. He was the first-known dying/resurrecting god/hero figure. Other later figures were the Egyptian Osiris, the Syrian Adonis, the Phrygian Attis, the Greek Dionysus, and the Christian Jesus. According to Weston, Dumuzi/Tammuz was the central figure of what she refers to as a Life Cult, with secret rituals that, like the mystery religion tradition, were devoted to celebrating the source of life. In the Eleusinian Mysteries, the central cult figures were goddesses, Demeter and Persephone. As I explained previously, Persephone was also known as the subterranean fire goddess Brimo, who gave birth to a child called Brimos. This divine child had other names, one of which was Iacchus, who, like Brimos, was linked with the dying/resurrecting god Dionysus, referred to as his son.

In her discussion of the history of the cult of Dumuzi/Tammuz, Weston refers to the ancient myth that chronicles his death and resurrection. When he suffered a death, the people of the upper realm wailed and lamented over his passing since after his departure the entire world became an infertile waste land, a motif that parallels the grail legends that speak of the desolated land surrounding the dying king of the grail castle. After his death, Dumuzi/Tammuz returned to the *abzu*, the Mesopotamian name for the abyss. His original name was *Dami-zi, ab-zu*, "'Tammuz of the nether sea,' *i.e.*, 'the faithful son of the fresh waters which come from the earth.'"[32] In my previous comments about the abyss, I mentioned that this was where the Tree of Life grew, and where the god of wisdom Ea/Enki dwelled; it was also the source of fresh water—the water of life.

Dumuzi/Tammuz was rescued from the *abzu* by a goddess—the Sumerian/Babylonian goddess Inanna/Ishtar, who is herself a supreme life source figure. After he returned to the upper realm, Dumuzi/Tammuz performed what is known as a *hieros gamos* rite with Inanna/Ishtar, a sacred union or holy sexual coupling, after which the world became fertile once more. Such rites were known to have been performed in great public ceremonies by Mesopotamian king figures with a priestess who represented the goddess Inanna/Ishtar.[33] Weston links the secret rituals surrounding the cult of Dumuzi/Tammuz with the mystery religion tradition, and how these traditions influenced secret rites associated with the grail as a symbol of the source of life.

These tales illustrate the rich history of the archetype of the source of life. They also illustrate the psychological philosophy of Jung and his nineteenth century predecessors who looked upon the unconscious as the source of psychic energy, the life source of the human psyche. Like the legends and rites surrounding the origin of the life source, archetypal symbols and motifs from the unconscious infused with psychic energy have the power to restore health and homeostasis to a traumatized psyche.

---

[32] Weston: 36

[33] Kramer: 124.

The source of life archetype is of primary importance to understanding the Otherworld since, as I have indicated, it is this nonrational realm from which the source of life originates. The unconscious is, in itself, an energy system, and archetypal images, therefore, are images of this energy system with the Self as the central archetype, the equivalent of a god power or the concept of god.

Symbols of the life source illuminate the difference between how ego consciousness interprets life from primarily a rational perspective and how the unconscious expresses life experiences and concepts with nonrational or irrational symbols. As Sonu Shamdasani explained while quoting from Jung's *Psychological Types*, Jung "used the concept 'irrational' 'not in the meaning of *against reason*...but in the sense of *outside reason*, namely that which is not grounded on reason...' and the recognition that life exceeded representational consciousness."[34]

The unconscious expresses itself through a nonrational language that ego consciousness struggles to understand and sometimes gives up in frustration, condemning these bizarre images and motifs and experiences as nonsense. And yet, ego consciousness itself is hard wired to make cause-effect relationships between phenomena that are at times nonrational. Research involving the study of individuals suffering from a split brain, in which one brain hemisphere cannot adequately interpret information from the other hemisphere, illustrates how the brain is obsessed with interpreting phenomena and will make nonrational connections between phenomena which the ego then attempts to justify through the defense mechanism known as rationalization to protect the integrity of the ego.

Michael Gazzaniga, along with colleagues, has done extensive studies with split brain patients. Gazzaniga mentions that the brain's left hemisphere has:

> ... [the] propensity to construct a world that makes sense [and] is called the *interpreter*. This term means that the left hemisphere is interpreting what the right hemisphere has done with only information that is available to it...To give [an] example: If the command *Stand up* is flashed to a split-brain patient's right [hemisphere] side, the patient will stand up. But when asked why he or she stood up, the patient will not reply, "You just told me to," because the command is not available to the (speaking) left hemisphere [i.e. the side of the brain that controls a person's language and speaking

---

[34] Shamdasani: 229.

> functions]. Instead, unaware of the command, the patient will say something like, "I just felt like getting a soda." The left brain hemisphere is compelled to concoct a "makes sense" story that explains, or interprets, the patient's action after it has occurred.....[When] people act in ways that are inconsistent with their beliefs, they often rationalize their behavior or provide excuses. Some of these explanations are after-the-fact attempts to make sense of behavior.[35]

The split brain example illustrates how desperate the brain is to make cause-effect relationships with the information available to it. Barbara Ehrenreich did something similar for decades, attempting to find a rational explanation for her uncanny encounter with an incomprehensible force when she was a teenager; after she couldn't rationalize the experience, she tried to dismiss it as a mental breakdown, but ultimately had to admit that what she had experienced was "outside reason," linked to animism.

The hard-wired function of the brain to find cause-effect relationships applies to the precausal stage where a child endows life to inanimate objects and then provides explanations to justify giving life to these objects. In an example from an interview conducted by Piaget with an eight year-old boy, Piaget asked him a series of questions regarding whether or not certain objects had a type of conscious awareness:

> Can [clouds] feel the wind or not? *Yes, it drives them*....When the wind blows against the Saleve [Mountains], does it feel there is a mountain there or not? *Yes.* Why? *Because it goes over it.* Does a bicycle know it goes? *Yes*. Why? *Because it goes* [i.e. it moves]. Does it know when it is made to stop? *Yes*. What does it know with? *The pedals*. Why? *Because they stop [it from] going*....Can the sun see us? *Yes.* Have you thought of that before? *Yes.* What does it see us with? *With its rays.*[36]

The compulsion to give reasons for phenomenal events based on nonrational logic are vividly apparent in both the adult split brain and child examples. However, the explanations given by the boy differ from those of the adult by the fact that the boy never questions the cause-effect relationships. Unlike adults whose attempts to justify nonrational experiences are sometimes attempts to rationalize away a troubling or incomprehensible experience, the boy is not worried about looking foolish with his endowing non-living objects with a life of their own.

---

[35] Gazzaniga, Heatherton, and Halpern: 142-143.
[36] Piaget: 174-175.

This tendency to give a type of explanation to nonrational, phenomenal experiences relates to Jung's ideas about how irrational, archetypal experiences drive a person to explain the phenomena in some way, yet ultimately the experience or compulsion remains inexplicable. Jung used the example of Elgonyi natives of central Africa with whom he stayed to study their tribal habits, mentioning that every morning at dawn, tribal members would stand in front of the rising sun, spit into their hands and then display their wet palms to the sun. When he asked why they were performing this action, tribal members said they were offering their spittle to *mungu*, the name they gave to the rising sun. Jung mentioned that the word *mungu* had a relationship with the word *mana* from Polynesia, both referring to an object or substance infused with extraordinary power. After Jung asked for further clarification for their actions, they replied, "We have always done it. It has always been done when the sun rises."[37] Although the tribal members seemed unaware of why they were performing this action, Jung ultimately interpreted it as having to do with a ritualistic offering of their own *mungu* to the rising sun in recognition of their connection with this extraordinary power. Jung further explained the compulsion to perform actions that are habitual but cannot be explained by rational means:

> You may ask many civilized people in vain for the real meaning of the Christmas tree or the Easter egg. The fact is, they do things without knowing why they do them. I am inclined to the view that things were generally done first and that it was only a long time afterward that somebody asked why they were done….Superficially, such reactions and impulses seem to be of an intimately personal nature, and so we dismiss them as idiosyncratic behavior. In fact, they are based upon a preformed and ever-ready instinctive system that is characteristic of man. Thought forms, universally understandable gestures, and many attitudes follow a pattern that was established long before man developed a reflective consciousness.[38]

As previously mentioned, Jung referred to archetypes as images of instinctual patterns. And, as I have indicated, many of these images express an unconscious energy system regulated by the archetype of the Self, a power likened to a god force or source of life that is linked with the concept of animism. The nonrational aspect of these images expresses a mystery beyond rational explanation but which still compels us to provide an interpretation of them, leading sometimes to fantastic cause-effect relationships as well as to the creation of myths, folklore, and ritualistic expressions of these experiences.

---

[37] Jung 1964: 81.
[38] Jung 1964: 76.

In Chapter One, I included examples from my college students about their experiences with animism, and many of these accounts include examples of nonrational cause-effect relationships. Several of these examples also speak of encounters with taotaomona, the ancestor spirits of the native Chamorro of the Mariana Islands who live in certain areas of the jungle, usually haunting large banyan trees and always demanding respect for the natural world; if they do not receive this respect, they sometimes possess the offender, leading to wild displays of out-of-control aggressive behavior:

> My family is pretty superstitious. We believe in most of the Chamorro superstitions…. [One] instance was when my grandmother got possessed... [by a taotaomona spirit after] she used the jungle as a restroom….I remember they took her to the hospital where they strapped her to the bed but she broke the straps. Then almost ten people held her down or tried to hold her down but she got loose and punched my uncle. This went on until she passed out. Eventually, my uncle went to a siruhano [a traditional healer/shaman] and he told him to go to where she peed and throw a coconut into the forest. If there was no sound, she would be cured. He did it, and she's fine now. (Pangelinan, written correspondence to author, 2017)

> I was in the second grade, about six or seven years old. I was at my grandmother's house….. [The] house was secluded and surrounded by jungle. [I was] playing hide-and-seek in the dark [with my god sister] and back then I didn't know that it was bad to be playing when the sun sets because that's when the "bad spirits" come out. I was hiding behind a bush and felt something hit my eye. I remember running to my mom crying because my left eye was in pain. [Later] I remember being taken to a [woman] witch doctor [i.e. siruhana] for my swollen left eye. The witch doctor…wrote my name on a piece of paper. She then lit a candle and waited for it to be fully burnt out. The remaining wax formed an old man with a cane. She said the old man [was a taotaomona who had] wanted to play with me…. (Lina, written correspondence to author, 2017)

These student examples illustrate how nonrational causal relationships closely related to animistic belief systems are still prevalent in many societies throughout the world, and that respect for the powers of nature are of supreme importance to these societies. The examples also illustrate how numinous, life-infusing powers have a relationship not only with animistic belief systems but also with physical objects like special trees and other objects such as mountains and unique rock formations. Another example from the Mariana Islands is the famous rock on Saipan known as the Old Man by the Sea, situated in a remote beach area accessible only by a long walk through jungle terrain (Fig. 3-3).[39] The rock has features resembling the profile of a weathered old man.

Figure 3-3: Rock formation on the island of Saipan known as Old Man by the Sea. (Photograph by author)

Another student originally from the Philippines wrote about a corresponding example from her homeland, along with mention of forest spirits that inhabit jungle terrain:

> Raised in a culture with folklore and various superstitions, animism isn't a completely foreign idea to me. One prevalent way that animism is practiced in the Filipino culture is doing "tabi tabi po," which means, "Excuse me, please move to the side." We usually say this when passing by grassy areas or through forests because of the belief that there are duendes, or dwarfs, lingering around. We perceived that the land may be occupied by these creatures and that it is alive with magic. Another way animism is familiar to me is by seeing faces or bodily figures in inanimate objects like mountains or clouds, and rock formations. In the Philippines, there is this mountain called "Mount Tagapo," otherwise known as "Suson Dalaga" mountain, [which] translates to Young Woman's Breast. Like how the Old Man by the Sea [on Saipan] looks like an old man's head, this mountain is similar to the shape of a young woman's breast, and in my province many believe that the

[39] Photograph by author.

> reason for this is that an enchantress is guarding the mountain; that's why it took its shape. (Fauni, written correspondence to author, 2018).

It is quite obvious from these examples that animism is embraced by young and old minds, providing insights into a nonrational world view.

Physical representations of the animistic spirit are linked with numinous life powers associated with totems. Animism and totemism are inextricably interconnected. The word totem is derived from *odem*, a Native American term from the Ojibwa tribe. A totem is an object "signifying the mystic bond between the spirit, the place, and the people."[40] Native American totem poles, for example, illustrate these objects and symbols of tribal power. Many totem poles feature recognizable animals that represent the tribal spirit, while others feature fantastic otherworldly beings (Fig. 3-4).[41] Some of the poles have obvious shamanic references such as the motif of dismemberment by demons. Others refer to the creation of the tribe by their totem spirits.

Perhaps the greatest exploration of nonrational animistic and totemistic belief systems is James Frazer's thirteen-volume work, *The Golden Bough.* Frazer's monumental achievement centers around the motif of the god/king/hero figure who represents the totem spirit of his culture and who must be periodically sacrificed—either symbolically or physically--and succeeded by a more youthful representation to ensure the vitality of the cultural spirit he embodies.

Frazer gives thousands of examples from cultures all over the world and from time periods spanning recorded human history to illustrate the universality of this belief in a god-like power that can inhabit humans and also plants, animals, special locations, and man-made objects such as totem poles, dolls, statues, houses, and community gathering places. Mary Douglas, general editor of an abbreviated illustrated version of *The Golden Bough*, explained Frazer's intent:

> He was intent on revealing a particular bias, a concern that preoccupied our ancestors, this concern was age-long meditation on humanity as part of nature. It infused all nature with animate spirits and called for a sense of wonder, harnessing guilt and impossible hopes. It produced the prototype

[40] Debelius: 65.
[41] Creative Commons.

of all religion, the belief in God incarnate, dying to redeem his people and being resurrected in due course.[42]

Figure 3-4: Totem Pole from Stanley Park in Vancouver, Canada featuring a thunder bird, a fabulous being with supernatural powers sacred to numerous Native American tribes. (Creative Commons)

Frazer devoted most of his professional life to exploring this theme of the god-hero-king, "dying to redeem his people and being resurrected in due course." As Douglas explained:

> If ever a scholar had a one-track mind it was Frazer. He never wanders from the theme of the slain god….The core of Frazer's lifelong theme of the slain god appears in [his] first article on Totemism [written for the *Encyclopedia Britannica*] in which he describes a mimed death and revival in initiation ceremonies, and suggests that the totemic rites are really sacrifices in which the god dies for his people.[43]

Frazer's work influenced numerous early twentieth century scholars, artists, creative writers, and scientists including Jesse Weston's *From Ritual to Romance*, and T.S. Eliot's epic poem *The Waste Land,* as well as some

[42] Douglas, ed.: 12.
[43] Douglas, ed.: 10-11.

of the writings of Freud and Jung. Freud based his book *Totem and Taboo* on Frazer's insights, and Jung's first major publication, *Transformations and Symbols of the Libido*, also known as *Psychology of the Unconscious*, employs Frazer's use of the comparative method to explore the writings of a young woman suffering from schizophrenic-type symptoms and how her writings contain similar themes found in world mythology, religion, and literature.

Frazer delved deeply into the phenomenon of sympathetic magic, that an object, person, or animal could inhabit an enduring spirit and that this spirit-energy could be transferred to another object to effect an outcome. As Frazer defined the phenomenon: "Sympathetic Magic… [assumes] that things act on each other at a distance through a secret sympathy, the impulse being transmitted from one to the other by means of what we may conceive as a kind of invisible ether, not unlike that which is postulated by modern science for precisely similar purpose, namely to explain how things can physically affect each other through space which appears to be empty."[44]The use of dolls—Voodoo dolls, for example--as totem representations of an individual's spirit that can be manipulated to have an effect on the individual's health or even result in his or her death vividly illustrates the consequences involved when a culture embraces an animistic belief system.

As Frazer also mentions, sympathetic magic is essentially the idea of nonrational causation. He considered sympathetic magic as a less sophisticated version of the scientific method, implying that the compulsion to see and determine cause-effect relationships between phenomena is an archetypal thought and behavioral pattern:

> Thus we see that in sympathetic magic one event is supposed to be followed necessarily and invariably by another, without the intervention of any spiritual or personal agency. This is, in fact, the modern conception of physical causation; the conception, indeed, is misapplied, but it is there nonetheless. Here then, we have [a] mode in which primitive man seeks to bend nature to his wishes. There is, perhaps, hardly a savage who does not fancy himself possessed of this power of influencing the course of nature by sympathetic magic; a man-god, on this view, is only an individual who is believed to enjoy this common power in an unusually high degree… [and who] draws his supernatural power from a certain physical sympathy with nature. He is not merely the receptacle of a divine spirit. His whole being, body and soul, is so delicately attuned to the harmony of the world that a

[44] Frazer (1890) 2018: 27-28.

> touch of his hand or a turn of his head may send a thrill vibrating through the universal framework of things.[45]

Although Frazer uses the pejorative word "savage" to describe "primitive" peoples who embrace the idea of sympathetic magic, he is referring to anyone who has this tendency to believe that they can manipulate life through nonrational methods, and gives many examples from his fellow citizens of Great Britain to illustrate how very much alive this belief system is. I once encountered an alcoholic homeless man in Portland, Oregon, who stood out in traffic and began waving his arms around as if he were shooting power beams out of the tips of his fingers. When the driver of an oncoming car saw the man and hit the brakes, the homeless man turned to me and said, "See? I have the power to slow down traffic. That's my job: to slow down the pace of life so people can enjoy life more." I realized that, like so many people, he was making the attempt to give meaning to his nonrational acts in order to protect the integrity of his ego; even though he was homeless and suffering from alcohol abuse, from his perspective, he was still performing an important function for his community by manipulating the animistic forces inherent in the natural world.

Frazer's comments about the man-god endowed with totemic power are such a common idea that contemporary people who swoon over a rock star or display a frenzied loyalty to a political figure or pay millions of dollars to possess items from a celebrity or works of art from a creative artist have little conscious awareness of how their actions are expressing the animistic and totemistic belief system. While Frazer referred to individuals possessed with "an unusually high degree" of totemic power as god-men, Jung referred to them as possessing a mana-personality, with *mana* once again referring to someone or something that is "extraordinarily potent."[46] Jung also warned against modern individuals becoming too "potent," which could lead to ego inflation or worse: ego identification with the archetype of the Self, the equivalent of a god power:

> …the mana-personality is a dominant of the collective unconscious, the well-known archetype of the mighty man in the form of hero, chief, magician, medicine man, saint, ruler of men and spirits, the friend of God. This…collective figure who now rises out of the dark background and takes possession of the conscious personality entails a psychic danger…by inflating the conscious mind….The ego has appropriated something that

---

[45] Frazer (1890) 1981: Vol. 1, 12.

[46] Jung: (1928) 1972: 233.

> does not belong to it....Thus he becomes a superman, superior to all powers, a demigod at the very least.[47]

One can easily recognize the dangers inherent in becoming a god-man in modern times, when such charismatic figures are worshipped for their successes and, in many cases excesses, living comfortable lives until their natural deaths. As Frazer indicates, for traditional cultures, these god-men who embodied the totemic power of the culture were sacrificed when it appeared their powers were waning, then replaced by a more "extraordinarily potent" successor to ensure the vitality of the entire community. Unlike many modern god-men possessed by a mana-personality, the traditional figures were extremely aware of their responsibility to serve as the nation's totem power rather than use it for personal fame and glory.

Frazer's thirteen-volume masterwork is named after one of the most profoundly numinous totem objects in mythology: the mysterious golden bough referred to in Roman poet Virgil's epic poem *The Aeneid*. The poem is a celebration of the founding of ancient Rome by the hero figure Aeneas. At one point in the poem, Aeneas descends into the underworld to converse with the soul of his dead father who dwells in an area of the underworld known as the Elysian Fields, a type of paradise or realm of rebirth within the land of the dead. Before he descends, he meets with a prophetess called the Sibyl for guidance on how to successfully traverse the underworld without ending up lost and condemned to a torturous death. The Sibyl tells Aeneas that she will guide him through the underworld, but first he must pluck a branch from a sacred tree, and this branch—the golden bough—will keep him safe from perishing in the underworld (Fig 3-5).[48]

One of Frazer's main concerns was to identify the sacred tree as an oak, representing a totemic god power associated with a king who was the incarnation of the animistic power inherent in nature.

Frazer also strove to identify the golden bough as mistletoe which grows on oak trees and flourishes on the tree all year round, a fitting symbol of the eternal soul of the oak as well as a totem object representing the soul of the king and his relationship with the powers of the natural world.

---

[47] Jung (1928) 1972: 228-229.

[48] Creative Commons.

Figure 3-5: Aeneas carries the golden bough as the Sibyl leads him through the underworld to the Elysian Fields. Painting by Jan Brueghal the Elder, circa 1630. (Creative Commons)

Although he provides numerous examples of sacred trees representing the power of a king and how mistletoe symbolizes the soul of the tree and the king, Frazer does not mention an aspect of the golden bough that is linked with the mystery religion rites. As already mentioned, the underworld goddess Persephone was a central figure of the Eleusinian Mysteries along with her mother, the earth goddess Demeter. In *The Aeneid*, before he was allowed to enter the Elysian Fields to converse with the soul of his father, Aeneas had to give Persephone—referred to in the poem as Proserpine--the golden bough. Some scholars familiar with the mystery rites mention that all initiates participating in the rites had to do something similar: carry a totem object with them as they participated in the rites. The ancient Roman philosopher Servius refers to this aspect of the mystery rites: "…those who are said to have written about the sacred things of Proserpine assert concerning this branch that it is something related to the mysteries…and one was not able to approach the sacred rites of Proserpine without the carried-away branch."[49] The significance of this totem object must have

[49] Smith: 12.

been linked with the idea of carrying an object symbolizing their own eternal soul and giving over this object to Persephone in preparation for experiencing a rejuvenation of their soul, resulting in rebirth from the land of the dead.

Although Frazer identified the golden bough with mistletoe from an oak tree, it could have also been an object made from a fig tree. The fig tree was sacred to Dionysus, the Greek's premier death/resurrection god figure. Keep in mind that the holy child born from Persephone was called Brimos, also known as Iacchus, the latter considered the son of Dionysus. A myth featuring Dionysus tells of him descending into the underworld carrying an object made of fig wood. This object was carved into the likeness of a phallus.[50] The implication is that initiates carried a phallic object representing the enduring power of the Greek god of death and resurrection, and became one with this object which resulted in their rebirth from the land of the dead. Many of the death and resurrection god figures—Osiris, Attis, and Adonis as well as Dionysus—were dismembered and suffered a loss of their phalluses resulting in their deaths. After their phallic essence was restored by a goddess figure, they rose from the dead. This appears to have relevance to the mystery rites and could also relate to Aeneas' own descent and return from the underworld.

Frazer does not explore in any detail the mystery religion tradition, but he does provide numerous examples of similar rites which might have inspired the mystery rites. These were puberty rites. As Frazer explained:

> Amongst many savage tribes, especially such as are known to practice totemism, it is customary for lads at puberty to undergo certain initiatory rites, of which one of the commonest is a pretense of killing the lad and bringing him to life again. Such rites become intelligible if we suppose that their substance consists in extracting the youth's soul in order to transfer it to his totem. For the extraction of his soul would naturally be supposed to kill the youth or, at least, to throw him into a death-like trance, which the savage hardly distinguishes from death. His recovery would then be attributed…to the infusion into him of fresh life drawn from the totem. Thus, the essence of these initiatory rites, so far as they consist in a simulation of death and resurrection, would be an exchange of life or souls between the man and his totem.[51]

[50] Kerenyi (1951) 1995: 206.
[51] Frazer (1890) 1981: Vol. 2, 342-343.

Jane Harrison, one of the early twentieth century classical scholars highly influenced by Frazer's writings, noted the link between these types of puberty rites and the mystery religion tradition, specifically in regards to the mystery religion in which Dionysus was the central god figure. She also noted how the theme of dismemberment, which permeates puberty rites as well as myths associated with dying/resurrecting gods, is linked to shamanism. In one of the myths associated with Dionysus, he was dismembered when he was a youth by ancestor god figures called Titans, mimicking many traditional puberty rites in which adult tribal members adorn themselves with demonic attributes of ancestor spirits and then symbolically dismember the young participants. After the youthful Dionysus was attacked and killed by the Titans, his "heart" survived the dismemberment and was hidden in a gypsum statue made into his likeness.[52] This statue was then revived and Dionysus came back from the dead. I put quotation marks around "heart" because according to Hungarian mythologist Carl Kerenyi, this word in Greek—*kradios*--is closely associated with "phallus."[53] As I indicated earlier, many death/resurrection gods suffered dismemberments and the loss of their phallic essence which was later restored by a goddess figure, resulting in their revitalization and resurrection. I also mentioned previously that during the secret Eleusinian rites, participants were either veiled or covered in a clay-like substance infused with asbestos to protect them during an encounter with a holy fire representing the underworld goddess. The myth of Dionysus having his phallic essence preserved in a gypsum statue could relate to the practice of initiates being covered in clay—mimicking the gypsum statue of Dionysus--and carrying the Dionysian totem object, a phallus made from fig wood, in preparation for an encounter with Persephone/Brimo, the subterranean goddess of fire, with fire symbolizing the primal, animating life source. After their encounter with this life source, they became the divine child Brimos/Iacchus, the embodiment of the inexhaustible Dionysian spirit: the old renewed and become young again.

Jung recognized the universality of all initiation rites, that they follow an archetypal pattern illustrating the transformation of an initiate's primal life source, linked to the developmental stages of life, of which puberty is a primary stage of transformation:

> …fantasies from the impersonal unconscious…are not so wild and unregulated as a naïve intelligence might think; they pursue definite,

[52] Harrison (1912) 1962: 15, 18-19.

[53] Kerenyi (1951) 1995: 255-256.

> unconscious lines of direction which converge upon a definite goal. We could therefore most fittingly describe [certain]…fantasies as processes of initiation….All primitive groups and tribes that are in any way organized have their rites of initiation, often very highly developed, which play an extraordinarily important part in their social and religious life…..They are clearly transformation mysteries of the greatest spiritual significance. Very often [initiates] are subjected to excruciating treatment and at the same time the tribal mysteries are imparted to them, the laws and hierarchy of the tribe on the one hand, and on the other the cosmogonic and mythical doctrines. Initiations have survived among cultures. In Greece, the ancient Eleusinian mysteries were preserved…right into the seventh century of our era. Rome was flooded with mystery religions. Of these Christianity was one, and even in its present form it still preserves the old initiation ceremonies, somewhat faded and degenerated, in the rites of baptism, confirmation, and communion. Hence, nobody is in a position to deny the enormous historical importance of initiations….*The fact is that the whole symbolism of initiation rises up, clear and unmistakable, in the unconscious* (italics for emphasis).[54]

Because of Frazer's avalanche of examples of animistic and totemistic beliefs from cultures around the world throughout all time periods, and Jung's insistence that these beliefs originate in the collective unconscious, one must again raise the question: what is the origin of archetypal reality? Why does the unconscious express itself in these types of nonrational, symbolic motifs, many of them illustrating an inexhaustible power linked to death and resurrection, life enduring death? Certainly, we can see how this cycle of life-death-rebirth expresses itself in the natural world, linked to the cycle of the annual seasons. As Jung states, humans impulsively act and create rites simulating the cycles found in nature, and these rites are, no doubt, inspired by "fantasies from the impersonal unconscious," experienced by individuals, most notably shamans in a trance-induced state. The unconscious, therefore, is expressing an Otherworld reality accessible through the REM dream state and other altered states of consciousness.

A most extraordinary folk tale from Russia illustrates a type of puberty initiation rite complete with a totem object representing the protagonist's soul essence linked to an ancestor spirit; the tale also features an encounter with a fire goddess who represents the powers of nature. The story, called "Vasilisa the Beautiful," is also a variation of the Cinderella folk tale, one of the most universal of all folk tale motifs. Vasilisa is the beautiful daughter of a farmer who, after his first wife dies, remarries a woman with two daughters of her own. Vasilisa's stepmother and stepsisters are cruel to her

[54] Jung (1928) 1972: 230-231.

and force her to do all the house chores which she does without questioning their overbearing demands. Vasilisa finds comfort in a doll that she keeps hidden from everyone, carrying it with her wherever she goes. The doll was a gift from her real mother, and when Vasilisa gives it food, it comes to life and communicates with her. It also assists her with her endless chores.

One evening when the father is away and the stepmother is in bed asleep, Vasilisa and her stepsisters are spinning yarn and knitting late into the evening when the fire goes out and they are left in total darkness. The stepsisters then insist that Vasilisa go fetch more fire from the great cannibal witch Baba-Yaga who lives deep in the forest in a hut made from human bones. Baba-Yaga has powers that control the forces of nature—sunrise, daylight, and the blackness of night; she is also in control of the source of fire. Comforted by her doll, Vasilisa travels through the night and the next night, during which she sees various horsemen, one red, one white, and one black, who represent the rising sun, daylight, and night. She finally reaches Baba-Yaga's hut which is surrounded by a fence decorated with human skulls with fire glowing from their empty eye sockets. Baba-Yaga suddenly appears flying through the air in a giant mortar and whipping the sky with a pestle. When Baba-Yaga catches sight of Vasilisa, she swoops down and threatens to eat her. Luckily, after Vasilisa introduces herself and tells her where she lives, Baba-Yaga realizes Vasilisa's stepmother is a kinswoman, so the witch invites her into her hut made of human bones. Not long afterward, the witch puts her to work performing impossible tasks, telling Vasilisa that if she fails any of the tasks, she'll eat her. Vasilisa calls upon her doll for help and after feeding the doll some scraps of bread, the doll comes to life and agrees to help her. The doll beckons to the birds of the forest to help with one task—picking out black bits of dirt from a huge sack of millet--then calls to all the mice in the surrounding fields to take another huge sack filled with poppy seeds and peas and separate them into two piles. After these tasks are completed, Baba-Yaga is infuriated and decides to eat Vasilisa anyway. With help from an enslaved maid, Vasilisa manages to escape while Baba-Yaga is taking a nap. Before she escapes, she steals one of the skulls emitting fire from its eye sockets, sets it on a stick, then runs off into the night (Fig 3-6).[55]

When she returns home the following evening, her stepmother and stepsisters berate her for taking so long to return with the fire. Vasilisa enters the house and as the light from the eyes of the skull permeates the interior,

---

[55] Creative Commons.

it sets the stepmother and stepsisters ablaze, engulfing them in flames until they are burnt to smoldering ash piles. Afterwards, Vasilisa feels liberated. She decides to journey to a nearby town and start a new life spinning yarn and making clothing. The clothes she weaves are so stunningly beautiful, they impress the prince of the Tsar. When the prince calls Vasilisa to the palace to praise her work, he immediately falls in love with her, and soon afterward, they marry.[56]

Figure 3-6: Vasilisa returns home from Baba-Yaga's hut carrying a skull emitting fire from its empty eye sockets. Illustration from "Vasilisa the Beautiful." (Creative Commons)

The story of Vasilisa is infused with motifs from puberty initiation rites in which youths are isolated in a forest or in an initiatory hut and put through a terrifying simulation of death and dismemberment by cannibal demons.

[56] Yolen, ed.: 335-342.

Sometimes these rites include threats of being burned to death. Jane Harrison, for example, refers to an Aboriginal Australian rite, reported by Frazer, featuring a fierce ancestor spirit called Dhuramoolan who "…pretended that he always killed the boys, cut them up and burnt them to ashes, after which he molded the ashes into humans and restored them to life as new beings."[57] Vasilisa goes through a similar rite, first threatened to be eaten, then forced to perform certain tasks in an initiatory hut made of dismembered humans. She passes her initiation and returns with a purifying fire that destroys her old way of life, resulting in new life as an adult.

Mircea Eliade commented on the archetypal significance of the secluded hut used for initiations:

> The memory of the secluded initiatory hut, far away in the forest, was preserved in popular tales, even in those of Europe, long after puberty rites had ceased to be performed. Psychologists have shown the importance of certain archetypal images; and the cabin, the forest, and darkness are such images—they express the eternal psychodrama of a violent death followed by rebirth…. [The] cabin is the maw of the devouring monster, in which the neophyte is eaten and digested, but it is also the nourishing womb, in which he is engendered anew. The symbol of initiatory death and rebirth are complementary.[58]

The doll Vasilisa carries is a perfect example of a totem object as a guiding ancestor spirit, the eternal soul of her mother, who, like Baba-Yaga, is an animating force of nature with the power to control aspects of the natural world to help with Vasilisa's transformation from maiden to young woman. The doll is an extremely common totem object for both traditional and contemporary cultures as this example from one of my students illustrates:

> I have given life to my Barbie dolls throughout my childhood years. I had…two female dolls and one male, a Ken doll. I had my dolls go through daily life activities and always kept them consistent with my story lines. When I would change my clothes, I would be sure to cover Ken's eyes because boys cannot see girls naked. At night, I made sure that my dolls were also tucked into bed because I believed they also needed sleep. When I would accidentally drop a doll, I would apologize so they would not be angry with me. It even came to the point where I would be afraid of my own dolls. Sometimes, I felt that they were plotting to hurt me in my sleep. I think these fears grew from me reading books about ventriloquist puppets

[57] Harrison (1912) 1962: 18.

[58] Eliade (1958) 2005: 36-37.

> coming to life and killing people. As I grew older, this fear subsided… [but] I also had a fear my entire life of mannequins….I am [also] currently afraid of statues. (Tarkong, written correspondence to author, 2018)

This student's love for, and also fear of, her dolls, as well as a fear of puppets, mannequins and statues—a fear known as automatonphobia--demonstrates the numinous dimension of these types of objects. Folklore and especially films have embraced this motif of dolls and puppets endowed with life, sometimes with benevolent intent, such as the brilliant *Toy Story* series of films featuring an array of different types of toys and dolls becoming animated and conversing with one another whenever humans aren't around. Most often, however, animated dolls and puppets are featured in horror films. A personal favorite is a ventriloquist's dummy that terrorizes its alleged master, played by Michael Redgrave, in the anthology horror film *Dead of Night*, released in 1945 (Fig. 3-7).[59] In many of these types of ventriloquist dummy films, the puppet is a demonic alter ego of its master, or a demon itself that drives the ventriloquist insane.

Figure 3-7: A ventriloquist, played by Michael Redgrave, is terrorized by his dummy in *Dead of Night*, 1945. (Creative Commons)

Demon dolls, such as the ones featured in the *Annabelle* and *Chucky* series of films—the latter of which *Child's Play* is the first and best in the series, released in 1988--are totem incarnations of mass murderers, serial killers, and malevolent spirits from the Otherworld who terrify and threaten

[59] Creative Commons.

to kill or possess their youthful owners, replicating traditional puberty rites, except in the films, whoever dies remains dead.

The same fate holds true for film characters—usually pubescent teenagers or young adults--who go off on adventures into the dark woods and end up spending the night in abandoned cabins where demonic forces dwell. Unlike the initiatory huts of traditional cultures where ritual dismemberment is always followed by transformation and resurrection, the teens and young adults in such films as the *Friday the 13$^{th}$* series, and the *Evil Dead* films, end up dismembered and either permanently dead or transformed into a zombie possessed by a cannibal spirit. If anyone is left alive, it is usually a young woman—sometimes referred to as the "final girl"—most often a virgin, echoing the archetypal motif of the Kore or Maiden, who became Persephone, queen of the dead, after she was raped by Hades.

One of the most potent and terrifying film examples of the initiatory hut motif is the original *Texas Chainsaw Massacre*, released in 1974. Like Baba-Yaga's hut, this cinematic cabin in the woods is decorated with human body parts, leftovers from victims of the cabin's regular occupants who are cannibals that run a local barbecue featuring meat with a very unique taste. The film features a group of young visitors to the cabin who end up bludgeoned and dismembered by Leatherface, a chainsaw-wielding maniac. Like so many adult leaders of traditional puberty rites, Leatherface wears a gruesome mask, this one made from human skin (Fig. 3-8).[60] The last one left alive in the group is a young woman who, after being sadistically terrorized and nearly tortured to death by the cannibal family, manages to escape from the hut with Leatherface pursuing her through the woods and finally into the path of an oncoming truck. The motorist ends up another victim, but the young woman manages to jump into the truck and escape, leaving Leatherface sorely frustrated.[61]

To a very large degree, watching these types of horror films featuring demonic dolls and creepy cabins located in dark forests is a type of contemporary initiatory rite. Because modern societies do not normally have puberty rites that subject participants to a visceral experience of ritual death followed by rebirth, these films serve as a cinematic alternative. Like the traditional rites, most of the victims are young people brutally

---

[60] Creative Commons.

[61] Hooper, dir.: Vortex/Bryanston Distributing Co.

slaughtered by demons. Although the cinematic victims stay dead, the audience members who, for the most part, are made up of mostly teens and young adults, survive the ordeal. Whether these films result in a transformative experience, a temporary adrenaline rush, or psychological trauma depends upon the individual viewer.

Figure 3-8: The Leatherface character from *Texas Chainsaw Massacre*, 1974. (Creative Commons)

Some of the most popular films of all time feature the animistic force, most notably the *Star Wars* film series. "May the force be with you" has become such a common phrase in popular culture that many do not fully realize its connection with animism. Characters in the film who are "extraordinarily potent" with this animating force are the Jedi who are essentially shamans with Samurai training. Like traditional shamans, the Jedi can manipulate the force for either benevolent or malevolent purposes. Unlike the victims in teen slasher films, Jedi killed in battle never really stay dead; they live on in an Otherworld reality.

Another extremely popular film featuring the animistic force is *Avatar*, released in 2009. The film, set on an alien planet called Pandora, has a strong emphasis upon animism linked with the powers of nature, and features a traditional culture called the Na'vi that lives in harmony with this power. Like the ending to the "Search for the Magic Lake" folk tale, greed and exploitation in the form of U.S. Marine forces and a big-business mining operation, destroy the link that the Na'vi tribe has with the animistic spirit. It is restored when one of the exploiters, a Marine called Jake Sully (Sam Worthington), sides with the Na'vi. Sully communes with the tribe in an artificial Na'vi body—a type of totem-animated mannequin—referred to as an avatar. When it appears that the Marine forces and the corporate powers will destroy the Na'vi, Sully makes an emotional appeal to the source of the animistic power, a sacred tree called the Tree of Souls. Every living entity on this intergalactic planet, including all ancestor spirits, is linked to the Tree of Souls. Sully's appeal is heard by the Tree of Souls which sends out a telepathic command to all the animals of the planet, compelling them to rise up en mass and destroy the opposing Marine forces. Sully ultimately sacrifices his life to help bring about the defeat of his fellow Marines. Unlike the horror films that revel in gruesome, permanent deaths for their teen victims, the sacrifice made by Sully is followed by his rebirth after his human and avatar bodies are placed within the pulsating roots of the Tree of Souls, resulting in the transference of his human vitalist life force to the avatar/totem object.[62]

Animism has been called the most primal form of religion. However, as it has--I hope--become apparent, belief in animism is still very much a part of modern life, and is hardly reserved for religious-oriented individuals. Animism permeates all belief systems, including atheism. It is embedded deep within the human psyche in the form of psychic energy. It enlivens all of life, empowering and pulsating throughout the universe. In fact, certain scientists and philosophers have proposed a theory—called panpsychism—that explores the possibility of the universe having a type of consciousness or "proto-consciousness field."[63] Such a theory has very much in common with animism.

Even though the animistic force enlivens every form of matter, it remains one of the most mysterious of all forces. Perhaps if someone like Sumac were willing to make a journey into the Otherworld, and find the lake at the end of the world that holds the waters of life, we might be able to solve this greatest of all mysteries, the mysterious origins of all physical matter, as well as life itself.

---

[62] Cameron, dir. and screenwriter 2009: Twentieth Century Fox.

[63] Powell: n.p.

# CHAPTER FOUR

# THE OTHERWORLD AND WAKING WORLD OVERLAP

In addition to having my students write about their experiences with animism, I also have them write about significant dreams. One student reported the following dream, first mentioning that she believes it is an example of a phenomenon known as sleep paralysis:

> The night that I experienced sleep paralysis was when I was in a deep sleep and in my sleep I was dreaming that I was in the woods walking at night. I could hear the small noises like the leaves moving because of the wind. As I started to feel scared, I felt as if someone was watching me and started to chase me. I ran as fast as I could but then when I turned around to see if someone was there, that someone was standing right in front of me. I could still remember his severe burnt face and blood sliding down it. I screamed and he knocked me to the ground and got on top of me with his hands covering my mouth so nobody could hear me screaming. I was screaming so loud that I "woke up." My eyes were wide open but I could still feel him on top of me. I thought I was screaming but not a sound was coming out of me. I couldn't move because the pressure of him was so strong that it maintained me motionless. I could hear his creepy laughter until finally he let me go and left. I was scared out of my mind and simply just covered myself. I told my mom about the dream and she said it was because I needed to be nicer and needed to add Jesus more in my life since that only happens to people who are evil. (Marcelo, written correspondence to author, 2018)

Another student reported a similarly themed dream:

> I personally suffer from frequent episodes of sleep paralysis....Through these episodes, I have encountered numerous memorable dreams. Dreams that terrified me, dreams that showed me a glimpse of any troubles I was going through. One significant dream I vividly remember...was a typical routine from my normal episodes of sleep paralysis. I would feel awake in my dream. I woke up to the sight of my bedroom. It was dark, felt normal; I thought I was actually in my room. Sometimes I can't tell whether what I'm experiencing is real or not. At some point, my mom who was apparently in the room, was just roaming back and forth. At this point, I knew

> something was definitely odd. Things in the room started to disappear into the darkness. My mom, however, or who I thought was my mom, tackled me as I lay in my place. She started to choke me and was throwing my neck vigorously against the surface I was laying on. I started to lose breath. I looked into my mom's eyes and they were red, glowing out of the darkness. I had to become conscious and realize that it was all a dream. I do this by repeating "This is not real," and start moving my body in my dream to actually move it in real life. As soon as I awoke to the movements of my body, I started to cry. I realized that the idea of getting choked and suffocated related to what I was going through in real life. I had so much on my plate and basically was suffocated by the amount of responsibility and obligations I had in my life. (Espino, written correspondence to author, 2018)

These student accounts of what they call sleep paralysis are consistent with what is known about this phenomenon. Sleep paralysis is essentially the experience of either being on the verge of falling asleep—called the hypnagogic state--or emerging out of REM sleep—called the hypnopompic state--sometimes with eyes open, and feeling physically paralyzed while conscious of the presence of a foreign intruder, usually in the dreamer's bedroom. While the dreamer lies in bed unable to move or make a sound, this entity roams about the room, sometimes approaching, attacking, and sitting on top of the dreamer, then at times choking, smothering, and in some cases sexually assaulting the helpless person before vanishing. At that point, the sleeper is able to move again and is usually left in a state of emotional trauma.

Sleep paralysis has been documented throughout the ages and has been given different names from various cultures. The most significant name given to this phenomenon is the original meaning of the word "nightmare:" "The 'mare' element of the English [word] 'nightmare' derives from the same root as the Germanic *mahr* and Old Norse *mara*, [referring to] a supernatural being, usually female, who lay on people's chests at night, thereby suffocating them."[1] Nightmare, in other words, referred specifically at one time to a nocturnal encounter with a female demon, sometimes referred to as an old hag, witch or succubus, although many times the demon is male--a warlock or incubus. During the witch hysteria of the Middle Ages, it was quite common for people to report being visited by a witch in their dreams; these witches usually wanted to trigger nocturnal orgasms in males. The witches would then use the semen from the orgasms to create more demons (Fig. 4-1).[2] Incubi had the same agenda: to arouse women to orgasm, then impregnate them and breed more demons.

---

[1] Davies: 184.

[2] Creative Commons.

As I mentioned, the origins of sleep paralysis are widespread and most often associated with demonic spirits from an Otherworld reality. Owen Davies gives numerous examples in his examination of the link between sleep paralysis, witchcraft, and folklore:

> In Japan, some people believe sleep paralysis is caused by evil spirits, and the traditional term for the experience, *kanashibari*, meaning "to tie with an iron rope," derives originally from the belief in the magic powers of a Buddhist god….The *kokma* of St. Lucia [in the Caribbean] is attributed to the spirit of a dead baby, which jumps on sleepers' chests and chokes them….In Indonesia the *tindihan* (meaning "to be weighted down") is attributed to spirit assault, and, in Hawaii, sleep paralysis is said to be caused by supernatural "night marchers…." Amongst the Syan tribe of Uganda, it was believed that the *emisambwa*, spirits of the dead, were responsible for pressuring and throttling sleepers at night…. At least some nightmare experiences in Zanzibar are attributed to…the *popabawa*, a nocturnal humanoid, bat–winged demon that rapes men as they lie in their beds….In Poland, the nightmare experience was sometimes attributed to the *strzyga* (from the Latin *striga*), which in Polish came to be associated with dead people's souls….In parts of southeastern and central Europe, the experience also has associations with *revenants* and members of the living dead….[3]

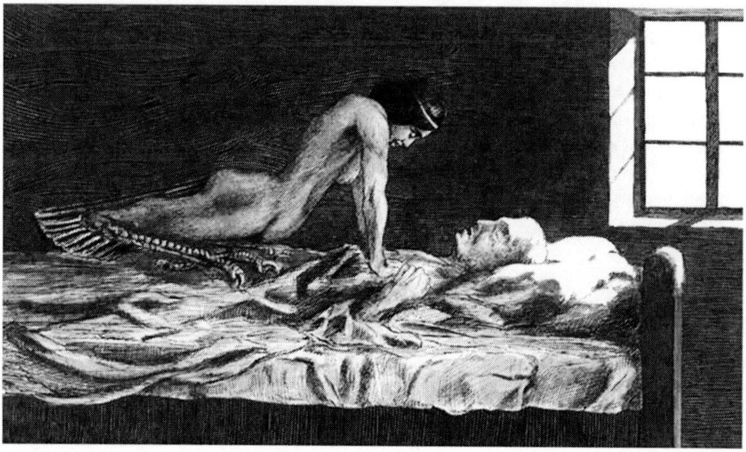

Figure 4-1: A succubus straddles a sleeper. Image by Fritz Schwimbeck, entitled "My Dream, My Bad Dream," 1915. (Creative Commons)

[3] Davies: 198.

The most ancient of all night demons comes from the Sumerians, with the great goddess figure known as Lilith identified as the first succubus figure. According to Jewish legend, Lilith was also considered the first wife of the Biblical Adam; however, she refused to be subservient to him, as Yahweh demanded. She insisted, for example, on straddling Adam during intercourse, the traditional position of the succubus. When both Adam and Yahweh demanded obedience from her, she learned the secret name of Yahweh and uttered it in his presence, which freed her from the Garden of Eden. She then fled to the wilderness and set up her own kingdom among the wild animals of the world. She also created demonic followers—incubi and succubi--and sent them off to invade the dreams of the offspring of Adam and Eve.[4]

Lilith, therefore, is the first wild, untamed goddess figure, the personification of the human psyche's link with raw, instinctual nature. As Barbara Black Koltuv describes her:

> Lilith, an irresistible, long-haired she demon of the night, flies through Sumerian, Babylonian, Assyrian, Canaanite, Persian, Hebrew, Arabic, and Teutonic mythology....Among the Semites of Mesopotamia, she was...a night demon who lays hold of men and women who sleep alone, causing erotic dreams and nocturnal orgasm....Lilith, the Winged One and Stranglerless, became known throughout the world... [as] witch, hag, snatcher, and enchantress. She was...the soul of every living creature that creepeth. She was Adam's first wife, the female of [the sea beast] Leviathan, the wife of Samael the Devil...and even the consort of God himself while the Shekinah [the female companion of God] is in exile. Attempts to suppress and deny her date from the sixth century B.C., but she returns evermore, as a seductress... and will continue to do so until the Messiah comes.[5]

The figure of Lilith is important to understanding the rich history of sleep paralysis. As Koltuv also mentions, Lilith as succubus was associated with shamanic practices and mystery religion rites. She refers to a famous image from Greece, circa fourth century B.C., of a naked man lying in a trance-like sleep with a winged succubus straddling him; in the background are icons associated with the cult of Dionysus.[6] Koltuv also references Jung who called Lilith a "shamanistic anima" figure.[7] In other words, succubi and

[4] Koltuv: 19-20.
[5] Koltuv: xi.
[6] Koltuv: 41-42.
[7] Koltuv: 49.

incubi are the spirit brides and spirit grooms of shamans who, while in ecstatic trance states, converse and couple with these supernatural figures in order to learn secrets of the Otherworld.

In Chapter Two, I mentioned the studies done by dream researcher Antti Revonsuo and his theory about how nightmares are emotionally-charged rehearsal scenarios that help individuals prepare for life and death situations in their waking lives. One of the most common of all dream scenarios is to be menaced by a stranger or demonic figure with the dreamer attempting to run and hide from this menacing figure or grappling with it but usually failing to subdue it or kill it so it stays dead. One can see how this common dream scenario relates to sleep paralysis; the student example that opens this chapter vividly illustrates this connection between sleep paralysis and nightmare rehearsal scenarios. However, the key difference is that with sleep paralysis, the person is in a state of "paradoxical sleep," nearly awake but at the same time in the REM stage of sleep. In this state, the demon appears to be in the room with the sleeper. The emotional intensity of such an experience is heightened to the point of hysteria. One is experiencing what Marie-Louise von Franz called a "waking hallucination;" and, according to von Franz, such experiences are the origins of myth and folklore.

Sleep paralysis blends waking consciousness and the REM dreaming state when muscle tension is nonexistent—giving the person a feeling of being paralyzed; the person is also in a state of sexual arousal with the person's memory and emotional centers of the brain highly active. The memories, however, are similar to those who have reported near-death experiences: they are not usually from the personal sphere. The memories tapped by the dreaming brain during these episodes might have references to one's personal life but are dominated by archetypal motifs from the collective unconscious. The student who reported being strangled by her mother, for example, also mentioned that this "mother" figure was not a representation of her real mother but a demon who had taken on the persona of her mother.

People who are terrorized by their bouts with sleep paralysis are reacting to archetypal figures--succubi and incubi--while in a state of panic. Not understanding what they are going through increases the panic, and the demonic figures they see become living representations of their panicked state. It is important to keep in mind that panic is an instinctual survival response to physical danger. It is also important to remember that the word panic is related to the Greek's nature god Pan, depicted as half-human, half-goat, and sporting an erection. Pan himself was an incubus figure; he could appear in dreams to cause terror and panic, but also to provide insights into the secrets of the natural world.[8]

Some people experiencing sleep paralysis report a sense of not only being oppressed by a demonic figure but also feeling a sense of floating. As one person described the experience:

> As I was floating above myself, I saw two shadowy figures that gave off a silvery light ... They seem to have entered the room by passing through the window ... They drew my prone body on the bed to them as if by magnetic pull ... I found myself following them without effort or conscious intent through the window into the open night sky.[9]

The similarities between this type of dream experience with descriptions of the trance-flight of the shaman are apparent. There is also a strong link between these types of accounts with people who have reported being abducted by intergalactic aliens. Like the reported encounters with succubi and incubi, alien abductions sometimes include forced sexual intercourse with alien beings who also implant foreign objects into the abductee's body. Once again, these accounts have strong parallels with the shamanic tradition. Mircea Eliade, for example, described an Aboriginal Australian initiation ceremony in which the shamanic candidate was put through a symbolic death and resurrection:

> ...referred to [as] his rising to the sky....[The] initiatory master [also] introduces rock crystals into the apprentice's body and makes him drink water in which such crystals have been placed; after this the apprentice succeeds in seeing spirits....The rock crystals that play an important part in the initiation of the Australian medicine men are [considered]...celestial [in] origin.... All this is as much as to say that one becomes a shaman when one is stuffed with "solidified light," that is, with quartz crystals; this operation changes the initiand's mode of being by making him mystically akin to the sky. He who swallows one of these crystals flies up to the sky.[10]

Sleep paralysis, therefore, is a waking hallucination that, depending upon the culture in which a person experiences this trance-like state, is associated with assaults by a succubus, incubus, old hag, or a witch; an encounter with spirits of the dead; a rapacious violation by a demonic

---

[8] Hillman (1972) 2000: 26-27.

[9] Davies: 201.

[10] Eliade (1951) 2004: 135-138.

humanoid bat or inhuman baby; a confrontation with a god; or a visitation from an alien from another planet. Most dramatically, sleep paralysis is linked to the long tradition of shamanic visionary flights to the Otherworld. In all of these accounts, the waking hallucination features something beyond the personal sphere, an archetypal experience infused with numinous energy both terrifying and enthralling.

Sleep paralysis is just one example of what psychologist William James called an experience of the "unseen reality," essentially a sensing of the presence of the Otherworld: "It is as if there were in the human consciousness a sense of reality, a feeling of objective presence, a perception of what we may call 'something there,' more deep and more general than any of the special and particular 'senses' by which the current psychology supposes existent realities to be originally revealed."[11] Like von Franz, James states that the unseen reality is like a waking hallucination and describes it in terms similar to the experience of sleep paralysis: "…the person affected will feel a 'presence' in the room, definitely localized facing in one particular way, real in the most emphatic sense of the word, often coming suddenly, and as suddenly gone…."[12] James gives the example of an acquaintance whose description of his experience is identical to sleep paralysis:

> After I got into bed and blown out the candle, I lay awake…when suddenly I felt something come into the room and stay close to my bed. It remained only a minute or two. I did not recognize it by any ordinary sense, and yet there was a horribly unpleasant "sensation" connected with it. It stirred something more at the roots of my being than any ordinary perception. The feeling had something of the quality of a very large tearing of a vital pain spreading chiefly over the chest…and yet the feeling was not pain so much as abhorrence. At all events, something was present with me, and I knew its presence far more surely than I have ever known the presence of any fleshly living creature. I was conscious of its departure as of its coming; an almost instantaneously swift going through the door, and the "horrible sensation" disappeared.[13]

Although this experience of the unseen reality was "horribly unpleasant" for this person, James gives other examples in which this reality is a benign, even comforting and exhilarating experience:

---

[11] James (1902) 1982: 58.
[12] James (1902) 1982: 59.
[13] James (1902) 1982: 59-60.

> Whenever I had any trouble, especially when I had conflict with other people, either domestically or in the way of business, or when I was depressed in spirits or anxious about affairs, I now recognize that I used to fall back for support upon this curious relation I felt myself to be in to this fundamental cosmical *It.* It was on my side, or I was on Its side, however you please to term it, in the particular trouble, and it always strengthened me and seemed to give me endless vitality to feel its underlying and supporting presence….What I have spoken of as It was…my own instinctive and individual God, whom I relied upon for higher sympathy….[14]

In this example, one can see how a person who experiences the unseen reality can develop a personal relationship with a supernatural being likened to a benevolent god entity.

An intimation of a cosmic force that strengthens, supports, and comforts in times of need is similar to what Michael Ventura called the Watcher. Ventura described the Watcher in a series of correspondences with Jungian psychologist James Hillman:

> …don't you sometimes feel accompanied, especially when alone, in a way that you usually take for granted…? I'm thinking of something I now call "the Watcher…." [It's] that sense of a common companion, which is you and yet more than you, and who seems always with you, watching from a slight distance….It's not exactly passive but rarely active. Its action is to watch….[My] experience of the Watcher is that it's not within you, it's a little off to the side….(Or it's above; a friend of mine told me that as a child he pictured his Watcher as a television camera that followed him off to the side….) [Some] people have endured horrors because their Watcher is…a companion….You may not like yourself at all, yet your Companion is calm and doesn't disapprove, and your solitude can be sweet at times because of this….[My] Companion, my Watcher, is patient—not condoning nor even reassuring, just patient….[According] to the people I compare notes with, the sense of a Watcher is so common it's taken for granted. My conviction is that during a bad time one's relationship with one's Watcher is crucial; it may be all one has….[15]

After reading Ventura's description of the Watcher for the first time when I was in my mid-forties, I had a strong emotional reaction to this idea of a "companion" entity that reassures and never condones. His mentioning that one of his friends had described the Watcher as a television camera that followed him around and objectively filmed his life related directly to my

---

[14] James (1902) 1982: 64-65.
[15] Hillman and Ventura: 83-89.

own life since I had played around with this same fantasy for decades. My television camera fantasy changed when I was in my late twenties and I began keeping a personal journal. The journal allowed me to personally address this "companion" who, like the TV camera, never questioned my actions or confessions. It accepted everything without passing judgment. In this regard, it was a cherished companion that comforted me during personal crises and personal triumphs.

What is interesting about my experience with journal writing is that it was only after I read Ventura's description of the Watcher that was I able to identify my journal writing "audience." Before that, this audience went unrecognized, which might at first seem strange since the audience of the journal writer is the writer. However, since we are all endowed with various personas, complexes, and other dimensions of self-identity, it is of crucial importance to identify which "self" to whom one is confessing these most intimate thoughts and passions. In many cases, because a person fails to identify his or her writing audience as the non-judgmental Watcher, some journal writers censor themselves or write in code to hide these confessions from their writing audience, i.e. themselves; in other words, they don't fully trust or sense a hostile relationship with their core sense of self-identity. In this regard, the Watcher must be recognized as one's personal writing audience. As Ventura states, "you may not like yourself at all," but the Watcher does, and during a personal crisis, having this type of "relationship with one's Watcher is crucial; it may be all one has." Liking or not liking what I call one's core sense of self identity could relate to how people who sense the unseen reality react to it, since the Watcher is an aspect of one's psyche that Jung, no doubt would link to the impersonal psyche of which the archetype of the Self is the central organizing power. The Watcher, therefore, corresponds to what James' confessor intimated about his relationship with an "instinctive and individual God," the god image inherent in every individual.

Depending upon how our egos interpret this god-like power within us, we can have a relationship with a benevolent "cosmical *It*" that is always on our side, or feel the presence of an abhorrent thing that threatens to strangle us in our sleep. Most importantly, as Ventura and James indicate, a great number of us have felt this unseen reality. And it is not usually a sense of a presence coming from within. In other words, the unseen reality—the Watcher--is both within us and outside of us. The impersonal psyche is linked with the world around us, an animistic power that infuses the material world and interconnects all of life.

Jung's ideas about personal and impersonal complexes—emotionally charged dimensions of one's self-identity--apply to the Watcher concept and the unseen reality. In his essay, "The Psychological Foundation of Belief in Spirits," which he wrote as a speech given to the Society for Psychical Research in 1919 and later revised it in 1948, Jung explored the concept of belief in the spirit world and how prevalent this belief is. Jung made a crucial distinction between soul and spirit and how they relate to personal and impersonal complexes:

> It is impossible to speak of belief in spirits without at the same time considering the belief in souls….[According] to primitive belief, a spirit is usually the ghost of one dead….[For] the primitive, the soul is something that seems normally to belong to him, but spirits seem to be something that normally should not be near him. He avoids places haunted by spirits, or visits them only with fear, for religious or magical purposes….We therefore have to postulate the existence of unconscious complexes that normally belong to ego and those that normally should not become associated with it. The former are soul-complexes, the latter spirit-complexes.[16]

As Jung states, a soul-complex is an inherent part of our ego identity. A spirit-complex is linked to the impersonal psyche or collective unconscious, associated with instinctual thought and behavioral patterns beyond the control of ego. Therefore, when a spirit-complex erupts into ego consciousness, it feels as if something foreign and invasive has overtaken one's psyche:

> …when…a complex of the collective unconscious becomes associated with ego, i.e., becomes conscious, it is felt as strange, uncanny, and at the same time fascinating. At all events the conscious mind falls under its spell, either feeling it as something pathological, or else being alienated by it from normal life….The irruption of these alien contents is a characteristic symptom marking the onset of many mental illnesses. The patients are seized by weird and monstrous thoughts while the whole world seems changed, people have horrible, distorted faces, and so on. While the contents of the personal unconscious are felt as belonging to one's own psyche, the contents of the collective unconscious seem alien, as if they came from outside.[17]

Jung emphasizes how spirit-complexes from the impersonal psyche have an autonomous life. They usually invade ego consciousness during times of stress and turmoil, or during times "when the individual is ripe for

---

[16] Jung (1920) 1969: 112, 116-117.

[17] Jung (1920) 1969: 118-119.

conversion," that is, when "a new insight breaks through with violent emotion."[18] Jung's comments relate directly to what Barbara Ehrenreich experienced, explored in Chapter Three. As a teenager, Ehrenreich was obsessed with finding the meaning to "everything," or a purpose to life beyond the mere biological mode of existence. While on her quest to find a meaning to life, she at one point had a disturbing dream that underscored her atheistic view of life as merely a biological system of sexual reproduction to ensure the survival of a species. Then, not too long after this disturbing dream, she had a waking hallucination, a "new insight" that broke through with "violent emotion." The eruption of this experiential insight was so violent, she compared it to an inhuman violation from a wild, god-like power. This power seemed to originate from outside of her, but also penetrated her, connecting her with her surroundings. Ultimately, she concluded that this experience was the answer to her search for meaning.

The emotionally invasive experience of the spirit-complex relates directly to what religious scholar Rudolf Otto called an experience of the *mysterium tremendum*, the "tremendous mystery" of a religious experience, a blending of abject terror and horror with an overwhelming sense of awe and wonder. As Otto described it:

> It may burst in sudden eruption up from the depths of the soul with spasms and convulsions, or lead to the strangest excitements, to intoxicated frenzy, to transport, and to ecstasy. It has its wild and demonic forms and can sink to an almost grisly horror and shuddering. It has its crude, barbaric antecedents and early manifestations, and again it may be developed into something beautiful and pure and glorious. It may become the hushed, trembling, and speechless humility of the [individual] in the presence of—whom or what? In the presence of that which is a *mystery,* inexpressive and above all creatures.[19]

The religious experience is the invasion of the unseen reality or Otherworld into waking consciousness. As Jung mentions, such invasions happen when there is a need for it, when we need to be shaken to our core of being in order to experience new insights into life and the workings of the world. The quote from William Roll from the Introduction expresses how the need for transformation triggers something within and from without to satisfy the need. Roll's comments relate to the animistic spirit permeating the material world as having a type of primordial consciousness, linked to the impersonal psyche.

[18] Jung (1920) 1969: 114.
[19] Otto (1923) 1958: 12-13.

This "need" is what Jung considered the reason behind the rise in sightings of UFOs, which began not long after the catastrophe of World War II and the threat of nuclear annihilation during the height of the Cold War. It was during this time of psychic turmoil that he wrote his famous extended essay, "Flying Saucers: A Modern Myth of Things Seen in the Sky," first published in 1958. As he emphasized in the essay, a psychological necessity in the collective psyche of humanity resulted in eruptions in the impersonal psyche, leading to mass psychological projections of an archetypal image interpreted as a god image symbolizing wholeness and homeostasis:

> If the round, shiny objects that appear in the sky be regarded as visions, we can hardly avoid interpreting them as archetypal images. They would then be involuntary, automatic projections based on instinct….Anyone with the requisite historical and psychological knowledge knows that circular symbols have played an important role in every age; in our own sphere of culture, for instance, they are not only soul symbols but "God images." There is an old saying that "God is a circle whose center is everywhere and circumference nowhere." God in his omniscience, omnipotence, and omnipresence is a totality symbol *par excellence,* something round, complete, and perfect….On the antique level, therefore, the UFOs could be conceived as "gods." They are impressive manifestations of totality whose simple round form portrays the archetype of the Self, which we know from experience plays the chief role in uniting apparently irreconcilable opposites and is therefore best suited to compensate the split-mindedness of our age. It has a particularly important role to play among the other archetypes in that it is primarily the regulator and orderer of chaotic states, giving the personality the greatest possible unity and wholeness.[20]

Jung's eloquent statement about the significance of UFO sightings essentially encapsulates his psychological philosophy. Jung based his psychology on what he perceived as the malign of modern society: its estrangement from a spiritual life. Rationalism had overpowered a belief in the importance of the nonrational, the realm of soul and spirits. Jung's emphasis upon acknowledging the archetypal substratum of the human psyche was an attempt to counterbalance the too rational-minded thinking of modern man, which had resulted in the near annihilation of all life on Earth with the creation and proliferation of the nuclear bomb, and continues to threaten the stability of the planet with wanton disregard for the ecological integrity of the environment. It was the need for spiritual depth and significance that resulted in mass sightings of a god symbol expressing

---

[20] Jung (1958) 1970: 327.

the reconciliation of the internal war between the rational and the nonrational, or scientific and fantasy thinking. These sightings continue to be reported with even more frequency. Although Jung emphasizes the psychical significance of UFO sightings, he still left open the question of whether there is a physical aspect to these sightings, since in many cases UFOs have been tracked on radar screens and also have left physical traces of their presence.

Jung's essay on flying saucers has the subtitle, "A Modern Myth of Things Seen in the Sky." Modern UFO sightings began in earnest in the 1940s and since then a rich mythological tradition with religious undertones has emerged. Hilary Evans describes some of the elements of the UFO phenomenon that have developed since the first modern sightings:

> As it has evolved, the phenomenon ranges across the spectrum from fact to fantasy, incorporating Nazi bases under the Antarctic ice, mutilated cattle in the American Midwest, Men in Black knocking on the doors of witnesses, circular marks in cornfields interpreted as cosmic messages, government conspiracies, abductees beamed up into spaceships for the purpose of intergalactic breeding, and more. It's a rich and wonderful myth, but it's not stuff of which science is constructed. Yet, it is important to bear in mind that, within the soft flesh of the myth, there remains a hard kernel of genuine scientific anomaly.[21]

Evans is correct to emphasize how the UFO phenomenon is a blending of traditional mythic themes with scientific and technological references, a perfect modern myth for our technologically sophisticated times.

Psychologist Clay Routledge echoed Jung's theory that people claiming to have seen UFOs were expressing a need to reinvigorate the inherent spiritual dimension of their psychic make-up. In a playfully-titled article, "Don't Believe in God? Maybe You'll Try UFOs," he noted the decline in people who reported belonging to an organized religious group, then emphasized how the decline didn't necessarily mean people were less spiritually inclined. The "religious mind" is still alive within all of us, "our concern with existential questions and our search for meaning."[22] In a series of studies he conducted with colleagues from North Dakota State University, Routledge discovered that there was a demonstrable "link between low religiosity and belief in advanced alien visitors [which] is at least partly explained by the pursuit of meaning. The less religious

[21] Evans: 89-91.
[22] Routledge: n.p.

participants were, we found, the less they perceived their lives as meaningful. This lack of meaning was associated with a desire to find meaning, which in turn was associated with belief in U.F.O.s and alien visitors."[23]

Routledge's findings underscore Jung's statement that people who are "ripe for conversion" are the ones most prone to an archetypal experience or waking hallucination that leads to an experiential breakthrough satisfying the need for spiritual meaning. Even some people experiencing the horrors of sleep paralysis have claimed that, after such experiences, their belief in a spiritual Otherworld grew into a certainty. In the documentary *The Nightmare* (2015), which chronicles the experiences of eight people suffering from sleep paralysis, two people from the group developed strong religious convictions, and all of them insisted that sleep paralysis was not merely a question of a REM sleep-related disorder; there was an archetypal Otherworld dimension to the experience.[24]

People who have a fervent belief in UFOs have also created organizations with a strong religious undercurrent. Robert Bingham from Los Angeles, for example, first saw a UFO when he was thirty-nine, and kept it a secret for nearly a decade before confessing it to a neighbor. The neighbor became engrossed in Bingham's claim and asked if he could invite friends over to discuss the existence of UFOs. From this impromptu meeting, a world organization of UFO enthusiasts developed. Bingham now holds regular UFO sighting sessions in which group members gather together and discuss their experiences. Their group has inspired other UFO enthusiast groups to form. Bingham's group also attempts to summon UFOs through mass prayer: "Everyone has a different method, but most agree that it's similar to meditating. Some say that they feel physical sensations when they do it. The most important thing…is to focus…."[25] If someone in the group senses the presence of a UFO or spots something in the sky during their summoning session, several members with telescopes and cameras equipped with high-powered telephoto lenses attempt to confirm and document its appearance.

What is most interesting about the Bingham group is that they are attempting to use psychic methods to influence the appearance of a physical object, a technique very much in the tradition of sympathetic magic,

---

[23] Routledge: n.p.

[24] Ascher dir.: Zipper Brothers Films.

[25] Rago: n.p.

discussed in Chapter Three. The technique also implies that UFOs are not necessarily from some other planet in the solar system; they are from another dimension of reality, indicating the relationship or overlap existing between the Otherworld and waking reality.

One of the most insightful theories about UFO sightings comes from astronomer and computer scientist Jacques Vallee and his landmark book *Passport to Magonia.* The book has a most intriguing subtitle: *On UFOs, Folklore, and Parallel Worlds.* Vallee convincingly makes the connection between modern UFO sightings and their relationship with similar reported sightings from folklore and myth involving alien creatures: elves, fairies, dwarfs, and other beings who sometimes appear in the sky in flying objects. To clarify his emphasis, he states:

> ...my basic contention [is]: the modern global belief in flying saucers and their occupants is identical to an earlier belief in the fairy faith. The entities described as the pilots of the craft are indistinguishable from the elves, sylphs, and lutins [i.e. goblins] of the Middle Ages. Through the observations of unidentified flying objects, we are concerned with an agency our ancestors knew well and regarded with terror: we are prying into the affairs of the Secret Commonwealth.[26]

Vallee's reference to the Secret Commonwealth is to a book written in 1691 by Scottish scholar Rev. Kirk of Aberfoyle, entitled *The Secret Commonwealth of Elves, Fauns, and Fairies.* Vallee refers to the book as "the first systematic attempt to describe the methods and organization of the strange creatures that plagued the famers of Scotland."[27]

Vallee includes an amazing collection of anecdotes from ancient to modern times that documents sightings of alien beings and their actions which mirror in many cases the actions of the figures reported by sufferers of sleep paralysis and those who have claimed to have encountered extraterrestrial aliens: these uncanny beings attack, abduct, terrorize, seduce, and sexually couple with victims. And then they vanish. This latter aspect of the "fairy folk" is a main component of Vallee's argument about the otherworldly origins of UFOs. He mentions that many UFO enthusiasts report the physical presence and physical traces left by certain UFOs. However, Vallee indicates that many of these same enthusiasts fail to report the sudden disappearance of these physical objects:

---

[26] Vallee (1969) 1993: 57.
[27] Vallee (1969) 1993: 64.

> Unidentified flying objects, they argue, leave physical traces and behave like space probes. It is obvious to them that UFOs are scientific devices having nothing to do with the mystico-religious content of medieval apparitions, and nothing to do with the creatures studied by Kirk, since…these latter could appear and vanish at will. This view is no longer tenable. The reports of recent observations do describe objects that appear and vanish. It is just that such reports are not published. Students of UFOs are reluctant to publish them. And the witnesses themselves are not eager to come forward with stories they know are unbelievable.[28]

Vallee, therefore, acknowledges the Otherworld as an alternate reality that exists in parallel with waking reality, one that has always existed, and one that complements, and sometimes invades the consciousness of people who are more susceptible to seeing and experiencing this other reality. Victims of sleep paralysis are such individuals.

Vallee uses the word Magonia to describe this Otherworld reality, a reference to a case reported in the ninth century by Agobard, the Archbishop of Lyons, France. Agobard rescued four individuals from being burned to death as witches by a mob who claimed these individuals fell from the sky out of a flying ship. When these individuals were questioned, they insisted they were fellow humans who had been abducted by creatures resembling sylphs—winged fairies--from a nether region called Magonia.[29] Vallee describes the various characteristics of Magonia which he considers a realm comparable to Elfland:

> The physical nature of Magonia…is sometimes…a remote country, an invisible island, some faraway place one can reach only by a long journey. Indeed, in some tales, it is a celestial country….This parallels the belief in the extraterrestrial origin of UFOs so popular today. A second—and equally widespread—theory, is that Elfland constitutes a sort of parallel universe, which coexists with our own. It is made visible and tangible only to selected people, and the "doors" that lead through it are tangential points, known only to the elves. This is somewhat analogous to the theory, sometimes found in the UFO literature, concerning what some authors like to call the "fourth dimension"—although, of course, this expression makes much less physical sense than does the theory of a parallel Elfland. (It does sound more scientific, however!)[30]

---

[28] Vallee (1969) 1993: 67-68.
[29] Vallee (1969) 1993: 12.
[30] Vallee (1969) 1993: 102.

Vallee's description of this "parallel universe which coexists with our own," reminds me of a significant dream I had, which occurred not long after the death of a close friend. This friend's death left me with a deep, emotionally devastating sadness, since he was the epitome of someone with a fervent love of life. He was an amazing cook, and he loved to hold mass barbecues in his expansive backyard for his many friends, sometimes manning several barbecue grills at once while racing around to make sure everyone was having a great time. After he died, I had several dreams of him, and this one had the strongest effect on me:

*Journal Entry: Wednesday, February 8, 1995, 4:20a.m. (Northridge, California)*

I had a very vivid dream of Steve. It occurred shortly after a small earthquake; it wasn't too strong, but strong enough to wake me up and get the neighborhood dogs barking. The dream was set in a restaurant. For some reason, I think I was in Australia. Steve was suddenly there in the restaurant with me. We had a long and intimate conversation about "the other side." He told me that he could talk and appear to other people besides myself. Before he went about proving this, I asked him what the other side was like. He didn't really answer, just gave me an analogy of a city with two parts to it: an old, ghostly part from the past, sort of existing along with the modern part. I said, "You mean like New Orleans?" I was thinking about how New Orleans has that wonderful old section preserved in the heart of the newer, more modern section. Steve didn't answer. I think what he was trying to get across was that the other realm, the one he is in right now, exists right along with the waking world. He gave me the impression that the two realms are exclusive from one another, that the other side is everywhere yet completely autonomous from the waking world and very foreign from it.

As he tried to explain the differences between the two realms, I saw an image of an ancient city superimposed on a modern-day city, with the ghostly city overpowered by the noise and bustle and indifference of the modern city's inhabitants. There was a kind of place or border or marking where the old ghostly city sort of took over. The border area was very intense, the change from old to new was abrupt. It appeared as an underground stairway with ghosts walking up and down along with the modern live people. As the live people moved up the stairway, the hustle and bustle of the modern city became more intense and the ghostly realm became more transparent. I think this border area might have to do with how the different realms can be accessed: there *are* borderlines between the two realms where one can see into each realm. But these access areas are hazardous and abrupt and tricky.

I'm sure one of the ways a person can peek into the other realm is through dreams. But there are other ways too.

> During our talk, I asked him if anyone in the restaurant other than myself could see him. He said yes, then got up and started asking other people if they could see and hear him. Several other men responded and Steve invited them over to our own table for an impromptu dinner, something Steve typically would do when he was alive. But then when it came time to pay for the dinner, Steve got very upset. I think he wanted to pay for the dinner but couldn't. Not because he didn't' have any money. Apparently, he was pretty well off in his realm. But his "riches" couldn't be transferred to pay for such things as food and material goods. Steve finally got so upset that he stormed out of the restaurant and disappeared. After he left, the dinner guests and I took a ferry boat back home. Apparently, the guys I was travelling with were frequent visitors to Australia. They had discount passes for travelling from this area to their homes.
>
> When I got back home, there was a beautiful woman whom I had never seen before waiting for me. I told her about my experiences with Steve. I also mentioned that I had found some belongings of Steve's in the ferry boat I'd taken back. These belongings consisted of a journal, a book on Eastern philosophy, and some other miscellaneous papers. When I had been in the ferry boat and had found Steve's belongings, I casually glanced at the journal and after reading a couple sentences which were handwritten in a very sloppy style, I realized they were Steve's descriptions of the other side.

The dream has obvious archetypal elements, most notably its setting: the "other side" of the world in Australia, which is also known as the land down under or "underworld." It is in this setting that I converse with a recently deceased person, a setting that could be considered the equivalent of the Elysian Fields, the paradise realm of the underworld of classical Greek mythology. Just as Aeneas conversed with the soul of his dead father in this area of the underworld, I converse with my friend Steve who, because he is now a spirit rather than a flesh and blood human being, cannot communicate in the same manner as someone alive. He uses images and mental projections which I then interpret as best as I can. The overall significance of my conversation with him is that the underworld, or Otherworld, exists in parallel with waking world consciousness. It can be accessed more readily in certain locations and by certain individuals, like the "tourists" who have discount passes to this realm and visit it often. These tourists are probably shamans. It is also interesting to note that the journey to this realm is over a body of water, similar to the Greek, Sumerian, and Native American examples from Chapter Two. I also love the idea that I took a ferry or "fairy" boat to and from this Otherworld realm. When I return to my residence, I am greeted by a beautiful woman with whom I am not familiar, but to whom I confess the details of my journey. This woman is certainly a spirit bride or anima figure. It's too bad that I can't remember what Steve wrote in the journals I found in the "fairy" boat I took back from this realm. But, what I did come back with is a view of the "other side" comparable to Vallee's insights into Elfland and Magonia.

My dream also refers to certain people like the shaman tourists who are more aware of the Otherworld than most people, and that this realm can be accessed or seen more easily in certain parts of the world, at what I refer to as border areas. Vallee mentions the same characteristics about Elfland: "It is made visible and tangible only to selected people, and the 'doors' that lead through it are tangential points, known only to the elves."

An excellent folk tale that illustrates the Otherworld-waking world overlap and how certain people are granted permission to see this reality by a spirit who then leads the visitor through a door into this realm, is the Scottish tale, "A Vision of the Dead." The tale begins with a woman spinning wool in her house when she is approached by a beautiful woman dressed in green who asks the woman if she can care for her baby for a while. The woman agrees, and the lady in green disappears. After months pass, the woman becomes concerned that she might never see this lady again. During the lady's absence, the woman periodically receives new clothes and food from a mysterious source. Finally, the lady returns, and when her baby reaches up to touch the lady's shimmering green dress, its hands pass through the fabric. The woman immediately realizes this lady is a fairy from the Otherworld. The lady thanks the woman for taking such good care of her child, and in gratitude offers to show the woman her own house. After the woman agrees, they walk into the forest and climb a hill where the lady utters strange words and suddenly an opening in the hill appears. Inside the opening is a door. After they enter the door, the opening in the hill closes and the woman finds herself in a dimly-lit chamber. The lady then takes a goblet containing green liquid and sprinkles it into the woman's left eye, and says, "Look now." The woman looks and sees a beautiful countryside with a deep forest, along with lakes, streams, rivers and fields of barley. The lady then puts drops into the woman's right eye and again says, "Look now." This time, the woman sees a multitude of men and women tending the fields of barley and picking fruit from fruit trees. Looking closer, she realizes these people are all citizens she knows who have died. After the woman marvels at this vision of the land of the dead, the lady passes her hands over the woman's face and she finds herself back in the dark chamber underneath the hill. The lady gives the woman gifts of food and medicine, then utters more strange words, and the opening in the hill appears, after which the woman passes through the door leading to the upper realm and returns to her home. For a while she is still able to see people from the Otherworld moving through her own world, until one of these phantoms realizes the woman can see him. He then breathes upon her eyes, and the woman is never able to see this realm again.[31]

Just as my dream illustrates, this tale emphasizes how the Otherworld is a concurrent reality with the waking world; it overlaps and complements waking consciousness. The difference is that it is inhabited by timeless beings and spirits of the dead. Eighteenth century philosopher Immanuel Kant made similar observations about these two realms of existence:

> Since the soul has through the body a sensuous [i.e. physical] view of the corporeal world, when freed from the sensuous view of the body [after physical death] it will have a spiritual view, and this is the other world. In going to the other world, one does not enter a community of other things, as it were on another planet, one stays in this world but has a spiritual view of everything.[32]

Kant does not specify what a "spiritual view of everything" might look like. However, sleep paralysis sufferers, UFO enthusiasts, shamans, and anyone who has had an emotionally charged dream infused with mesmerizingly bizarre images have had insight into this spiritual view of everything. Barbara Ehrenreich's experience as a teenager in which she saw the world, along with herself, consumed and enlivened by a fiery force is a vivid example of seeing the material world from the point of view of spirit or soul--its eternal aspect. Also, many people claiming to have had a supernatural experience might have caught a glimpse of this reality. The Scottish folk tale illustrates such a glimpse, and features one of the most universal of all supernatural figures: the Green Lady.

Folklore abounds with examples of this figure. One of the most recognized examples appears in Shakespeare's *A Midsummer Night's Dream*: the figure of Titania, queen of the fairy world. Like the Green Lady from the Scottish tale, Titania is essentially the great Earth Mother, similar to the Greek's Demeter. The Green Lady in the Scottish tale leads the mortal woman into the earth where she reveals to her the Otherworld reality. Something similar happened during the Eleusinian Mysteries: initiates made a symbolic descent into the earth to confront Demeter's daughter Persephone, queen of this underworld realm.

---

[31] Mackenzie: 122-125.

[32] Jaffe: 167.

In addition to the Green Lady, other female figures of various hues appear throughout folklore and myth, including the Gray Lady, but most notably the White Lady. White Ladies usually haunt borderline areas, those marking the end of a rural village and the beginning of a wooded area. They also frequently haunt abandoned buildings or houses with a history of tragedy or some injustice inflicted upon a woman. The following legend potently illustrates the link between this spectral figure and a house where a tragedy occurred. It is also an example of what is perhaps the most frequently reported legend, documented in great depth by folklorist Jan Harold Brunvand in his landmark book on urban legends, *The Vanishing Hitchhiker.*[33] The vanishing hitchhiker is a variant of the White Lady since this figure commonly appears as a young woman dressed in a white gown—usually a wedding gown or prom dress--haunting deserted urban roads. In most variations of the legend, she is picked up by a traveler who agrees to take her to her home, but before they arrive, she vanishes (see Fig. 4-2).[34]

Figure 4-2: The vanishing hitchhiker is one of the most universal of all legends, usually featuring a young woman commonly dressed in white, a variation of the White Lady, another supernatural figure found in numerous folk traditions. (Creative Commons)

[33] See Brunvand.

[34] Creative Commons.

The following version of this legend was recorded in the early twentieth century, set along a rural rather than an urban highway. A young man traveling by horseback comes upon a young woman standing by the road near a decimated house. The young man offers the woman a ride home if she doesn't mind riding double. She agrees and he swings her up behind him and they ride off. When they come to a graveyard, the woman, whose name is Lucy, asks to be let down, so the man helps her down from his horse and watches her disappear into the graveyard.

Not far up ahead is a house, and the man figures Lucy wanted to cut through the graveyard to the house in order to avoid being spotted by her parents riding at night with a stranger. Curious, the man stops at the house and is greeted at the door by a man who introduces himself as a local judge and invites the young man to have supper with him and his wife. The young man agrees, hoping to have supper with Lucy to whom he's become attracted during their ride together. Lucy, however, never appears. Because it is late, the judge invites the young man to bed down for the night. In the morning, around the breakfast table, the young man, still anxious to catch sight of Lucy, learns that the couple recently moved to this house after their older house was hit by lightning and burned to the ground. The young man realizes their previous house is the one where he first spotted Lucy. The judge continues to talk about the tragedy, mentioning that his young daughter, who was sick during the time, died that same night. "We buried her in that graveyard," says the judge. "You can see her stone from the front gallery." The young man is speechless and remains quiet for a time, but then finally asks, "What was your daughter's name?" The judge says, "Her name was Lucy."[35]

In virtually all of the hundreds of variations of this tale, the vanishing hitchhiker is associated with an area where her death occurred. This emotional factor relates to many examples of ghost and spectral sightings, reflective of William Noll's comment in the Introduction about how events triggering strong emotional responses impact the environment in which the response occurred: "Events that would give us strong memories in our minds—death, accidents, and so forth—are the same kind that are strong outside our bodies." In other words, these supernatural figures are archetypal images of our instinctual responses to emotional events that have occurred in a particular environment.

[35] Yolen, ed.: 430-432.

Aniela Jaffe, a colleague of Jung's, examined a series of letters written by Swiss citizens in response to a local publication's request for examples of supernatural experiences. Jaffe collected numerous examples of the White Lady appearing to many of these citizens. The following was written by an elderly woman whose experience occurred when she was a young girl. In the middle of the night, she woke up thirsty and called to her mother for a glass of water:

> Then I heard a soft sound from the bedroom as if footsteps were approaching—was it Mother already? I raised myself in bed… [and] kept my eyes on the threshold… [Then] something appeared on the threshold and it was not Mother. It was a completely strange figure, a woman, tall, beautiful, in a flowing white robe, with long black curls hanging down. She moved very, very slowly past the bed of my sleeping brother and came towards me, with her large, dark eyes fixed on me. I remained transfixed… [and] stared at the approaching phantom and tried to scream, but I could not utter a sound. The apparition came to a standstill at my bedside, to the left of my pillow. Mute and motionless, the woman stood there, looking down at me neither kindly nor unkindly, neither gaily nor sadly, just strangely, and I stared back at her, for I could do nothing else. For a minute or two she remained there, then slowly moved round the head of my bed and again I could not, just could not do anything but gaze up at her petrified….[Then she] reached the threshold [again and] she came once more to a standstill, and once again turned her strange face towards me. At that moment, my mother appeared with the glass of water. I saw the two figures quite distinctly side by side—my tall mother looked small beside the apparition—then suddenly vanished as if dissolved in air….It was only much later, long after I had grown up, that I learned how it was said in the village that the house we had lived in was haunted, and that the grey lady walked there. But the phantom which terrified me as a six-year old child was dazzling white.[36]

This evocative example of the appearance of the White Lady has much in common with sleep paralysis, occurring in the middle of the night with the spectral figure appearing beside the sleeper's bed, leaving the sleeper paralyzed and unable to utter a sound. What makes this account different from sleep paralysis sufferers is that the young girl, although terrified, is never really menaced by the figure. The White Lady appears more like a Watcher figure: she simply appears and stands over the girl; she is a benign observer, a Great Mother figure. In fact, she could be interpreted as the Great Mother archetype since the girl was expecting to see her mother rather than this archetypal figure who appears as a giant next to her tall mother. It

---

[36] Jaffe: 89-90.

is also interesting to note that the mother never sees the figure; it only appears to the girl, again, a characteristic of sleep paralysis sufferers.

In one of my assignments to students, I ask them to relate any supernatural experiences they or someone they know might have had. I was inspired to create such an assignment by Jaffe's collection of letters from her Swiss citizens, and also by a study conducted in 1989 in which college students were asked if they believed in some sort of supernatural or paranormal experience. The response was impressive: 100%.[37] The percentage of my students who believe in the supernatural is perhaps closer to 80%, but this is still an impressive number. Within that number are students who have a much stronger belief, based on personal and familial experiences since many of the students in the Northern Mariana Islands have relatives who are siurhanos or siurhanas, traditional medicine men and women linked to the shamanic tradition. As some of the previous student responses indicate, certain areas of the islands are more conducive to having such experiences, usually jungle areas where banyan trees grow and in locales where latte stones were erected by the original Chamorro inhabitants of the islands thousands of years ago. Also, the main cemetery of the island of Saipan is another area where one might likely see an otherworldly spirit. One student reported the following experience:

> As a child, I would stay at my grandmother's place and work in her reflexology shop during the summers. Her house was behind her shop and is what we called a "barracks" where people rent out rooms in one big home. What should have been a backyard is our parking area that gives us a close view of the cemetery. The cemetery was literally just a few steps away separated by a small gravel path. I was about 8 years old when one night my grandmother wanted to go clubbing with her friends, but had no one to watch me for the night. So what happened was, I was advised to hide in her car for the two hours they spent in the club (forgive the minor child neglect). When we got back to her home, in the parking area near the light post, I saw a man. It was a perfect black silhouette of a man. I asked my grandmother who he was, but she didn't seem to notice him yet. He was standing at the driver's side of a truck parked near a light post. At the time, it didn't occur to me that although he stood there facing the light post, no light reflected on his face. He was pure black. I kept pointing again and said the same thing I said just moments earlier, "He's right there." She still didn't see him. At the time I was really confused why she couldn't because he was clearly there, no fuzz, just a solid silhouette. It didn't occur to me either why the man didn't respond despite all the fuss I made about him. She then grabbed my hand and said, "Never mind, let's go inside…." It took me years later to

[37] Santrock: 9.

> really dig into what I actually saw and found that other people saw these things and called them "Shadow People." (Cayabyab, written correspondence to author, 2018)

This student's account reflects sleep paralysis sufferers who see similar shadowy figures in their bedrooms. In fact, this student also reported seeing such figures in her bedroom when she was sleeping with her mother. In both instances, only she was able to see these shadowy figures, indicating that the student has a heightened sense of awareness of phenomena that others fail to recognize.

Another student reported an encounter with a traditional jungle spirit, referred to previously by a student from the Philippines:

> When I was around eleven, my mom woke me up one morning and told me to take the spoiled food out to the back of the house so I could feed it to the chickens and ducks that we have. It's not unusual for me to do that since it's part of my regular chores. I took the pot of spoiled food and brought it to the back of the house where the ducks were at. I called the ducks because I wanted to feed them first. While I dropped the food on the ground for the ducks, I was looking at the chickens and realized they didn't even want to come near the food. I was like, "Wow, that's weird." Then all of the sudden the chickens started to make some loud, weird noises. I got irritated and tried to calm down my chickens by throwing them some food from the pot. But, that didn't help. I then looked over to where the chickens were and saw the most horrifying sight I've ever seen: three little people, wearing dark short pants and triangle-shaped hats, staring at me with their small faces and black eyes. They were about two feet tall, and one waved at me and smiled. I got scared and threw the pot down as fast as I could and ran straight back to my house, all the way to my room and stayed there until my mom checked on me. She asked what happened, and I said, "I saw duendes." My mom said they're just a myth, but I wouldn't believe her because I saw them with my two eyes. My mom, dad, and brothers all checked the backyard but there were no duendes. It was just chickens and ducks fighting. Then a few days after the event, I got sick at night and couldn't sleep because I was full of bad dreams. I also shook with fear in my eyes because I thought the duendes were going to bring harm to me and my family. I was sick for almost two weeks. My dad decided to call a witch doctor if he could check on me. After all the spiritual prayers, the witch doctor said that duendes were just trying to help me by holding the chickens away from the ducks and me. So I guess this whole time they were trying to help me. Being able to hear that from the witch doctor made me more relaxed. So from that time, every time I go to the backyard I just say excuse me and thank you, letting the duendes know I don't bring them harm. That's also why every time I'm out in the jungle,

> I always respect the path I'm going on, to let them know I don't bring them no harm. (Cabrera, written correspondence to author, 2018)

After the student shared this account with me, I asked him for further details and he mentioned that while he was being treated by the witch doctor, or siruhano, the traditional healer told him that he was one of those individuals endowed with a special ability to perceive these types of entities. Duendes have much in common with mischievous elves from other cultures. They are especially attracted to children, and rumors abound about duendes luring children into the jungle where they become lost and disappear for significant periods of time, reemerging dazed and disoriented. In one of the most traumatic events to occur on the island in recent history, two young sisters, nine year-old Maleina Luhk, and ten year-old Faloma Luhk, disappeared on the morning of May 25, 2011, while waiting at a school bus stop located near their home in the As Teo village which is surrounded by deep jungle. The largest manhunt in the island's history resulted in which hundreds of citizens participated, led by the FBI. No trace was ever found of them. Although the most logical explanation for their disappearance is child abduction by a human predator, many islanders couldn't help but wonder whether duendes were responsible.[38]

Another student reported an exceptionally interesting phenomenon:

> One night I was giving my friend a ride home at nearly 3am. My friend lives in Kagman, a long drive for me, and I fought to keep myself awake. As we were getting close to my friend's house, I noticed a lady who appeared to be dressed as a nun walking along the sidewalk. I never got a clear look at her face, but I saw the lady as we approached and descended into the area she was in. A few minutes later, we arrived at my friend's house and he looked at me as if he was in shock. He asked me if I had seen the nun along the pathway, and I agreed and commented on how strange that was. My friend then said that the nun appeared to be floating, without any legs, and he couldn't make out a face, even with having a clear and good look at it. I was in shock and ended up staying at my friend's house until the sun came up so I could go home without feeling paranoid. (Kautz, written correspondence to author, 2018)

What makes this example so intriguing is that the apparition in the form of a nun appeared to both of these young men, with one reporting that he got a clear look at the figure which appeared to be floating across the road. Although this figure seemed to be a nun, nearby Kagman is the Santa

[38] De Guzman: n.p.

Lourdes Shrine, dedicated to the Virgin Mary. The Virgin Mary is one of the most frequently reported supernatural figures, sharing a close affiliation with the White Lady who has also been seen on the islands by numerous people, usually on the island of Tinian near a well, located in Taga Park, as a student in a previous account reported about her experiences with animism.

The following student caught a quick glimpse of the White Lady while playing outside after dark, the traditional time when spirits are most active:

> I remember my friend and I were playing outside the house. It was a full moon, so very bright. We played hide and seek that time. When I was hiding behind a coconut tree, I saw a white lady standing near another tree. I was frightened and scared. I heard my friend calling my name but I was speechless. I couldn't even talk because I was so nervous. What I did was to close my eyes and then later opened them. She had disappeared. So I said to myself, "Oh my God, I don't want to play again during the night time, because the white lady comes out during the full moon time." (Loverlas, written correspondence to author, 2018)

It is significant that the student mentions a connection between seeing the White Lady during a night when the full moon was bright and clearly visible. The White Lady has close affiliations with the figure of the White Goddess, or goddess of the moon. The moon has traditionally been considered a maternal symbol since it is associated with a woman's menstrual or "moon" cycles, both of which follow a twenty-eight day cycle. One of the most significant appearances of the White Goddess occurs in *The Odyssey* when Odysseus is thrown into the sea after his boat sinks. As he clings to the wreckage, the White Goddess, called Leuocothea, appears to him out of the raging sea and throws him a purple sash, telling him to wrap it around him and it will protect him from drowning until he reaches land. She then disappears. Odysseus does as he is told and is saved from drowning (see Fig. 4-3).[39] In this mythic example, someone in a life and death situation has a waking hallucination of an archetypal image linked to the survival instinct that ultimately saves his life. This example mirrors the real-life incident described in the Introduction, featuring the young Laotian boy lost in a jungle in the middle of the night who then sees a glowing white rabbit that leads him to safety. The rabbit, most notably the white rabbit, is an animal that also has close affiliations with the moon.[40]

---

[39] Creative Commons.

[40] Fisher: n.p.

Figure 4-3: Odysseus has a vision of Leuocothea, the White Goddess, during a life and death crisis and is saved from drowning. (Creative Commons)

The purple sash that the White Goddess gives to Odysseus has a relationship with a mystery cult on the Aegean island of Samothrace where the White Goddess played a part in their rites. After members of the cult were initiated, they received a purple sash to affirm their connection with the goddess.[41] Also, as the scene from *The Odyssey* illustrates, the White Goddess was closely associated with the sea, since the moon plays a part in affecting the tides of large bodies of water. She was also known to come to the aid of sailors, again exemplified in the scene from *The Odyssey*.

An historical incident from 1955 involved a sailor who experienced a waking hallucination during a life and death crisis that mirrors the mythic example from *The Odyssey*:

> On Christmas Eve, 1955, after celebrating the festive season rather too well, Arne [Nicolaysen] fell from the deck of his ship into the waters of the Gulf of Mexico. No one saw him fall, and his ship steamed away into the dark without him. For hours he kept himself afloat, but could not attract attention from any of the ships he saw passing. The following night, he saw two sailors walking across the water towards him. They told him that if he swam towards the moon, he would reach safety. He did as they directed, and a few

[41] Cole: 29.

> hours later he was picked up by a tanker after surviving more than thirty hours in the water.[42]

The "two sailors" that Nicolaysen saw walking across the ocean to tell him to swim towards the moon for safety have a rich mythic heritage, closely related to two brothers known as the Dioscuri, "sons of Zeus." Like the White Goddess to whom they were devoted, the Dioscuri were also god figures who appeared to sailors in need of rescue and had many cult sanctuaries throughout Greece and surrounding environs, including the island of Samothrace.[43]

Perhaps the most common of all supernatural experiences is a precognitive dream or waking hallucination in which a person sees the figure of a close relative or friend, then learns soon afterwards that this person has died. Aniela Jaffe records dozens of such experiences and variations of them in the letters she examined from her Swiss citizens. Several of my students have also reported these types of experiences, of which the following is a variant example:

> My first and only experience with the supernatural was quite unnerving. It was during my late father's funeral in the Philippines. I was only 11 years old and his funeral was held at his home town province of Ilocos. I remember it quite vividly. It was the night just before his burial. I was sleeping in the same bed with my mom. When I was laying down facing my mom it felt normal, but when I turned to change my position (my back facing her), that's when I could smell a sweet floral aroma. I was half asleep but the scent woke me up. I turned back to face my mom and the scent vanished. I turned my back towards her once more and I could smell that sweet fragrance. I did this a couple times until my mom woke up. I told her in an uneasy voice that I could smell a soft, sweet floral fragrance. I smelt a mixture of plumeria and vanilla with a very slight musk. My mom sat up and started praying and eventually started talking to someone (no one was there). Then she said, "Mar," which was the nickname my mom used to call my dad. My mom said in Ilocano, "We'll be fine, you may cross over, we love you." With a confused and despaired look, I turned and asked "What's happening?" She then told me that it was just my dad next to me in spirit for the last time, saying goodbye. With that, I started crying, knowing that I would never see my dad again. (Pagaduan, written correspondence to author, 2017)

---

[42] Evans: 167.

[43] Cole: 79.

It is quite common for people to have supernatural sensory experiences other than visual, as this very vivid and moving example illustrates. The emotional factor is also quite apparent, as all of the examples illustrate, most notably those involving the death of a loved one.

I also had what I believe to be a type of supernatural experience on the island of Saipan, one that was auditory rather than visual, and one that left me more baffled than terrified. I once lived in a small apartment complex on Lao Lao Beach Road, a one-lane dirt road that offers a spectacular view of the ocean on one side and deep jungle on the other side. I frequently walked the road but for quite a while avoided walking up an offshoot of the main road that led uphill to an abandoned restaurant. I had a desire to inspect this old restaurant because I had heard from a lot of people that it had once been a beautiful and quite popular place, and offered an amazing view of Lao Lao Bay. However, I was hesitant to walk up the trail leading to the restaurant because, frankly, it looked spooky as hell, overgrown with tall weeds and thick jungle foliage. Finally, I got up the courage to walk up the trail. It was a creepy, deathly quiet walk, but it finally led me to the abandoned restaurant, or what was left of it. Only large wooden beams, a crumbling roof, and cracked walls remained with everything covered in vines. The interior was infested with rats, wasps, and feral cats. However, after I cut my way through overhanging jungle vines, I was afforded a gorgeous view of the bay below. I spent a half hour poking through the remains, then started down the trail again but didn't get far before I stopped in my tracks. I distinctly heard a man's voice talking in a language I was not familiar with; the voice was coming from deep within the jungle. I knew that no one would choose to stand in thick jungle in this remote area and talk out loud, so I immediately sensed that I had heard a taotaomona, a Chamorro ancestor spirit, calling to me, beckoning me to enter into deeper jungle terrain. I said out loud, "Excuse me," then bowed, and hurriedly scuttled down the trail to the main road. I cannot completely rule out the possibility that somebody was there talking out loud while standing in thick jungle terrain. But, I cannot also completely rule out that I had heard an ancestor spirit of the Chamorros. There is also the very strong possibility that the unsettling, "haunted house" environment—the animistic spirit--evoked such a response (see Fig. 4-4).[44]

[44] Photograph by author.

Figure 4-4: Abandoned (haunted?) restaurant along Lao Lao Bay Road on the island of Saipan. (Photograph by author)

As I indicated in the chapter on animism, many names have been given to this energetic power that infuses the material world and unites all life forms. One of these names comes from medieval philosophy: *Anima Mundi*, the world soul. This soul of the material world is most commonly symbolized by a beautiful naked woman, a variant image of the White Lady or White Goddess, who acts as an intermediary between God and humanity. Jung would call her an archetypal anima figure, a soul guide that helps ego consciousness develop a more unifying relationship with the Self (see Fig 4-5).[45] What this figure also signifies is the collective unconscious which Jung considered a maternal source of power since it gives birth to consciousness itself and is the source of archetypal energies that take the form of universal images and influence behavioral patterns linked to instinct. As C.G. Carus noted in Chapter Three, within the unconscious is a primordial god image representing the "primordial source of life." Although the god image within has infinite representations, I can think of no better image to represent this primordial life source than Anima Mundi.

---

[45] Creative Commons.

Aniela Jaffe indirectly refers to the connection between Anima Mundi with the White Lady or White Goddess when she discusses Great Mother and Earth Mother figures and their relationship with the alchemical figure known as *femina alba* (white woman).[46] Since one of the most famous depictions of Anima Mundi is by the seventeenth century alchemist/philosopher Robert Fludd (Fig. 4-5), the connection between Anima Mundi and *femina alba* seems to be an obvious one. Jaffe emphasizes the dual nature of the Great Goddess: she is both creator and destroyer, birth giver and life taker. Her appearance as a succubus who strangles and a White Lady who watches over the sleeper or haunts areas where a death or injustice has occurred illustrates her dual nature. She is the animistic spirit with an infinite variety of forms. People sensitive to this spirit, especially those in the throes of a psychological crisis or primed for a psychological breakthrough, activate the unconscious forces within them which in turn activates complementary forces within the environment. The result is the appearance of an archetypal energy taking the form of a spirit, ghost, elf, fairy, "Chinese Gentleman," Bigfoot, Pan, E.T., or the Great Goddess herself as a hitchhiker dressed in a prom dress walking along a deserted road, a lady dressed in green, gray, or white gliding over a lonely stretch of land, or a beautiful naked woman floating upon a raging sea.

Just as certain areas of the natural world evoke archetypal specters, certain times of the year also loosen the boundaries between this world and the Otherworld during which time ghosts and spirits of the dead are more likely to appear. The most obvious time of the year is All Hallows Eve. A film, *Pay the Ghost* (2015), dramatically illustrates the connection between this time of year with the appearance of a female specter, once a caring mother of three, but due to a terrible injustice, becomes a demonic child snatcher, known by many names in mythology and legend, one of which is the Lamia from Greek myth. The film is set in New York on the eve of Halloween. Eight year-old Charlie Lawford (Jack Fulton) is anxiously awaiting Halloween night when he can dress up as a pirate and go trick-or-treating with his parents and the neighborhood kids. Charlie is especially excited to go out trick-or-treating with his father, Mike (Nicholas Cage), who has been preoccupied too much lately with his work as an English professor hoping to secure tenure with his university. On Halloween night, Mike arrives home too late to accompany Charlie and his mother Kristen (Sarah Wayne Callies). To make up for his tardiness, Mike takes Charlie to a Halloween street carnival not far from their home filled with colorfully

[46] Jaffe: 93.

masked partygoers and street entertainers. While Mike stops to buy Charlie an ice cream cone, Charlie looks up at his father and says, "Dad, can we pay the ghost?" Mike is confused by Charlie's comment and turns instead to the ice cream vender to pay him for the cone. When he turns back to Charlie, his son is nowhere to be found.

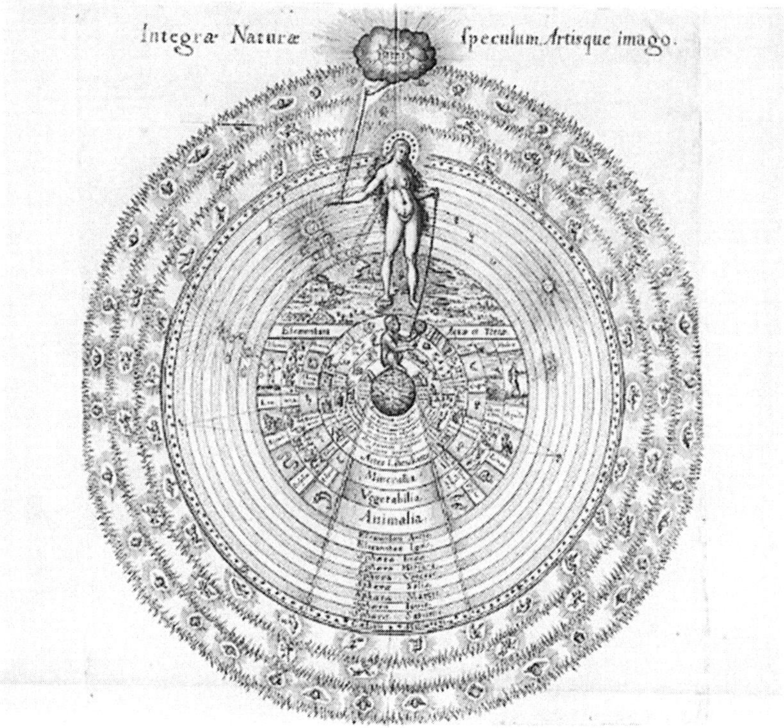


Figure 4-5: An image of Anima Mundi, the soul of the material world, depicted as a beautiful naked woman who unites God with humanity, the latter depicted as a feral, ape-like being. Image by Robert Fludd. (Creative Commons)

Frantic, Mike races through the street carnival looking for Charlie, then when he can't find him, he runs back to his house where Kristen is waiting for their return. When he asks if Charlie has returned home and she looks at him perplexed, both run back to the carnival and search among the crowd with no luck. Finally, they call the police who try to calm down the couple by telling them such cases are usually resolved within twenty-four hours.

One year later, Charlie is still missing. Mike is now living alone in a one-room apartment. Kristen has demanded a separation, furious with Mike for not protecting Charlie. Mike has become obsessed with finding his son. His apartment is littered with articles about children who have disappeared, and he repeatedly puts up flyers everywhere throughout the city with a photo of Charlie and a plea for help from anyone who might have seen him. Mike also mercilessly hounds the police for more information about any progress they have made in finding his missing son.

On the day before Halloween, as Mike is putting up more flyers, he spots Charlie dressed in his pirate costume riding on a passing public bus. Mike chases after the bus, but when he boards it, Charlie is not there. Mike exits the bus and is astonished when he spots an abandoned building with a graffiti scrawl upon one of its walls: "Pay the Ghost." Mike enters the building and finds a stairway leading down into a cavernous warehouse. Upon descending, he is nearly attacked by a large black dog, but manages to dodge it and explore the area which he finds inhabited by homeless people. When he asks about the graffiti scrawl and what it means, no one speaks to him. Then everyone cowers when the sound of a wailing woman pierces the interior. A blind homeless man (Stephen McHattie) appears and when Mike asks him about the graffiti scrawl, he leads Mike to another wall with the same phrase written hundreds of times all over it (Fig. 4-6).[47] The blind man claims he knows nothing about the meaning of the phrase, but Mike suspects he knows something about it that he is hesitant to share with a stranger.

Both Mike and Kristen begin to experience unnatural events. When Mike looks at a video that Charlie took while they were at the street carnival, the carnival footage is suddenly interrupted by an image of an old farmhouse surrounded by a forest. Mike catches a glimpse of the farmhouse's interior: it is full of children dressed in strange costumes. Kristen also sees Charlie's scooter moving by itself around the interior of the house. The two get together and talk about what they have experienced, and Mike tells her he believes Charlie is trying to contact them. He shows her a computer file he has of children who have disappeared and tells her most of the children eventually are found, except those who disappeared on Halloween. After they find the name of a girl who disappeared on Halloween a year ago, they track down her residence and find the father living in squalor and nearly out

[47] Creative Commons.

of his mind with despair. He tells them, "I should have paid the ghost. That's what my daughter said just before she disappeared: 'Papa, pay the ghost.'"

Figure 4-6: Mike (Nicholas Cage) confronts a blind seer (Stephen McHattie) in an underground warehouse who shows him a wall covered with the phrase, "Pay the Ghost." Scene from *Pay the Ghost*, 2015.

Mike and Kristen return together to their house and while Mike is downstairs, he hears strange noises coming from upstairs where Kristen is getting ready to sleep. When he investigates, he finds Kristen speaking in Charlie's voice while she carves up one of her arms with a pair of scissors. He immediately grabs the scissors from her which knocks her out of her trance-like state. The arm she has disfigured bears a strange marking, a type of symbolic image. They show the scar to a sympathetic colleague of Mike's at his university who recognizes it as a Celtic symbol of the Great Mother Goddess; the symbol appears as a two crescent moons facing in opposite directions with the full moon in the center (Fig. 4-7):[48]

[48] Creative Commons.

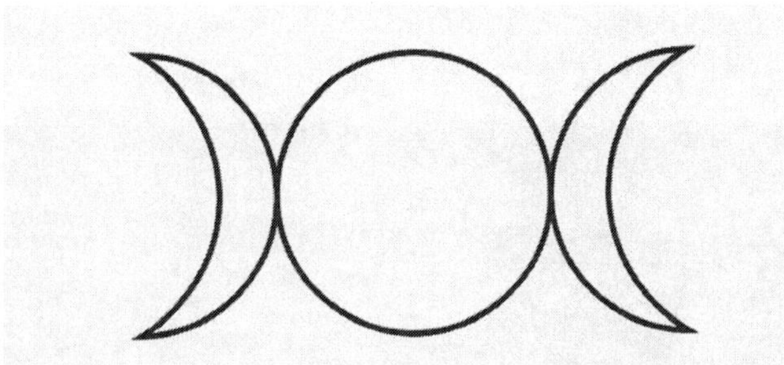

Figure 4-7: Triple moon symbol featured in the film *Pay the Ghost,* 2015. (Creative Commons)

The symbol represents the various phases of the moon—waxing, full, and waning--and their corresponding representations of the Great Goddess as Maiden, Mother, and Crone, or witch. Mike and Kristen learn of a Celtic community inhabiting an old part of the city, one with ancient roots. They also learn that, on the night of October 31, 1679, a woman from the Celtic community was accused of practicing witchcraft and burned to death with her three children in a public ceremony. They decide to visit this old community and when they do they find the inhabitants celebrating Halloween, known as Samhain, in the ancient Celtic tradition: boys and girls dressed in colorful costumes circle around a bonfire and throw totem dolls into the fire. When the couple asks one of the adult participants what the significance of the ceremony is, the woman tells them the children are offering a sacrifice to the Celtic goddess in her crone or waxing moon phase. Mike and Kristen show the woman Kristen's scar, and she confirms that it is a symbol of the Great Celtic goddess. She also tells them that the crone or witch phase of the goddess is her destructive phase. On Halloween, she has been known to snatch children and take them with her to the Otherworld, which is why the children are offering a totem sacrifice to her: they are paying her an offering so they will not be snatched by her. The woman also tells them that access to the Otherworld becomes available to mortals on the night of Halloween, but ends at the stroke of midnight. They ask her if she knows where this access point is, but she has no idea, only that on the night before Halloween, people can sometimes hear her wailing for the lost children.

Mike then realizes he knows where the access point is: in the abandoned warehouse. He and Kristen race to the area, and Mike enters the warehouse, only to find it completely abandoned, except for the homeless blind man. Mike begs the man to show him the access point, and the man leads him to

Figure 4-8: Some of the children snatched by the witch on Halloween in *Pay the Ghost*, 2015. (Creative Commons)

an underground bridge. "The portal is open," he says. "But it closes at midnight." Mike walks carefully across the bridge which spans across an abyss covered in a dark, impenetrable fog. On the other side of the bridge, he finds a wooded area with the old farmhouse he glimpsed on the video footage that Charlie took at the street carnival. When he enters the farmhouse, he finds a basement leading to a huge, cavernous room filled with thousands of children, all dressed in decorative costumes (Fig. 4-8).[49] The multitude of children gaze at him as if in a stupefied trance. Mike calls for Charlie, and all the children raise their hands. As he passes through the crowd, he also passes through their upraised hands, all except for one: it's Charlie's hand. Charlie stands dressed in his pirate costume. Mike hugs him, then takes him by the hand and begins leading him out of the crowd of phantom children. Two other children appear, an Asian girl and Hispanic boy. Charlie says they all arrived in the farmhouse together. Mike remembers that the Celtic woman told him that only the most recently snatched children can return; the rest are spirits of their former selves, lost forever. He tells the three children to follow him but they must hurry because midnight is approaching. They race across the open field to the bridge and begin to cross it but only get half way. The ghost of the Celtic woman burned as a witch appears, the incarnated spirit of the Great Goddess

[49] Creative Commons.

in her demonic crone aspect. She attacks Mike and begins strangling him like a succubus as they fly into the air above the bridge. Charlie calls out for help, and suddenly the souls of the thousands of snatched children emerge out of the farmhouse and fly up to where the witch is strangling Mike. They fly in a frenzied swarm around the two of them, and the witch finally screams and drops Mike back onto the bridge. He grabs the children and as the bridge begins to crumble underneath them, they run to the other side just before the bridge finally collapses.

The film's final scene is Mike and Charlie returning home and Kristen bursting into tears as she hugs her son and thanks Mike for saving him.[50]

Although a commercial and critical flop, *Pay the Ghost* nevertheless is an excellent depiction of the relationship between this world and the Otherworld and how these worlds collide during significant times of the year. It is also infused with references to folkloric traditions surrounding the Great Goddess and her association with the phases of the moon, along with references to child snatching demonesses from folklore. Most notably, it illustrates the emotional factor, how a horrific injustice against a woman and her children left an indelible trace upon the landscape. *Pay the Ghost* also has references to a journey to the underworld, complete with descent into this netherworld where the hero figure first encounters the fierce guardian to the entrance: in this case a black dog, modeled after Cerberus, typically depicted as a three-headed dog, the animal equivalent of the Great Goddess. The hero figure also usually has a guide through this netherworld and in this case it is a blind "seer," modeled after the famous blind prophet from Greek mythology Tiresias, who acted as a guide for Odysseus when he called up the spirits of the dead at one of the entrances to the underworld in one of the most famous scenes from *The Odyssey*. The film also emphasizes how people desperate for a need to be fulfilled are those most susceptible to experience the Otherworld reality.

Numerous other films dramatize the waking world-Otherworld overlap. One of the most skillful and successful of all is *The Sixth Sense* (1999), about a boy with the ability to see the ghosts of people who have suffered from a traumatic death or one involving an injustice. Although at first terrified of these specters who act as if they are not dead, he ultimately learns how to help them understand their condition and finally find peace as spirits

---

[50] Edel dir.: Voltage Prod.

in the land of the dead. In this regard, he acts as a shaman, helping to appease the wrath and suffering of these ghosts from the Otherworld.[51]

*ParaNorman* (2012) is an animated film with the same theme as *The Sixth Sense:* the young character of Norman can see the spirits of the dead walking around his neighborhood. Although he has been ridiculed for his claim to be able to see dead people by his father and kids from school, he has grown accustomed to seeing the ghosts and happily greets them all every morning as he walks to school. The film also has a theme similar to *Pay the Ghost*: Norman's New England city is haunted by the specter of a young witch burned at the stake during America's early history. On Halloween, she must traditionally be appeased by someone reading to her a story from her childhood just as her mother did, but when the person familiar with this tradition dies before Halloween, she unleashes her wrath upon the city, resulting in the emergence of zombies rising out of their graves and terrorizing the community. Norman learns that these zombies are actually the ghosts of those who condemned the young girl to death long ago. On Halloween night, he finds the location of her gravesite and, like a young shaman, passes over into the Otherworld in an attempt to appease her wrath by telling her that she is just like him, someone with a special power that no one else understands. He asks for her forgiveness, and she accepts his sympathetic plea, which gives her and the zombie judges a final eternal peace in the Otherworld.[52]

*Midnight Special* (2016) is another fine film with a strong waking world-Otherworld overlap theme. Like so many of these types of films, the person who is aware of the Otherworld is a child. In this case it is an eight year-old boy, Alton (Jaeden Lieberher) who has grown up in a religious cult. This cult has recognized Alton's special powers and all the members consider him a prophet. Alton is snatched by his father, Roy (Michael Shannon) and taken to his mother, Sarah (Kirsten Dunst), both former members of the cult. They are determined to transport Alton to a location he says he needs to be on a certain date. Because it appears Alton has been kidnapped, and also because the cult where Alton has grown up has lately been purchasing and stockpiling weaponry, the FBI becomes involved with the affairs of the cult, as does the National Security Agency due to the revelation of Alton's ability to predict events that compromise national security. After the NSA and FBI learn of the location where Alton's parents are taking him, they converge

[51] Shyamalan, dir. and screenwriter: Hollywood Pictures.
[52] Fell and Butler, dirs.: Laika.

upon this location in the Florida swamps. Along with them are cult members determined to return Alton to the cult's confines. While Roy tries to act as a decoy, leading the other forces astray, Alton and Sarah race to the special locale. When they reach it, Alton sends out an energy force that triggers the emergence of an Otherworld physically imposed upon and encircling the material world in this area and surrounding environs. Millions of citizens in this region are stunned to see this Otherworld which appears as an advanced civilization populated by beings filled with luminous energy. The Otherworld is everywhere, winding around buildings in rural and urban areas and sprouting up in open fields. As a group of luminous beings from this realm approach Alton and circle around him, he suddenly disappears and the Otherworld vanishes with him.[53]

Like the numerous examples given throughout this chapter, the cinematic ones have essentially the same underlying intent: to acknowledge an unseen reality that many of us have felt some time in our lives, an emotional resonance that haunts and calls into question the strictly rational view. All of the examples attempt to validate Kant's spiritual view of life, one that complements our material world and yet illuminates another dimension to it.

Jung emphasized how these types of experiences invigorate the spiritual dimension which has for too long been dismissed as inferior to the rational view. In the Prologue to Jaffe's book about the supernatural experiences of Swiss citizens, Jung echoed the comments of Rudolf Otto in regards to the *mysterium tremendum*, that all such experiences have one main purpose:

> An integral component of any nocturnal, numinous experience is the dimming of consciousness, the feeling that one is in the grip of something greater than oneself, the impossibility of exercising criticism, and the paralysis of the will. Under the impact of the experience, reason evaporates and another power spontaneously takes control—a most singular feeling which one willy-nilly hoards up as a secret treasure no matter how much one's reason may protest. That, indeed, is the uncomprehended purpose of the experience—to make us feel the overpowering presence of a mystery.[54]

I would only add that the purpose of such experiences is to make us feel the overpowering reality of the Otherworld, and how these types of experiences encourage the development of what Kant called a spiritual view of life, one illuminated by folklore, myth, and intensely visceral dreams that challenge our view of the reality we see as we struggle to shake off the overlap.

---

[53] Nichols, dir. and screenwriter: Faliro House Prod.

[54] Jaffe: 9.

# CHAPTER FIVE

# THE OTHERWORLD AND THE BENDING OF TIME, SPACE, AND CONSCIOUSNESS

In the science-fiction film *Interstellar* (2014), director and co-screenwriter Christopher Nolan, uses some of the known and speculative properties of gravity and its effects on time to give the film's storyline a deeply emotional resonance (Fig. 5-1).[1] The film is, at its core, a father-daughter relationship drama, set in the near future when Earth has been nearly destroyed by climate change. The film's protagonist, Joseph Cooper (Matthew McConaughey), a trained engineer and former pilot, now works on a farm with his ten year-old daughter Murph (Mackenzie Foy), fifteen year-old son Tom (Timothee Chalamet), and father-in-law Don (John Lithgow). Like the rest of the farmers in the area, the crops they grow are threatened with heat, blight, and massive wind storms. Cooper hates farming and longs to return to his former life as a pilot for NASA. He gets his chance when he learns that NASA has been exploring new planets for sustainable life since it is apparent that Earth is doomed. NASA has already sent out astronauts who journeyed through a wormhole near Saturn to explore three planets deemed potential worlds for reestablishing an Earth colony. NASA is also attempting to develop a massive space station, essentially an artificial Earth, but has yet to solve the question of gravity for this man-made Earth. In the meantime, NASA needs to send another space ship through the wormhole to learn the fate of the three previous astronauts, whose transmissions to Earth have stopped, and determine whether any of the planets to which they were sent can be colonized.

Cooper agrees to be one of the astronauts, even though he knows he might never return, and if he does, he could be gone for decades. When he tells his family about his decision, Murph begs him not to go. He tries to tell her that the fate of the entire Earth depends upon his success, but she rails against him for choosing to abandon her. Before he parts, he gives her a

[1] Creative Commons.

watch and he synchronizes its time with his own so they will be "in synch" all the time he is gone. She responds by throwing the watch against the wall.

Figure 5-1: Promotional poster for *Interstellar,* 2014. (Creative Commons)

After Cooper leaves Earth with his fellow astronauts and they successfully navigate the wormhole, they explore the first planet on their agenda. This planet, covered in a sheet of water, is situated next to a massive black hole. The astronauts know that the black hole has the ability to bend time, and by descending upon this planet, every hour they are on its surface equals seven Earth years. After they reach the planet via a landing craft, they quickly realize the planet is inhospitable and the previous astronaut is dead. A massive tsunami threatens to destroy their craft, and it ends up killing one of the astronauts. By the time they are able to recover from the tsunami and return to the mother ship, twenty-three Earth years have passed.

In his absence, Cooper has received transmissions from his family, specifically his son. In the film's most emotionally wrenching moment, Cooper watches the series of transmissions. He breaks down while he sees his fifteen year-old son Tom age before him, transforming into a young man (Casey Affleck) who at one point claims he has fallen in love, then later proudly holds up a baby son for Cooper to see. He listens as Tom tells him that Grandpa Don has died. Then, finally, he hears Tom, now a middle-aged man, tell Cooper that this will be his last broadcast because, after twenty years of these messages with no response from Cooper, he fears his father is dead. Unable to send any transmissions back to Earth to let his son know he is still alive, Cooper weeps in despair.

Cooper barely has time to recover from these series of transmissions when a new one begins to play. It is from a young woman whom he at first does not recognize, but then looks on in stunned amazement at his now-adult daughter Murph (Jessica Chastain), the first time he has seen her since he left Earth. Although two decades have passed, she is still furious over his having abandoned her. She tells him she is now the same age he was when he left.

Cooper is left emotionally devastated over the transmissions. He at first wants to abandon the mission and return to Earth; he even contemplates using one of the landing crafts to drive through the black hole in the hope that it can somehow bend time backwards. Finally, he agrees to continue to investigate the two remaining planets. When the crew descends to the second planet, they find the astronaut alive in a sleep chamber but ultimately realize the planet is also inhospitable. After they revive the astronaut, he tries to kill Cooper and escape from the planet in Cooper's landing craft. When he reaches the mother ship, he kills another astronaut and nearly destroys most of the mother ship with his botched attempts at docking, ultimately killing himself in the process. Cooper is rescued in another landing craft by the one remaining fellow astronaut, but because the mother ship has lost most of its fuel, they must jettison much of the remaining equipment. Cooper then suddenly jettisons one of the landing crafts with him in it, telling the remaining astronaut to continue to the final planet alone, while he drives his craft into the black hole.

As Cooper descends into the black hole, his craft is torn apart, leaving him floating in his space suit through the black hole into another reality. This reality is a tesseract, a cube-like Othcrworld, where he floats in suspended animation, separated from Earthly reality. The Earthly reality he can see is a scene from his life on Earth: he can see the bedroom of Murph from various time perspectives while he floats from a vantage point situated behind her bookcase.

Cooper's presence in this time-view perspective was established in the film's beginning when ten year-old Murph often complained of her bookcase being haunted, with books and other objects sometimes falling from the shelves along with other peculiar happenings. No one believed her complaints, most notably Cooper. But, now he realizes he was the ghost, or more accurately a poltergeist, haunting her bookcase. As he is able to see her bedroom from different moments in time, he rages against his inability to communicate in any real effective way with her except to cause a book to fall off a shelf on occasion with his aggressively emotional outbursts.

Murph as an adult has been involved in NASA's attempts to create a sustainable artificial Earth by solving the problem of gravity. As Cooper rages behind her bookshelf and sees her in various stages of development through her life, he finally realizes why he is seeing this moment from the vantage point of her bedroom. "I brought myself here!" he shouts. Through his experience with the wormhole, he is now living in a physical representation of time and has unconsciously willed himself to this vantage point. Since his mission was to save the world, he realizes his desire to do so has brought him to this physical perspective to help Murph solve the gravity problem.

When he survived the descent into the black hole, Cooper was accompanied by one of his computers, and the computer has made computations about gravity based upon its experience inside the black hole; this is the information needed to solve the gravity problem. Cooper finally figures out how to communicate with Murph from his Otherworld: by manipulating the watches he synchronized with her before he left. Through these manipulations, he is able to send her Morse code messages on her watch. In her adult status, Murph finally notices the strange, code-like movements on the hands of the watch, and realizes her father is the ghost that plagued her as a child and who has been attempting to communicate with her for decades from his Otherworld vantage point from behind her bookcase.

As Cooper continues to send her Morse code messages based upon the information gathered by his computer companion, Murph solves the gravity problem. When she announces the solution to the world, Cooper's tesseract

Otherworld vantage point dissolves, and he finds himself floating in space near Saturn where there is a massive space station. This station is the artificial Earth, called Cooper's Station, named after its creator: Murph. Cooper is rescued from space and taken to the space station. Almost ten decades have passed since he left Earth, yet Cooper has only aged a few years. When he is reunited with his daughter, she is nearly one hundred years old and in failing health. Their reunion marks the second most emotionally wrenching moment of the film. As he holds her hand and looks into her eyes, she tells him that he shouldn't have to watch his child die. She encourages him to go back into space and attempt to rescue the one surviving astronaut from his mission. After a final emotional parting, he begins to prepare for another voyage into space.[2]

Upon its initial release, *Interstellar* was a major commercial success, due in large part to the reputation of its director Christopher Nolan whose *Batman* film trilogy earned high praise from viewers and critics alike. Certain critics were less praiseworthy of *Interstellar*, with many rightly claiming that the film's too-technical presentation of a futuristic space mission with speculations about wormholes, tesseracts, and the effects of black holes on gravity and time made it hard to follow. Dennis Overbye, science writer for the *New York Times*, mentioned that he initially watched the film with an astronaut who ended up as confused as he was over the film's high-tech science references. Overbye saw the film again after reading the book, *The Science of Interstellar*, written by Nolan and the film's technical advisor, gravitational theorist Kip Thorne. He enjoyed the film more during the second viewing, but still noted: "I wonder if a movie that requires a 324-page book to explicate it can be considered a totally successful work of art."[3]

I was also highly critical of the film's over-reliance on scientific explanations that, at times, seemed absurd. I was most upset by the scenes taking place in the tesseract. Up until that point in the film, I felt I pretty much understood the semi-logic behind the scientific jargon used to explain certain plot developments. But, when Cooper flew through the black hole in nothing but a space suit and landed behind the bookcase in the bedroom of his ten year-old daughter, I nearly threw my watch at the screen and left. However, I couldn't deny the emotional intensity of the scene in which Cooper watches in despair as his son ages in time from a fifteen year-old to

---

[2] Nolan dir. and co-screenwriter 2014: Legendary Pictures.

[3] Overbye: n.p.

a middle-aged man, then weeps over the sight of his now-adult daughter still fuming over his abandoning her at age ten. I couldn't help thinking about how I might react if I were in a situation that prevented me from watching my own son, his wife, and their children passing through the various life stages without my being able to experience these life moments along with them. And then there was that final reunion scene at the film's end between a middle-aged Cooper and his near-one hundred year-old daughter. The love and calm understanding expressed between them after having been kept physically apart for decades made a deeply emotional impression on me.

It was not until I saw the film a third time that I was able not only to tolerate the tesseract scene but actually understand it; however, it was not from a scientifically speculative understanding, but from the perspective of one of Jung's own most confounding theories: the theory of an acausal connecting principle, known as synchronicity. If one takes into consideration the theory of synchronicity along with what is known about black holes, the film's tesseract scene makes more sense. In the film, the scientific explanations about how a black hole can bend time is based on sound theoretical evidence. A black hole is made up of dense matter; both time and space in the vicinity of the black hole are affected by the density, with space bending and time slowing down.

As Cooper's computer explains to him while they are stuck in the tesseract, they are in a physical representation of time, a result of their experience with the black hole, the "bender" of time and space. Time has become a physical entity, and they are stuck in it at a particular point in Cooper's own personal experience of time. The time-memory he is stuck in has been triggered by his emotional bond with his daughter and their combined efforts to save the world. They are linked—in synch--together in emotion, in time, and in crisis. This type of situation—a life and death emotional crisis--is when the principle of synchronicity is most likely to become a reality.

Cooper's excited shout, "I brought myself here!" is his realization that he has bent time and space through the emotional bond he shares with Murph. He has willed himself to this moment to help prevent a catastrophic disaster affecting the fate of the planet and all life on Earth. In a sense, Anima Mundi, the soul principle permeating and enlivening all matter, has responded to Cooper's psychological crisis: masses of matter infused with a primordial consciousness and linked with the Self which regulates the human psyche and synchronizes with the rhythms and principles of the natural world.

Synchronicity is essentially a split between physical and psychical space and time; the split is triggered by the emotional factor, a disaster or life and death crisis. The many examples that Aniela Jaffe presents in her analysis of supernatural experiences of Swiss citizens illustrate over and over again the principle of synchronicity, most dramatically in the examples of dreams in which a loved one appears to the dreamer and says goodbye, then the dreamer wakes up to learn that the loved one has just passed away:

> [In a dream] I saw my cousin under a tree; she looked at me sadly and beckoned to me. I asked her why she was so sad, and she replied that she had to go away on a long journey, I should probably never see her again. Two days later I received news that my cousin had been killed by lightning under a tree.[4]

> I dreamt that my sister came into my room from the balcony, wearing a long white dress. I hurried to her with great joy; at that moment, there was a loud knock at the door. I asked her to wait a moment, and ran to the door, but there was nobody there. I swung round, overjoyed by my sister's visit, but the room was empty. Two days later the announcement of my sister's death was in my hands.[5]

In these types of examples, it is obvious that the dreamer has not caused the death of the loved one by dreaming about the person dying. And yet, there is an obvious connection—a meaningful coincidence--between the psychic reality of the dream and the physical reality of the event that occurs not long afterwards. As Jaffe states: "The principle of synchronicity applies to all the pairs and groups of events which cannot be explained by causality, but which are experienced as related because they are bound together by meaning."[6]

Jaffe quotes medieval philosopher and theologian Albertus Magnus regarding the emotional factor in such experiences:

> ...a certain power to alter things indwells in the human soul and subordinates the other things to her, particularly when she is swept into a great excess of love and hate or the like. When therefore the soul of man

---

[4] Jaffe: 51.
[5] Jaffe: 81.
[6] Jaffe: 177.

> falls into a great excess of a passion, it can be proved by experiment that it (the excess) binds things (magically) and alters them in the way it wants, and for a long time I didn't believe it, but… (then) I found that the emotionality of the human soul is the chief cause of all these things.[7]

The quote from Magnus relates to the emotional bond between Cooper and Murph: this bond which transcends space and time originating from an Otherworld reality—the tesseract—effects an outcome in Earthly reality, a cinematic example of the principle of synchronicity. Jaffe specifically mentions the primal importance of the parent-child bond in synchronistic experiences, that such bonds are infused with a numinous power because they are based upon archetypal behavioral patterns:

> The unconscious forms the foundation of every kind of interpersonal understanding. In some human relationships, the unconscious bonds are far stronger because they are based on an archetype….In such relationships, based on an archetype, the knowledge of one partner concerning the thoughts and experiences of the other is more easily established, and may be drawn more readily into the relativity of time and space categories.[8]

When the emotional tension that binds Cooper and Murph together is loosened after the life and death crisis has been resolved, the tesseract Otherworld dissolves with it, and Cooper reintegrates back into the material universe where he is physically reunited with Murph. The implication is that while Cooper was in the tesseract, he was viewing Earthly reality in a manner similar to the way the unconscious does: from his vantage point, he views a static moment of physical reality—Murph's room—from multiple time perspectives. The unconscious has a similar view of waking reality: it can take personal experiences and mix them up with other experiences, jumping from one perspective to another in a flash, giving the dreamer multiple ways to view a particular situation or concern that transcends a linear time frame. Like the tesseract scene, past, present, and future bend and blend together in the unconscious.

An even more dramatic and impressive film example of synchronicity featuring an elaborate and emotionally charged dream is *The Night My Number Came Up* (1955). Jung referred to the film in his essay on synchronicity, written and revised several times in the early 1950s.[9] Actually, to be more precise, Jung referred to the factual incident that inspired the

---

[7] Jaffe: 172.

[8] Jaffe: 181.

[9] Jung (1951, 1952) 1969: 526.

film. This incident involved a near-fatal plane crash that occurred in 1946. The crash had been predicted by the dream of someone not involved in the incident but reported to the air marshal riding in the plane, Richard Goddard, the former senior commander of the Royal Air Force during World War II. The dreamer, an English officer with the last name of Dewing, told Goddard the details of his dream at a dinner party they both attended the day before Goddard was involved in the near-fatal accident.[10]

The film is quite faithful to the details of the dream and to the factual event. The film begins in Hong Kong as a commercial plane, a Dakota airliner, is scheduled to fly to Tokyo in the morning. During a dinner party prior to the flight and attended by several of the passengers, many of the attendees watch a Chinese celebration occurring from below their vantage point, referred to as the Ceremony of the Returning Spirits, similar to All Soul's Day ceremonies in which relatives honor the memories of their dead ancestors. One of the attendees, Owen Robertson (Alexander Knox), makes condescending remarks about the superstitious beliefs of the Chinese, mentioning, for example, that the Chinese believe in predestination, and that dreams are visions of future events which they receive and interpret as ways to guide them to their preordained destinies.

Another attendee, Commander Lindsay (Michael Hordern) turns pale as Robertson ridicules the idea that dreams can predict future events. He reluctantly relates a dream he had the night before, telling the guests that it was pretty nonsensical and probably a result of eating too much lobster. The details of the dream are about the Dakota they are scheduled to fly to Tokyo. He tells them in descriptive detail about how the plane flies into a major storm and becomes lost; radio transmission dies as the plane struggles through the storm, flying into the night in search of a place to land; the wings ice up, and they run out of fuel, forcing them to attempt an emergency landing on a rocky beach on an island off the coast of Japan. During the landing attempt, the plane crashes. After he finishes relating the details of his elaborate dream, many of the passengers scoff at the idea that a dream can predict such an event.

In the morning when all the passengers have boarded the plane, some review the details of Lindsay's dream, with several of them becoming quite agitated while others continue to laugh at such a possibility. One passenger, Lord Wainwright (Ralph Truman) chastises Air Marshal John Hardie

[10] Greenhouse: n.p.

(Michael Redgrave) when Hardie acknowledges the possibility of the dream becoming a reality. Wainwright becomes belligerent toward Hardie, telling him that modern, civilized humans cannot give in to such superstitions, otherwise they become slaves to witchcraft and black magic. "We can't do these things in the middle of the twentieth century," he says. "We must brush these primitive things aside and behave like intelligent and common sense men in the age of reason." He also rails against the idea of predestination, saying that such a belief is intolerable to those who firmly embrace free will and are the masters of their own fates.

However, during the flight, the details from Lindsay's dream begin to occur. A storm overtakes the plane, the radio transmission dies, they become hopelessly lost and fly into darkness as the plane's wings ice up and they run out of fuel. Another detail from the dream also occurs: as the dream's prediction of the plane crashing becomes more of a reality, one of the passengers becomes hysterical and has to be restrained. Finally, the pilot spots land, then is shaken when he realizes he is flying over an island off Japan's coastline. When he sees a rocky beach, he attempts a landing, but at the last moment pulls up, realizing the beach is too small. He frantically searches for another possible landing area and spots a field covered in snow and surrounded by huge cliffs. Carefully maneuvering between the cliffs, he brings the plane down and it plows into the snow. However, unlike the dream's ending, the plane remains intact and everyone survives. Because the details of Lindsay's dream are so explicit regarding the area in which the plane set down, an emergency rescue crew is able to quickly locate the plane and bring all of the survivors back to safety.[11]

As I mentioned, the majority of the film's details of the dream and the flight match the factual events reported by Richard Goddard. Jung commented that the event is just one of many of the recorded modern examples of synchronicity, how a psychic reality becomes a physical reality, demonstrating a link between the human psyche and the physical world, confounding scientific ideas about causality and the relationship between time and space.

One of the most engaging aspects of the film is the emotional turmoil caused over the idea of dreams having a relationship with future events, indicating that the future is somehow already set and we are fated to live out this future. However, as one of the characters points out when ridiculing the

[11] Norman, dir.: Ealing Studios.

Chinese belief in dreams as glimpses into the future, such dreams serve as guides; we receive guidance from the unconscious to help us fulfill our singular destinies. The pilot seemed to embrace this view of dreams since, after he realized he could not land the plane on the rocky beach, he refused to follow the dream's disastrous outcome. Thus, knowing the details of the dream gave him insight into how to avoid this fate, as if the dream were giving all the passengers crucial information about a fate that was not predestined but prospective, a *possible* fate if they refused to take seriously the details of the rest of the dream.

Jung would agree with this idea of fate and destiny. The Jungian concept of individuation is based upon this idea. According to Jung, we are born with archetypal patterns that make us human, all of us destined to follow a predictable path of human development. As he once famously said, "The acorn can become an oak, and not a donkey,"[12] meaning that all life forms follow predictable stages of development. In order to become fully human and understand our singular paths to achieve our singular goals in life, we must pay attention to the unconscious. Since the unconscious is grounded in instincts and universal archetypal patterns beyond rational control—patterns linked with the rhythms and laws of the natural world--we are indeed fated to follow a certain predictable, or more accurately, a prospective, path in life. To resist following such a path results in psychological disorientation. The more we stray from our human path linked with the rhythms of the natural world, the more we suffer from psychological malaise.

A common example of how all of us—in fact, all life forms--have a relationship with the cycles of nature, is how our inborn biological clock, which follows a twenty-four hour cycle reflective of Earth's rotation around the sun, becomes disrupted when we fly from one part of the world to another over various time zones. Anyone who has suffered from jet lag knows how disruptive flying over multiple times zones can affect sleep and eating patterns as well as the ability to think straight; people become fuzzy-headed and disoriented for days until their biological clocks can reset themselves to the new time zone. Humans were not designed to fly, nor were they designed to climb mountains like Everest or descend into deep areas of the ocean like the Marianas Trench. We must rely on technologically sophisticated artificial enhancements in order to do these activities better suited for birds and fish. To rephrase Jung's previous comment, a human

[12] McGuire and Hull, eds.: 347.

embryo becomes a mature human being and not a chicken hawk. The mythical youth Icarus tragically learned the lesson of hubris when his father, the genius inventor Daedalus, fashioned artificial wings for the two of them to escape from the Cretan labyrinth and the youth, exhilarated over his new ability to soar through the sky, flew too close to the sun and perished.

Psychic disorientation is already happening on a massive scale. As *Interstellar* illustrates, we are slowly destroying the world around us because we continually emphasize our lordship over the natural world and every creature that lives upon it. Also, the characters in *The Night My Number Came Up* who ridicule and berate those who believe in superstitious nonsense ultimately learn that if they are relying upon technology as a means to escape from a life and death situation—in their case a flying machine built with humanity's amazing innovative scientific thinking abilities—they must still rely on intuition, instinct, and even precognitive dreams when dealing with the forces of nature in order to navigate a safe landing.

Holding on to a strictly rational view of life and denying the existence of an Otherworld reality is a betrayal of the animistic soul inherent in the physical world. As I mentioned in the chapter on animism, philosophers and scientists have posited a theory about the universe having a type of proto-consciousness field. Since all matter and all life forms are made up of the same basic elements, all of us must embody this same pan-psychic proto-consciousness. As biologist Neil Shuman remarked upon the human connection with the primal elements of the universe: "…the elements that compose us are derived from the birth of stars and the explosion of supernovae. These events are only the beginning of our deep connections to the universe. Written inside of us is the birth of the solar system and workings of the planet itself."[13]

Synchronicity underscores the link we all have with the world soul that acts to guide us in times of crisis. It can give us futuristic clues that keep us on our singular paths to fulfilling our destinies. And in many cases, these types of experiences help keep us alive by giving us clues about how to avoid a catastrophe. The experience of synchronicity is also linked with the religious experience. It is a shattering, numinous experience that destroys logical thinking and encourages a belief in an Otherworld reality. In his essay on synchronicity, Jung gives the example of a woman patient with an

[13] Shubin: SR8.

ultra-rational attitude that was seriously affecting her therapeutic progress. During one session, she described a dream she had recently in which someone had given her a piece of expensive golden jewelry in the form of a scarab beetle. As she was concluding her description of the dream, Jung heard a tapping sound coming from the window directly behind him. When he turned to see what was making the tapping sound, he spotted a scarab beetle flying against the window. He quickly opened the window, grabbed the beetle, then turned and handed it to the woman, saying "There is your scarab." The effect this physical representation of a dream image had upon her shattered her rationalistic attitude, resulting in a therapeutic breakthrough.[14]

Jung also mentions that synchronistic events are usually connected to archetypal patterns, and the example of the woman patient and her scarab beetle experience underscores this idea. Jung points out that the golden scarab is an Egyptian symbol of rebirth and renewal, and the effect the dream and physical appearance of the scarab had on his patient resulted in the renewal of her psychological well-being.[15]

I had what I believe to be a synchronistic experience during a time when I was conducting research on a book-length project. The subject of the project dealt with the film history of silent film comedian Buster Keaton.[16] One of the aspects of Keaton's film history that I was interested in was locating the area of one of the earliest film studios at which he worked in Southern California. I was also interested in locating the area, or even exact address, where he had briefly lived; this residence and the former movie studio were both located near the downtown area of Long Beach, California, about twenty miles from where I was living at the time. I kept putting off this scouting trip to downtown Long Beach, until one night I had a dream about standing in a flat, open area and looking up in the sky at a full moon and laughing at it, after which the moon duplicated itself so there were two full moons in the sky, a sight that made me laugh so hard that I fell down on the ground in hysterics. Because I rarely have dreams in which I laugh, I thought maybe the spirit of Keaton, one of the greatest film comedians of all time, was encouraging me to do my Long Beach scouting expedition during the next full moon, which was only a few days away.

At around dusk on the day of the full moon, I started to get ready to drive into Long Beach. Right before I left, my wife asked if she could come along.

[14] Jung (1951, 1952) 1969: 525-526.
[15] Jung (1951, 1952) 1969: 539.
[16] See Kline 1993.

The night was clear, and as we headed for the downtown area, the full moon began to rise--a magnificent site. By the time we arrived and I began looking for the address I had for the home where Keaton had lived, the moon was high above us. I then was able to find the exact address I was looking for, which made me feel ecstatic. Bursting with elation, I decided to run down to the beach area and get my feet wet, and as I ran, my elated feeling increased. Standing by the shoreline with my wife, I looked up at the dark sky with the brilliant moon shining down upon us and said, "This is fantastic! Isn't this an amazing night? Isn't the moon beautiful?" My wife looked at me smiling and said, "Well, you know, we *are* two moon children." She was referring to the fact that we were both born under the astrological sign of Cancer, a sign associated with the moon. Because she had never referred to us as moon children before, her remark struck me as peculiar, jarring a flashback to the memory of the dream of my laughing at the full moon and becoming hysterical when it became two moons. I then looked around and realized this flat, open expanse of beach replicated the landscape of my dream. After I realized this, I *did* become hysterical, screaming over and over again, "I dreamed this, and now it's happening! I dreamed this and now it's happening!" At one point during my rant, I looked back up at the moon, and it was almost as if it had become alive, looking down and winking at me as the past dream experience of a future event played out in the current moment: past, present and future blending into one. I ended up down on my knees pounding my fists into the sand still screaming my stupid phrase. Naturally, my wife thought I was nuts. By the time I'd lost my voice screaming, I was so emotionally exhausted that she practically had to carry me back to the car.

That's what a synchronistic experience can do to someone who doubts the possibility of such a bizarre, irrational phenomenon ever occurring to him or anyone else for that matter. As a dreamed event becomes a physical reality, with time bending and blending together, a person's hold on a rational view of the world is torn apart, and if the person is not prepared to accept the reality of such a possibility, his mental state can be torn apart as well. My hysterical reaction mirrored that of the character in *The Night My Number Came Up*, who broke down in hysterics as the details of the dream of the plane crashing became more and more of a reality.

In these types of nonrational experiences, a common physical object like the moon can suddenly become filled with a numinous power. Such moments give birth to a mythological view of life. The moon during my experience became a living incarnation of the White Goddess. After this incident, I became obsessed with mythic lore about the moon, which led me to one of Jung's colleagues, Esther Harding, and her book on moon symbolism, *Woman's Mysteries,* filled with references to many ancient societies viewing the moon as the incarnation of a god power associated with the female principle as life giver. Describing how a common physical object can become imbued with a supernatural power that inspires a worshipful reverence, she states:

> …man did not choose his gods in any comprehending way. The process of god-choosing, to coin a phrase, takes place entirely otherwise. The volition seems to be in the symbol, which obtrudes itself on man's consciousness. It has fascination for him, *mana,* it demands attention, worship…it has a peculiar power which insists that he do certain things in regards to it. The history of religion is the history of the power of such symbols. We now know that this power comes from the unconscious and that this is the secret of its fascination for the human being…. [The] symbol is the representative of an unknown truth. It rises spontaneously from the depths of the unconscious and expresses or manifests the hidden fact in an image whose meaning can only partly be grasped by consciousness.[17]

Harding's comments underscore the connection between physical reality and the unconscious. Synchronistic events involving a dream with a significant central image creates a meaningful relationship with a waking experience featuring that same central image; such an experience encourages and inspires a new view of that central object which has now become both a natural and a supernatural entity. In such moments, the unconscious, which transcends linear time, has invaded consciousness with its time-bending view of reality. In other words, synchronicity gives a person the experience of the timeless, eternal dimension of the human psyche.

The Biblical example of Jacob having the dream of a ladder reaching to Heaven, referred to in Chapter Two, relates to this experience with the supernatural. After he had his amazing dream of angels ascending and descending a stairway to Heaven and hearing Yahweh's voice blessing him and his ancestors, Jacob took the stone he had used as a pillow, set it upright, anointed it with oil, and made it a holy relic by establishing a sacred shrine on the spot where he had his dream, a spot he called Bethel, the House of God. The humble stone he used as a headrest had now become a totem object imbued with the power of God.

---

[17] Harding: 64.

Aniela Jaffe expressed the connection between a singular numinous experience with the eternal dimension of the unconscious:

> The space-time extension of [a singular] "moment" relative to the nearness or distance of consciousness, might be represented by a pyramid with a base extending to infinity, i.e., to the no longer knowable unconscious, while its apex would be the point of the "here and now" of consciousness…The deeper the layers of the unconscious involved, the further the field extends…until…the deepest, absolutely unknowable layer of the unconscious…extends to infinity. The [singular] "moment" [then] becomes identical with the unconscious.[18]

What connects the deepest, timeless layers of the unconscious with a singular conscious moment is the emotional factor, as Jaffe pointed out with her quote from Albertus Magnus. During highly emotional moments that threaten psychological equilibrium, the unconscious becomes more alive as if to remind the individual of the eternal dimension of life that transcends physical reality and mortality.

The unconscious is not the only dimension of the psyche that bends time. As I mentioned in Chapter One, the brain's default mode is daydreaming. A person who is not engaged in directed, logical thinking falls into the daydreaming mode in which a past experience can flitter through a person's endless stream of consciousness, only to be replaced moments later with thoughts of a future event, then suddenly combine with the person's current situation mixed with a fantasy from childhood. What is fascinating about this type of thinking is how closely it matches unconscious, nonrational dream logic, and how both reflect the language of cinema. The relationship the unconscious has with cinema is one of the key reasons why I have included so many references to films throughout this presentation.[19]

Buster Keaton was one of the pioneer filmmakers who instinctively recognized the relationship between the language of dreams and the language of the cinema with film's ability to cut from one scene to another, sometimes flashing forward in time, then flashing backward, and mixing incongruous scenes with others to create a surrealistic effect. No better example of Keaton's understanding of film logic and dream logic is *Sherlock Jr.*, made in 1924. The film is a riot of surreal events with much of the story line taking place while the Keaton character is asleep and dreaming. In the film, he plays a film projectionist who, while screening a

[18] Jaffe: 123-124.

[19] Another key reason is illustrated in the Conclusion.

particular movie, falls asleep in the projection booth and dreams a ghostly image of himself rising out of his sleeping form. This "ghost Buster" then watches the film being screened and begins to imagine people from his life taking the place of the film characters. When he realizes this, the Keaton specter runs down into the theater and jumps into the movie screen and begins engaging with the movie characters. After this happens, he is thrown from one incongruous scene to the next, with the film first abruptly cutting to a busy street scene where he is almost run over by passing motorists, followed by Keaton nearly walking off a cliff that has suddenly appeared in front of him; stepping back from the cliff, he finds himself in a jungle surrounded by lions; when he tries tiptoeing away from the lions, he tumbles into a hole in the desert; trying to get out of the hole, he is nearly hit by a train barreling through the desert landscape; as he sits down on a mound of sand, he ends up sitting on a rock in the ocean; attempting to dive off the rock into the water, the scene changes to a field full of snow and he ends up with his head stuck in a snowbank.[20] The entire scene is incredibly technically sophisticated, with Keaton's expert use of quick-cut editing that seamlessly weaves all these scenes together in rapid-fire. The result is not only comedy but an amazing example of the power of film to recreate the unconscious logic of dreams and how both dreams and cinema defy linear time and space.

Keaton learned much of his cinematic expertise and appreciation of the relationship between film language and dream language from silent filmmaker D.W. Griffith. Keaton's first feature film, *The Three Ages,* for example, was a parody of Griffith's monumental epic film *Intolerance,* released in 1916. *Intolerance* had the theme of man's inhumanity to man, inspired in part by the outbreak of World War I. The film interweaved four different stories from four different time periods and cut back and forth between these stories: the fall of ancient Babylon; the final days of Christ leading up to and including his crucifixion; the St. Bartholomew's Day Massacre taking place in Renaissance France; and a contemporary drama featuring a young man falsely accused of murder. Griffith's expert editing techniques coupled with his use of emotionally visceral scenes of outrage, slaughter, and injustice, came to an amazing climax in which he cut back and forth between these historical time periods at a feverish pitch, resulting in an astonishing example of film's ability to replicate dream language: how

[20] Keaton, dir.: Metro Pictures.

dreams defy linear time and combine past events with present concerns linked with strong emotions.[21]

Like Keaton, Griffith understood how both dream language and film language are made up of moving images driven by emotionally dramatic stories; like dreams, he considered the language of film, specifically silent film, a universal pictorial language that could speak to people no matter what their spoken or written language was. Echoing Jung's ideas about universal archetypal symbolism, Griffith stated that "A picture is the universal symbol, and a picture that moves is the universal language."[22] Lillian Gish, a frequent actress in many of his films, underscored Griffith's belief in the power of film to effect a mass emotional response in viewers: "He called [film] the 'universal language….' He wrote on celluloid a new formula to cure the ills of the world. Film was going to bring about the understanding of men on Earth—end wars and bring peace to the world."[23] Gish's remarks parallel those of humanistic psychologist Erich Fromm in his description of dreams, myths, and fairy tales as expressions of a universal symbolic language:

> Symbolic language is…the one universal language the human race has ever developed, the same for all cultures throughout history. It is a language with its own grammar and syntax, as it were, a language one must understand if one is to understand the meaning of myths, fairy tales, and dreams. Yet this language has been forgotten by modern man. Not when he is asleep, but when he is awake.[24]

Fromm rightly emphasizes the importance of understanding this universal language that parallels dream language when one is conscious; the pictorial language of silent cinema brought this symbolic language out of the realm of dreams and projected it upon movie screens for millions to see and understand from a conscious perspective.

One recurring image from *Intolerance,* for example--beautifully shot by Griffith's cinematographer Billy Bitzer—underscored Griffith's use of symbolic dream imagery; it featured actress Lillian Gish rocking a baby's cradle while three women symbolizing the mythical three fates—in this context the fate of humanity—sit placidly in the background (Fig. 5-2).[25]

---

[21] Griffith, dir.: Triangle Film Corp.
[22] Brownlow and Gill dirs.: Thames Television.
[23] Brownlow and Gill dirs.: Thames Television.
[24] Fromm (1951) 1957: 7.
[25] Creative Commons.

Figure 5-2: The use of symbolic imagery from D.W. Griffith's *Intolerance,* 1916. (Creative Commons)

Unfortunately, in the case of Griffith, his films suffered from an over-reliance upon torrid, melodramatic stories populated by hyperventilated actors which might have stirred up the viewer's emotions to heart-pounding overload, but the result was more of a sense of exhaustion rather than world peace. He was also a racist, as his 1915 Civil War epic *Birth of a Nation* graphically illustrated, with its depiction of African Americans as subhuman creatures who need to be prevented from corrupting the virtuous white race by the righteous actions of the film's hero figures: members of the Ku Klux Klan. The film triggered race riots across America in many cities where it played, a far cry from his desire to instill "understanding of men on Earth."

However, Griffith's insights into film as a universal language likened to the language of dreams remained an innovative approach to filmmaking and inspired countless filmmakers to follow his dynamic use of moving images to tell compelling stories which, in many cases, included images reflective of unconscious dream symbolism. Some of these early silent filmmakers include F.W. Murnau (*Nosferatu*, 1922; *The Last Laugh*, 1924; *Sunrise*, 1927), Erich von Stroheim (*Greed*, 1924), Fritz Lang (*Dr. Mabuse the Gambler*, 1922; *Metropolis*, 1927), Alfred Hitchcock (*The Lodger*, 1927), G.W. Pabst (*Pandora's Box*, 1929; *Diary of a Lost Girl*, 1929), and Carl Theodore Dreyer (*The Passion of Joan of Arc,* 1928).

The incorporation of dream logic into visual and other forms of entertainment is now so common, we take it for granted. Steven Johnson makes this aspect of storytelling a central point in an article about the default or daydreaming mode of the brain entitled, "The Human Brain is a Time Traveler." Johnson first mentions how certain forms of ancient and medieval storytelling incorporated the use of dream logic, weaving stories with other stories and doubling back on the original story. He refers to Homer's *Odyssey,* and *The Arabian Nights,* the latter also known as *The Thousand and One Nights*, as examples of this type of storytelling. *The Arabian Nights* is an exceptional example, with the central storyteller, Scheherazade, intermingling various stories and narrative perspectives to create a massive singular story structure that she relates to her husband each evening over a span of nearly three years. As Johnson mentions, "Analepsis and prolepsis--flashbacks and flash-forwards--constitute some of the oldest literary devices….[26]

Johnson then mentions how modern storytelling has far surpassed the ancient examples:

> A defining trick of recent popular narrative is the contorted timeline, with movies and TV shows embracing temporal schemes that would have baffled mainstream audiences just a few decades ago. The epic, often inscrutable plot of the TV show "Lost" veered among past, present and future with a reckless glee. The blockbuster 2016 movie "Arrival" featured a bewildering time scheme that skipped forward more than 50 times to future events, while intimating throughout that they were actually occurring in the past….These narrative developments suggest an intriguing possibility: that popular entertainment is training our minds to get better at cognitive time travel…Today's popular narratives zip around their fictional timelines with the speed of the default network itself.[27]

These narrative developments also illustrate how the unconscious logic of dreams is becoming more of an accepted way of viewing waking consciousness. As Johnson mentions, this type of approach to telling a cinematic story has only become more commonplace in the last few decades, specifically beginning around the time when the ultra-conservative Motion Picture Production Code that oversaw screen content was replaced in 1968 by the more liberal Motion Picture Ratings Code, allowing more freedom of expression for filmmakers. The result was more films with skewed storylines infused with flashbacks and flash forwards and a

[26] Johnson: n.p.
[27] Johnson: n.p.

character's inner thoughts abruptly invading the dramatic progression of events. An example of this approach to telling a story is *Petulia*, released in 1968 around the time of the introduction of the new Motion Picture Ratings Code. The film tells a fairly straightforward story of an affair between a young, rich, kooky socialite played by Julie Christie, and a successful middle-aged surgeon, played by George C. Scott. What makes the film nearly incomprehensible to follow at first are the numerous flashbacks to incidents that make no sense when they initially appear, followed later by scenes of future events that have not occurred yet in the film's basic linear storyline. Overall, however, the film's skewed storytelling approach works to illustrate the shattered lives being depicted on screen, and how desperate the two lead characters are to connect emotionally and romantically despite their age differences.[28]

A more recent film that uses flashbacks and flash forwards, this time to tell a story from the point of view of someone suffering from anterograde amnesia—the inability to form lasting new memories—is *Memento* (2000), another Christopher Nolen-directed film. To capture the disorientation of the film's main character (played by Guy Pearce), Nolan films a majority of the scenes by abruptly throwing the viewer into the protagonist's point of view: trying to figure out what he is doing in a certain situation interacting with people he doesn't recognize. In order to keep himself grounded in reality, he takes photos of key people he meets and labels them with descriptive information; he also tattoos information all over his body. All of his memory-jogging efforts are designed to help him find the person responsible for clubbing him on the head, causing his amnesia, and also causing the death of his wife during a botched house break in.[29] Like the structure of *Petulia*, the presentation of events is disorienting at first until the viewer adapts to the way in which the drama is unfolding. Both films illustrate how the psyche can adjust to these types of time-bending storytelling devices primarily because they mirror so closely the brain's default network and the non-linear language of the unconscious.

*Donnie Darko* (2001) takes a unique cinematic approach to presenting the world view of a schizophrenic high school student, played by Jake Gyllenhaal, who becomes obsessed with time travel after he begins receiving visitations from someone called Frank who appears to Donnie dressed in a rabbit costume to tell him the exact time the world will end and

---

[28] Lester, dir: Warner Bros.

[29] Nolan, dir. 2000: Summit Ent.

what to do to prepare for it. Filled with surrealistic moments that remain hauntingly ambiguous, the film's most perplexing scene is one from the future that literally crashes into the present moment: a jet airplane engine suddenly falls from the sky and lands in Donnie's bedroom. Fortunately for Donnie, at the time the engine destroyed his bedroom, he was meeting with his rabbit friend Frank on the grounds of a nearby golf course. While everyone remains baffled by the appearance of the engine—including investigators from the Federal Aviation Administration who cannot trace it to any known aircraft--Donnie realizes the significance of the engine crash after he reads a book about time travel, written by a former teacher from his high school, explaining how time travel works. The explanation remains incomprehensible for the viewer (at least for this viewer[30]). However, with his new-found ability to understand future events, Donnie accepts his fate and, with encouragement from Frank the rabbit, performs serious mischief around his community that exposes the hypocrisy embedded in his community's value system. After he secretly completes his major pranks, Donnie makes sure he is in his bed on the morning he knows the jet engine will once again fall from the sky, ensuring he will be killed. Thus, Donnie's world does end, and a new community--purified of pedophiles, wife stalkers, bigots, and bullies--begins.[31]

With a cinematic style that successfully captures dream logic from the point of view of someone suffering from schizophrenia, the film calls into question certain types of thoughts and behavior that are considered symptoms of a mental disorder but could in fact be the ability to see dimensions of reality that others can't. Jung, for example, took very seriously the comments made by his schizophrenic patients after he realized that some of their comments reflected mythic motifs and philosophical ideas beyond their personal experiences. By paying attention to their so-called unconscious babblings, Jung fashioned his ideas about archetypes and the collective unconscious. Marie-Louise von Franz also mentioned how certain people suffering from schizophrenia are, in a sense, possessed by unconscious dimensions of their personality which results in their ability to perceive hidden dimensions of the world, as well as dimensions of the personality of others normally kept hidden: "Psychotic borderline cases often have parapsychological gifts—knowing through the unconscious

---

[30] Like the criticisms leveled at *Interstellar*—that it would help if the viewer had a degree in gravitational theory before viewing it—one critic of *Donnie Darko* rightly stated that it would be helpful to have a Ph.D. in physics to even think about offering an opinion about its incomprehensibility. See Derisz.

[31] Kelly, dir. and screenwriter: Pandora Cinema/Newmarket Films.

things which they couldn't otherwise know."[32] In this light, Frank the rabbit who visits Donnie and tells him about future events is an archetypal figure--the shadow dimension of Donnie's personality--with the ability to detect the darker dimensions of those in his community and even predict future events.

There is also the widespread belief in cultures who practice traditional shamanism that symptoms of certain mental disorders such as bipolar disorder and borderline cases of schizophrenia are similar to the early indicators of a potential shaman. Dr. Maldoma Patrice Some′, a practicing shaman from the Dagara tribe of West Africa, states that people in Western countries are too eager to diagnose individuals exhibiting schizophrenic and bipolar symptoms as suffering from a disorder rather than a shamanic calling, noting that such persons are dealing with intimations, energies, and spirits from the Otherworld: "…they are called by beings from the other world to cooperate with them in doing healing work."[33] Some′ also mentions that the use of anti-psychotic drugs to deal with schizophrenic and bipolar disorder patients act to disrupt the communication between them and the Otherworld realm. It is interesting to note in the film that, even though Donnie is receiving medication from his psychiatrist, the psychiatrist ultimately confesses that she has been giving him a placebo, indicating that Donnie's contact with the Otherworld is at full potency. According to Some′, the most crucial connection between shamanism and certain types of mental disorders is that those diagnosed with these disorders "receive all kinds of information [from spirit beings] that they can make use of, so it's like they get some type of tangible guidance from the other world as to how to live their life."[34] Viewed from this perspective, Donnie willingly follows Frank's orders to perform destructive pranks because, like a shaman, he believes that by doing so, he is helping to heal his community from hypocrisy. At one point, during a Halloween party scene, Donnie wears a skeleton costume, the traditional dress of a shaman in recognition of the shaman's ritual experience with dismemberment and rebirth (see Fig. 5-3).[35] Ultimately, Donnie's actions ensure that his own fate and destiny come about and he dies on the day that Frank told him he would.

The unconscious is not only unbound by conceptions of linear time and space, but also constricts and expands experiences of time in dreams. Dream

---

[32] Von Franz (1974) 1995: 156-157.
[33] Gaddis and Marohn: n.p.
[34] Gaddis and Marohn: n.p.
[35] Creative Commons.

researchers have noted differences in the length of dreams in the REM and non-REM stages of sleep. Non-REM dreams are usually quick bursts of replays of recent life events, compressing a lived experience into sometimes seconds of time. REM dreams last much longer. People experiencing an elaborate and emotionally volatile REM dream sometimes feel as if the dream has lasted for hours, even days.[36]

Figure 5-3: Painting by Daekazu inspired by *Donnie Darko*, 2001. (Creative Commons)

The expansion and constriction of time in dreams relates to a rich subgenre in folklore: the "Rip Van Winkle" subgenre. Washington Irving's famous early American tale features a protagonist who experiences an expansion of time which, to the protagonist, feels as if no time at all has

[36] Coville, dir. and prod.: PBS/Nova.

passed. In Irving's tale, Rip Van Winkle is out hunting for squirrels in the Catskill Mountains and stops to rest, then comes upon a group of strangely dressed dwarfs playing a nine-pin bowling game. As they play, he helps himself to some of the strong alcoholic beverage being passed around, then passes out. When he wakes up and returns to his village, no one recognizes him, nor does he recognize anyone else. The village has also dramatically changed as well with all of the buildings he's familiar with, including his own home, now either gone or in ruins. Rip himself realizes he now has a long, gray beard. At one point, he spots his faithful dog who is old and decrepit and who growls at him as if he were a stranger. In desperation, he cries out, "Does nobody here know Rip Van Winkle?" Yes, someone responds, and points to a middle-aged man standing nearby. Van Winkle then recognizes the man as his own son who was a child before he left on his hunting trip.

Figure 5-4: Otherworldly time-bending scenes from "Rip Van Winkle." (Creative Commons)

Rip finally figures out that over twenty years have passed since he left on his fateful hunting trip. He also learns that the dwarfs he came across in the Catskills are Otherworld specters that have been seen by others from time to time in that area. Rip ends up living out the rest of his life with his now-adult daughter and her children, retelling his strange tale over and over again to anyone and everyone he sees[37] (Fig. 5-4).[38]

[37] Irving: 5-24.

[38] Creative Commons.

A personal favorite "Rip Van Winkle"-themed folk tale is from India called, "The Story of the King Who Would See Paradise." In this version, a king out hunting one day comes across a fakir, or Sufi Muslim ascetic, studying his Koran. When the king asks him what he is reading about, the fakir says he is reading about Paradise, praying he might be able to enter it after death. The king becomes curious and asks the fakir if it might be possible to get a glimpse of Paradise while still alive. The fakir tells him that to ask such a thing is dangerous to someone who has little faith. The king promises the fakir that if he can somehow give him a glimpse of Paradise, he will take care of the fakir for the rest of his life. The fakir thanks the king and says he will pray for guidance to see if he can grant the king's wish.

Years pass and the king makes good on his promise to supply the fakir with what he needs to survive while the fakir continues to pray for guidance. Finally, word reaches the king that the fakir is on his death bed. The king rushes to the fakir's bedside and once again asks if he might keep his promise before he dies. The fakir tells him to come to his impending funeral and after everyone leaves, to lay his hands upon the fakir's grave. So, after the fakir dies and is buried, the king waits until all the mourners have left, then approaches the fakir's grave and lays his hands upon it. Suddenly, the grave opens and the king sees the fakir sitting upright reading from the Koran. The fakir then beckons to the king to enter his grave. There is a crude flight of stairs leading down into the grave, and the king walks down the steps and stands in front of the fakir who turns and leads the king down a narrow corridor. Then: "…he stopped, turned solemnly to his companion, and, with a movement of his hand, drew aside as it were a heavy curtain, and revealed—what? No one knows what was there shown to the king…"[39] (Fig. 5-5).[40]

After that moment, the king staggers out of the grave. As he recovers from his descent, he tries to remember what the fakir revealed to him, but he can't remember anything about what he saw. When he returns to his kingdom, nothing seems familiar to him. Then, when he enters his palace, he is stunned to see another king sitting on his throne. He is even more astonished when he catches a glimpse of his reflection in a mirror: he appears in ragged clothes and now has a long, gray beard. A chamberlain approaches him and asks if there is something wrong, and the king says yes,

---

[39] Lang, ed. (1906) 1968: 27.

[40] Creative Commons.

demanding that the other king get off the throne since he himself is king. Everyone thinks he is crazy until he shows them a ring on his finger. When experts examine the ring, they tell him it is from a king who reigned over seven hundred years ago. Finally, the king realizes what has happened. He staggers off out of the palace and into the wilderness where he lives an ascetic life for twenty-five years, praying for forgiveness for having desired something forbidden to mortals "…until at last the Angel of Death came to him, and mercifully released him, purged and purified through his punishment."[41]

Figure 5-5: The fakir reveals Paradise to the king. Illustration by H.J. Ford for "The King Who Would See Paradise." (Creative Commons)

[41] Lang, ed. (1906) 1968: 28.

What makes this time-bending tale so fascinating is the motif of being able to see Paradise while alive but afterwards not being able to remember anything about what was seen. One has glimpsed the Otherworld, but it remains a mystery to those who haven't prepared in any way to understand or appreciate this realm. This motif corresponds to the mystery religion tradition, specifically the Orphic Mysteries. When people were initiated into this tradition, they were sometimes given small metallic tablets which they carried to their graves. The tablets were inscribed with instructions to help them traverse through the underworld to the Elysian Fields where they would await rebirth with hero figures and other worthy souls of the dead. The instructions included references to certain trees and rivers they would come upon, as well as guides they would encounter, and what they would have to say to these guides to make sure they received the right information that would help them choose the right path to the Elysian Fields. One such tablet had the following inscription:

> Thou shalt find on the left of the House of Hades a Well-spring, and by the side thereof…a white cypress. To this Well-spring, do not approach. Thou shalt find another by the Lake of Memory, cold water flowing forth, and there are Guardians before it. Say [to the Guardians]: "I am a child of Earth and Starry Heaven; but my race is of Heaven (alone). This you know yourselves. I am parched with thirst and I perish. Give me quickly the cold water flowing from the Lake of Memory." And of themselves [the Guardians] will give you drink from the holy Well-spring, and thereafter among the other Heroes [dwelling in the Elysian Fields] you shalt have lordship….[42]

As the inscription indicates, it is necessary to have been initiated into the Orphic mystery tradition in order to regain one's memory about the initiation process, that it was a preparation for this journey through the underworld to Paradise. An uninitiated soul might drink from the wrong well spring, forget everything, and become hopelessly lost, wandering aimlessly for eternity in the land of the dead. Something similar nearly happened to the king in the story. He was lost for seven hundred years after having seen something forbidden to an unbeliever.

An excellent cinematic example with the motif of time expanding and constricting is *Contact*, referred to in Chapter One. The astronaut Ellie Arroway blasts off from Earth and journeys through a wormhole to a distant planet where she meets with an alien who appears to her in the form of her dead father; after this meeting, the scene fades and she finds herself in her

[42] Harrison (1903) 1955: 573.

space ship on the launch pad back on Earth where she is told she was only out of contact with Earth for one second and therefore couldn't have made the journey she insists she experienced. Later, it's discovered that a recording device on board with her picked up and recorded eighteen hours of static, confirming Ellie's extended galactic journey that happened within a second's time on Earth.

Numerous other films with time-bending themes exist, of which *Interstellar* is a superlative example with its emotional scenes dependent upon black holes slowing down time, along with the scenes taking place in the tesseract depicting various time perspectives, and finally the film's climactic moments of a middle-aged Cooper reunited with his near-hundred year-old child. The extremely popular *Back to the Future* trilogy is another excellent time-bending cinematic example; like Cooper in *Interstellar*, the protagonist, Marty McFly (Michael J. Fox) visits past and future moments from his personal life and manipulates them to effect more positive outcomes.[43]

*The Terminator* film series also plays around with the idea of future historical time periods being manipulated by individuals—and cyborgs—from the future who travel back in time to either save the world from self-destruction or make sure it comes about, echoing the same theme as *Interstellar* as well as another film, *12 Monkeys* (1995);[44] the latter film has nearly the same premise as the *Terminator* series featuring scenes of the protagonist journeying back to moments in the Earth's past in order to stop those responsible for decimating the Earth's future time period. In the second and best film of the *Terminator* series, *Terminator 2: Judgment Day* (1991), the film's young hero-protagonist John Connor (Edward Furlong), expresses the guiding philosophy of the entire series as well as that of *Interstellar, 12 Monkeys,* and the *Back to the Future* films: "The future is not set. There is no fate but what we make for ourselves." This philosophy expresses the same view of fate as the Lord Wainwright character from *The Night My Number Came Up*: it is absurd to believe that all of us are not in complete control of our future destinies. This view of fate at first seems to differ from the attitude of Donnie Darko who goes about ensuring his ultimate fate will occur so he will die at the precise moment and manner in which Frank--his shadow self in the form of a giant rabbit--has indicated. However, like synchronistic experiences, as well as the attitude toward fate held by the Chinese according to *The Night My Number Came Up*, what *The*

[43] Zemeckis, dir. 1985: Universal Pictures.
[44] Gilliam, dir.: Universal Pictures.

*Terminator* and other time manipulating films emphasize is how we can get glimpses into our future that can help us better understand the life we are currently living and in doing so, ensure that we live the life we were born to live without destroying ourselves before we can do so. The director of the first two *Terminator* films, James Cameron, also emphasized this same theme in his film *Avatar*: the ultimate goal of humans is not to conquer the world but to understand our place within it and respect the fate of other living creatures that inhabit it in order to avoid self-annihilation.[45]

In other variations of these types of time-bending tales, one can enter a type of Earth-bound wormhole that propels the person into another dimension or another time period. There is a tradition--a series of stories, uban legends, and whispered taboos—about these types of portals, all of them involving either a green door or a green mound in the Earth. In the Rip Van Winkle tale, for example, Rip stops to rest upon "a green knoll covered in mountain herbage"[46] in the Catskills, and soon afterwards hears a dwarf calling his name; the dwarf then leads him to the community of dwarfs playing a nine-pin bowling game. In the tale, "A Vision of the Dead," from the previous chapter, a Green Lady leads a mortal woman up a vegetative mound in the Earth, then opens it with a secret incantation, revealing a door that leads to the underworld. Earthen mounds and hollow hills were the legendary dwelling places of such Otherworld beings as the Tuatha de Dannan and the Sidhe from Irish, Welsh, and Scottish folklore, all of them entities of a timeless era in which their knowledge of the secret, regenerative powers of nature endowed them with supernatural powers.[47]

One of the most famous references to this type of green mound or portal appears in the epic medieval poem *Sir Gawain and the Green Knight*. Sir Gawain is a knight of King Arthur's court, and one day the court of knights is visited by a giant green man who challenges any of the knights to cut off his head. Sir Gawain answers the challenge and decapitates the giant, who then calmly picks up his head which then speaks to Gawain, telling him he must now be subjected to the same deed one year from now. They will meet in a forest far away beside a Green Chapel. Gawain takes up the dare, and a year later travels into the forest looking for the Green Chapel. What he finds is the following:

[45] Cameron dir. and co-screenwriter 1991: Carolco/Tristar.
[46] Irving: 13.
[47] MacDonald: n.p.

> …he saw some way off what seemed to be a mound, a hillock high and broad, hard by the water, where the stream fell in foam down the face of the steep, and bubbled as if it boiled on its bed below. The knight urges his horse, and heads for the knoll; leaps lightly to earth; loops well the rein of his steed to a stout branch, and stations him there. He strides straight to the mound, and strolls all about, much wondering what it was but no whit the wiser; it had a hole at one end, and on either side, and was covered in coarse grass in clumps all without, and hollow all within, like some old cave, or a crevice of an old crag. "Can this be the Chapel Green? Alack!" said the man, "Here might the devil himself be seen saying [prayers] at black midnight! Now by heaven," said he, "it is bleak hereabouts; this prayer-house is hideous, half-covered with grass! Well, the grim man mantled in green hold here his orisons in hell's own style! Now, I feel it is the Fiend, in my five wits, that has tempted me to this tryst, to take my life; this is a chapel of mischance, may the mischief take it! An accursed a country church as I came upon ever!"[48]

This vivid description of the Green Chapel carved within a hill in the earth captures the sense of Gawain having entered another realm of reality. Like a shaman initiate, he has come to experience a ritual dismemberment, after willingly journeying to this Otherworld. The Green Chapel is a type of ritual hut located deep in a dark forest, the typical setting for such initiations, performed by an elder who represents an ancestor spirit, in this case the Green Knight. The figure of the Green Knight is related to the Green Man from folkore and myth; he is the male equivalent of the Green Lady or Earth Goddess, both of them incarnations of the inexhaustible regeneratvie powers of the natural world.

Green doors are featured in stories and urban legends about the "Secret Commonwealth," mentioned by Jacques Vallee: they are portals to forbidden knowledge, taboo desires, alien creatures, and other dimensions of time and space. "The King Who Would See Paradise," for example, is a tale in which forbidden knowledge appears behind a door within an earthen grave mound but cannot be understood by someone ill prepared to comprehend this knowledge. Perhaps the most infamous reference to a green door that leads to forbidden knowledge as well as the fulfillment of taboo desires is the 1972 pornographic film, *Behind the Green Door*. The film was inspired by a popular sexually explicit short story that discreetly circulated among service men during World War II, about a secret society of hedonists who kidnap women and subject them to a variety of sex acts

---

[48] Borroff (Trans.): 45-46.

on a stage while they indulge in a mass orgy among themselves.[49] During World War II and continuing through the Cold War, certain green doors were allegedly off limits to regular service men. According to legend, behind these doors were government agents involved in designing secret plans to combat Communist infiltration; or the agents were indulging in mind control experiments using mind-altering drugs like the one featured in the film *Jacob's Ladder*; or they were devising neferious methods of torture to inflict upon terrorists.[50]

In the early twentieth century, several literary works alluded to time portals found behind green doors. In 1911, H.G. Wells wrote a beautiful story, "The Door in the Wall," about a young English boy who gets lost in the West Kensington area of London and stumbles upon a green door embedded in a white wall. When he enters it, he is transported into an Eden-like garden where he plays with black panthers, frolicks with children his own age, and then is led by a beautiful young girl to an encounter with a sorrowful looking elderly woman dressed in purple and carrying a thick book. When the woman shows the boy the book, it comes alive, and he watches transfixed as animated images of significant moments from his young life play in front of him, ending with an image of him standing on a sidewalk crying. When he looks up from the book, he discovers he is indeed on a sidewalk in West Kensington; the green door in the wall has vanished. He is eventually found by his father and tries to tell him what he experienced, but his father calls him a liar and punishes him severely; he also takes away all of the boy's fairy tale books believing they are making him too imaginative for his own good.

As the boy matures, he catches glimpses of the green door and thinks about re-entering it, but his reasonable, practical upbringing gets the best of him and he avoids the temptation. He becomes a successful polititition and at one point tries to justify his refusal to re-enter the green door by telling himself, "Who wants to pat panthers on the way to dinner with pretty women and distinguished men?"[51] However, as much as he tries to demean his experience behind the green door, he remains obsessed with the memory. He longs to return to that experience of eternal time, beauty, and perfection: "…the door that goes into peace, into delight, into a beauty beyond dreaming, a kindness no man on earth can know. And I have rejected

[49] Baxter: 31.
[50] Safire: n.p.
[51] Wells: 16.

it…and it has gone….”[52] Finally, after having become a well-respected governmental minister, he wanders off one night into the West Kensington area in search of the green door. Instead, he mistakes a door leading to a ditch, falls into it, and dies.

The story is narrated by a friend of the man to whom the man confessed his obsession with the green door. His friend ends the tale with these musings:

> Was there, after all, ever any green door in the wall at all…? There are times when I believe [he] was no more than the victim of the coincidence between a rare but not unprecedented type of hallucination and a careless trap, but that indeed is not my profoundest belief. You may think me supersitious if you will, and foolish; but, indeed, I am more than half convinced that he had in truth, an abnormal gift, and a sense of something—I know not what—that in the guise of wall and door offered him an outlet, a secret and peculiar passage of escape into another and altogether more beautiful world.[53]

Like *The Night My Number Came Up*, Wells' story wrestles with the conflict between rational and nonrational views of reality. The green door in this instance is a symbol of the unconscious depths, the eternal realm that has given birth to so many mythical and religious ideas about Paradise, Eden, the Elysian Fields: perfection, beauty, and immortality. Many have constructed their lives around the hope of entering such a realm after death, following rules and moral constraints preached by religious and spiritual leaders who assure their followers that they know what the followers must do in this reality to ensure a blessed, eternal afterlife existence. However, like the story's protagonist, what might appear to be the portal to eternity could turn out to be a door leading to a ditch. In this regard, the so-called superstitious Chinese in *The Night My Number Came Up* seem to have the right attidude: know thyself. Pay attention to what your unconscious is telling you. Learn the language of the unconscious in order to find your own green door that leads to spiritual fulfillment.

In another story, one from 1910 entitled *The Green Door*, young Letitia Hopkins finds a green door in the basement of her Aunt Peggy's house. Although she is warned by her aunt not to enter it, she becomes obsessed over the idea of finding out what lies beyond it. One Sunday when Aunt Peggy is attending church, Letitia steals the key to the door and enters it. She is immediately transported in time to over one hundred years into the

---

[52] Wells: 18.

[53] Wells: 19.

past where she encounters relatives living in a log cabin and fighting off Indians. Letitia ends up living with her distant relatives for three months, during which time she learns how to spin yarn, darn socks, and load guns to keep the Indians at bay. Ultimately, she learns from one of her young relatives of the existence of another green door, one the adults have forbidden anyone to enter since it is a time portal leading to the future. Although Letitia is miserable and homesick, she at first balks at the idea of entering this green door, believing she might end up in a future existence worse than her current living condition: "Suppose she were to open the second little door and be precipitated into a future far from the one which had merged from the past, and be more at a loss than now. She might find the conditions of life even more impossible than in her great-great-great grandfather's log cabin with hostile Indians about it."[54] Finally, Letitia gets up the courage to enter the other green door. After she passes through it, she is transported back to her own time, having been gone for only a couple of hours.

Like the previous tale from H.G. Wells, the green door in this children's story represents the unconscious as time portal, first sending Letitia back in time and expanding this time period into a REM-like dream experience, before sending her back to her current time period and compressing time in the manner of a non-REM dream experience.

Finally, my favorite reference to a green door is this one: "…Winnie-the-Pooh went round to his friend Christopher Robin, who lived behind a green door in another part of the forest."[55] This quote from the classic children's book *Winnie-the-Pooh*, the first in the series by A.A. Milne, introduces a world inhabited by stuffed animals from an Otherworld reality that come to life and interact with a young boy who visits these animated figures by passing through a green door carved into an ancient oak tree. All of these green door experiences feature children who in each instance quickly adapt to the nonrational experience of having time expand and contract and extend into eternity. Also, in all the examples, the developmental stage of childhood is presented as one filled with time-bending enchantment, reflecting Jean Piaget's ideas about this stage as the one in which belief in animism and the mingling of conscious reality with the unconscious are most potent.

---

[54] Wilkins-Freeman: 34.
[55] Milne: 11.

These references to green doors and green mounds are associated with a reality inaccessible to those who do not have special permission to enter this forbidden realm. The green door leads to an Otherworld where one can expect to be transformed through dismemberment, taboo sex, and encounters with ancestor spirits from a distant past. It can also lead one back into an ethereal time of enchantment when black panthers and stuffed bears were one's most cherished childhood companions.

The green door, therefore, is a potent symbol of the unconscious and its connection with the Otherworld, both unbound by time, space, and morality, where one must be prepared to experience a transformation of consciousness. Like a tesseract, like a synchronistic experience, it links the Earthly realm with nonrational moments in time and space infused with emotional fervor. If one is not ready for transformation, intolerant of the idea that the nonrational view of life is of equal importance as the rational view, entering through the green door could result in madness, a schizophrenic state, where one becomes out of synch with one's normal state of existence, leading to an inability to distinguish between waking world reality and unconscious reality, a state of eternal wandering in the land of lost souls.

# CHAPTER SIX

# THE OTHERWORLD AND DREAMTIME

In the summer of 2006, a team of archeologists from the University of Oslo was searching for artifacts from the Middle Stone Age period—roughly dating from 250,000 to 40,000 years ago—in a region of Africa's Kalahari Desert known as the Tsodilo Hills. This area of Africa, in the country of Botswana, is known for having the largest concentration of rock paintings in the world. The hills are a sacred site for the indigenous San people who have lived in this region for at least 100,000 years; they refer to this area as the Mountain of the Gods and the Rock that Whispers.[1]

While exploring one of the caves embedded in the hills, the team came upon a rock carving on one of the walls of the cave; the carving was of a giant python nearly twenty feet long with hundreds of spear indentations gouged into the serpent's body. Upon further investigation, the team ultimately unearthed over ten thousand spearheads within the cave, many of them made from rocks transported from other regions hundreds of miles away; numerous spearheads, specifically ones with red coloring, showed signs of having been ritually burned.

There was little doubt that the cave had been used by the San people for religious ritual purposes. Commenting on the look of the rock carving and its significance as a religious icon, archeologist Sheila Coulson remarked, "You could see the mouth and eyes of the snake. It looked like a real python. The play of sunlight over the indentations gave them the appearance of snake skin. At night, the firelight gave one the feeling that the snake was actually moving."[2]

Further proof of the cave's use as a religious site was the discovery of a small chamber located behind the rock carving. The walls in the niche were worn smooth from frequent use. The investigators realized that the small

[1] Vogt: n.p.
[2] Vogt: n.p.

chamber was probably used by shamans as a way to speak in the voice of the python god. As Coulson remarked:

> The shaman, who is still a very important person in San culture, could have kept himself hidden in that secret chamber. He would have had a good view of the inside of the cave while remaining hidden himself. When he spoke from his hiding place, it could have seemed as if the voice came from the snake itself. The shaman would have been able to control everything.[3]

After conducting dating analyses of the spearheads and python carving, the archeologists concluded that the artifacts and carving were approximately 70,000 years old. This made the python carving the oldest religious relic ever discovered. Prior to the discovery, scientists had found religious relics from about 40,000 years ago in Europe, but now this serpent icon underscored the idea that religious rituals had first been performed by ancient ancestors in Africa, the same region of the world where humans were thought to have evolved. Obviously, the discovery was important in many regards, with perhaps the most significant having to do with ancient humans being able to perform sophisticated cognitive abilities involving abstract and symbolic thinking. However, what was equally amazing about the discovery was its depiction of the oldest-known god entity in the form of a giant serpent. According to San mythology in regards to their creation myth, "…mankind descended from the python, and the ancient, arid streambeds around the hills are said to have been created by the python as it circled the hills in its ceaseless search for water."[4]

For a multitude of Christians and other believers who accept the concept of god, the idea that this god power is likened to a giant serpent is blasphemy since they consider the serpent as the animal incarnation of the devil. However, numerous other cultures embrace the serpent god concept. In addition, as the San creation myth illustrates, many cultures consider humanity as descendants of a serpent god. How could such a widespread belief have come about? What is it about serpents that encourages so many cultures to endow this lowly creature with the powers of the supreme creator?

As I hope to illustrate, in order to understand this link between serpent and god, one must discount anything physically observable about the habits of serpents. For example, many believe the serpent became a symbol of

[3] Vogt: n.p.
[4] Vogt: n.p.

immortality because it cyclically revitalizes itself by periodically shedding its skin. However, numerous other animals shed their skins: lizards, frogs, crabs, and spiders to name a few. The link between serpent and god must therefore be archetypal: there is something in the collective psyche that insists upon this connection. However, having admitted that there is nothing physically observable about a snake that would inspire so many mythological traditions featuring serpents endowed with god-like powers, I believe there is a strong symbolic relationship between serpents and the workings of the human central nervous system.

Jane Harrison in her examination of Greek religion touches upon this relationship between snakes and the central nervous system when she explores the Greek's hero tradition. At one point, she refers to the Greek's founding hero figure, Cecrops, credited with the establishment of Greek culture:

> The oldest hero reverenced by Athens was Cecrops….He was the first king of Athens…a typical culture hero [who] softened and polished the rude manners of the inhabitants….He gave them laws and customs and taught them to cultivate the olive. He introduced the worship of Zeus…and forbade the sacrifice of living things….Cecrops the hero-king, the author of all these social reforms, Cecrops the humane, the benevolent, has a serpent's tail.[5]

It was not uncommon for heroes to be associated with serpentine characteristics. Like serpents, heroes were linked with the earth. While many serpents do live in the earth, heroes were actually considered *autochthonic*: they were born out of the earth itself. In many cases heroes were consorts of Earth Mother figures. There is, for example, an island off the coast of Greece called Salamis, where the serpentine hero-king Kychreus was born out of the earth and later became the consort of the earth goddess Demeter.[6] Athena, the Greek's wisdom goddess, had her autochthonic serpent-hero consort Erechthonius who succeeded Cecrops to become the second king of Athens. In fact, Harrison mentions that "each and every traditional Athenian king was regarded as being also in some sense a snake."[7]

Harrison probes the relationship between heroes, kings, and snakes, referencing the ancient Greek scholars Aelian and Plutarch:

---

[5] Harrison (1912) 1962: 261-262.
[6] Harrison (1912) 1962: 287-288.
[7] Harrison (1912)1962: 265.

> Aelian in his treatise "On the Nature of Animals" says that the backbone of a dead man, when the marrow has decayed, turns into a snake….Plutarch adds that "the men of old time associated the snake most of all beasts with heroes." They did this because, he says, philosophers had observed that "when part of the moisture of the marrow is evaporated and it becomes thicker consistency, it produces serpents."[8]

According to these ancient sources, the relationship between snakes and heroes was the result of an observable phenomenon: when a hero died, his backbone marrow produced a snake. This is an example of the irrational ancient belief in spontaneous generation, having much in common with the one previously mentioned regarding the bugonia tradition of bees being born from dead bulls. Ultimately, like the bugonia tradition, such a relationship can only be comprehended from a metaphorical point of view: we are speaking in the language of the unconscious.

The relationship between snakes and the backbone marrow of heroes closely resembles the Hindu concept of the kundalini snake. According to Hindu philosophy, the kundalini snake resides in a person's pelvic region and can be aroused through meditation. When it is aroused, it rises up the person's spinal cord and ignites energy areas within the body called chakras. When a chakra is energized, a person becomes filled with a type of wisdom or inner insight. The most significant chakra is located between the eyes—the person's so-called third eye. When this chakra is aroused by the rising kundalini serpent, a person achieves supreme insight and total awareness--pure consciousness. In other words, the kundalini serpent is a symbolic representation of a type of inner energy that, when activated, leads to an expansion of conscious awareness.[9]

In India, there is also a tradition surrounding mythical creatures called Naga serpents, also known as wisdom serpents. Naga serpents appear as snakes with human heads, similar in appearance to the Greek hero figures. If one can charm a Naga serpent, it will endow the person with secrets of the workings of the universe.[10]

---

[8] Harrison (1903) 1955: 330.
[9] Chowdhury: n.p.
[10] See Vogel.

All of these traditions feature serpents with human attributes, most notably serpent figures with human heads. This figure corresponds with the central nervous system: brain and spinal cord (Figs. 6-1 & 6-2).[11]

Figures 6-1 & 6-2: (Left) Kundalini serpent encircling the human spinal cord; (Right) the Hindu god Krishna charms Naga serpents while dancing on the head of the serpent Kaliya. (Creative Commons)

Like the kundalini serpent, the human nervous system comprised of brain and spinal cord is an energy system that transmits "wisdom"--sensory information necessary for keeping a person alive and aware of what's going on around him--as well as facilitating thinking processes. The transmission of information is through an internal communication system made up of billions of neuron cells that form highly complex neural networks. Each neuron cell is an energy cell that creates energy impulses through the release of chemicals called neurotransmitters. Because neurons create an energy impulse, they have been described as tiny batteries, "a store of potential energy" for transmitting information.[12]

An amazing characteristic of the central nervous system is how strikingly similar it is to these traditions that speak of human-headed Naga

---

[11] Creative Commons.

[12] Weiten: 69-71.

serpents endowed with secret wisdom, kundalini serpents rising up a person's spinal cord igniting consciousness awareness, and serpents born from the backbones of heroes. The central nervous system also has an uncanny physical resemblance to the kundalini and Naga serpents; the former is a physical reality, while the other two are archetypal.

Despite the similarities in the physical appearance of the central nervous system with Naga and kundalini serpents, as well as the relationship they have with transmitting knowledge, I seriously doubt that any culture embracing the mythic view of the serpent as a god entity based this view upon way the spinal cord and brain resemble a serpent endowed with a human head. Therefore, unless one prefers the idea of being descended from a king snake and thus having a royal lineage, one must accept the archetypal dimension of the relationship rather than it being a statement about the evolutionary history of humanity. Jung, however, might agree with the "humanity descended from serpents" view of evolution since he emphasized the strong link humans have with all other life forms; his two million year-old Self, referred to in Chapter Three, expresses this primordial link, as does his comment about how both the psyche and the body show "clear traces of the various evolutionary stages."

One of the most astonishing folk tales, perhaps my all-time favorite, illustrates the relationship between the human nervous system and inner serpent wisdom; it also provides a vivid example of a serpent entity endowed with god-like powers: *The Arabian Nights* tale, "The Queen of Serpents." Because of my strong affection for this story—which, in its unabridged version, is nearly one hundred pages long--I have created an abridged version based on several sources:[13]

> There was once a Greek wise man named Daniel who, with his wife, remained without a child until one night he prayed long and hard to God to bless him with a son. That night, when he lay with his wife, she conceived. As the day approached when she would give birth, Daniel, who was old, felt his day of death coming. Daniel died the day before his son was born. The mother named the son Hasib Karim al-Din and had high hopes for him to follow in his father's footsteps and become wise with knowledge. But, Hasib remained lazy and resistant to schooling. By the time he was a young man and married in his own right, he could only make a living as a woodcutter.

---

[13] Campbell, ed. (1952) 1962: 406-422; Lyons & Lyons, eds. and trans.: Vol 2, 363-453; Payne ed. and trans.: (1882) 2007: Vol. 2, 1054-1114.

One day as he and his fellow woodcutters labored in the forests outside of town, Hasib came upon a large flat stone embedded in the ground; attached to this stone was a metal ring. With help from his companions, they lifted up the stone and found a chamber filled with huge jars of honey. Hasib climbed down and began to haul up the jars to his companions. After the last one had been handed up, his companions were overcome with greed; knowing that they could make a fortune by selling the honey in town, and fearing that Hasib would claim most of the jars as his own since it was he who had found the chamber, they slammed the stone down, leaving Hasib trapped in darkness.

Hasib refused to remain trapped and began to explore the cave, finally coming upon a wall with a crack that emitted a faint light. By digging around the crack with his knife, he was able to open it wide enough to crawl through. The passage led to a huge door with a key in its lock. Turning the key, he opened the door and entered a large hallway that opened into a massive amphitheater.

A glittering lake shimmered in this amphitheater, and near one of its shores was a throne made of precious stones, surrounded by thousands of chairs made from granite. As Hasib marveled at these sights, he suddenly became aware of hissing noises coming from each direction, including the lake. The chamber then began filling up with writhing snakes slithering in from everywhere he looked. Hasib cowered behind the throne as the snakes slithered toward the chairs and seated themselves upon each one. Hasib then saw a giant serpent as large as a mule enter the amphitheater. Upon its back was a large golden dish, and seated on the dish was a serpent, shining brightly. This serpent had the face of a beautiful woman (Fig. 6-3).[14]

She was lifted down by others and placed upon the throne, after which she hissed at her fellow snakes and they hissed back in homage to her. Noticing Hasib cowering behind the throne, she smiled at him, and in perfect Arabic, greeted him, as if she had known him all of her life. "Have no fear of us," she said. "I am Yamlikha, the Queen of Serpents."

She then ordered her servants to fetch them food in the form of apples, grapes, pomegranates, nuts, and bananas. "Eat from these fruits and nuts," she said. As Hasib helped himself to the food, she encouraged him to tell her about his life. Hasib related the details of his humble and uneventful life, after which Yamlikha smiled and said, "Nothing but good shall come to you. But I want you to sit here with me for a time so that I can tell you events from my own life, which includes a tale of another human with whom I became acquainted. His name was Buluqiya."

[14] Creative Commons.

Figure 6-3: Hasib encounters the Queen of Serpents in her underground chamber filled with her writhing snake followers. (Creative Commons)

The queen then related to Hasib an elaborate tale of a young Jewish man who, at an early age, discovered a copy of the Koran in the library of his deceased father. After reading the Koran, he became enamored with the prophet Muhammad, and swore that he would travel the world seeking out knowledge of the prophet until the end of days when Muhammad would return to unite with his brethren.

Buluqiya's travels took him into uncharted regions where, on a distant island inhabited by serpents, he encountered followers of the Serpent Queen and learned of her whereabouts. He then traveled to Jerusalem and met a sorcerer named Uffan who was obsessed with finding the tomb of King Solomon, desiring to steal Solomon's ring which had the power the rule over all men, animals, and the jinn.

Uffan knew that the tomb of Solomon was hidden far away in a secret cave across the Seven Seas. He was also aware of a magic herb that, when smeared upon the bottoms of one's feet, enabled one to walk upon water. He knew that only the Queen of Serpents could lead one to this herb. When he discovered that Buluqiya knew of her whereabouts, he persuaded Buluqiya to lead him to her, telling Buluqiya that, if they found Solomon's ring, its power could reveal to them the whereabouts of the Ocean of Darkness where the Waters of Life flowed; if one drank from these waters, one could live forever, and in that way Buluqiya could live until the end of days when Muhammad would return. Upon hearing this, Buluqiya agreed to Uffan's plan.

After weeks of travel, they reached the land of the Queen of Serpents. Upon entering her secret chamber and finding her with her legion of serpentine followers, they pleaded with her to lead them to the herb. The queen finally agreed, after which the two gathered up the herb and approached the ocean. They squeezed out the juice from the herb, anointed the bottoms of their feet, then stepped upon the ocean and began to walk across its vast expanse.

Weeks passed as they walked upon the ocean's surface, living off the fish of the sea. Uffan finally led them to the secret cavern beyond the Seven Seas. Inside was a luminous dome, and within the dome was a royal throne, upon which sat the perfectly preserved corpse of King Solomon dressed in regal robes. Next to Solomon was a coiled serpent. As Uffan approached the throne, he began to chant incantations that would allow him to remove the ring from Solomon's finger. While he chanted, the serpent spoke: "Be gone or you will die." Uffan paid no attention to the warning. As he reached out to remove the ring from Solomon's finger, the serpent's eyes began to glow, then they shot out a blaze of lightning, and Uffan was reduced to ashes. At the sight of his dead comrade, Buluqiya fainted.

When he recovered, the archangel Gabriel was standing over him. "Go Buluqiya, far away from here" he said. "The time of Muhammad's coming is distant." Weeping, Buluqiya left the tomb of Solomon. He then traveled far and wide across the Seven Seas by the use of the magic herb. He encountered the daughters of the sea who led him to lands inhabited by wise men, demons, and angels, including the archangel Michael. Journeying beyond the farthest mountains, Buluqiya learned from another angel the secrets of creation, the origins of the jinn, and the various levels of hell.

After reaching one uncharted island, he came across a man weeping bitterly as he sat upon the shore between two grave stones. When Buluqiya asked this man who he was, the man replied, "I am Janshah, and I am waiting here until the day of my death." Janshah then related to Buluqiya how he had come to this island.

"I was out hunting in the forest of my own country," he said, "and was captured by pirates. They took me to their ship, and we sailed into a storm that tore our ship apart. I alone was able to survive after washing up upon the shores of a strange country.

"As I foraged for food, I stumbled upon a castle inhabited by a man who turned out to be the lord of the birds. Each year, all the birds of the world would gather at his castle and he would attend to them, listening to their tales since he knew their language. I stayed with him for a year, until one day, a flock of giant doves flew down and gathered around a secluded pool in an alcove of the castle. As I watched in secret, the doves removed their feathers, revealing themselves to be beautiful jinn maidens. I immediately fell in love with one of them, who was called Shamseh. When she was bathing with her companions, I stole her feather garment, and told her I would not give it back to her until she became my wife. After much persuasion and declarations of my love for her, she finally agreed.

"We were married by the lord of the birds, and lived in bliss for months until one day she discovered the hiding place where I had stored her feather garment. Before I could stop her, she donned her wings, and said, 'If you love me as much as I love you, seek me out at the Castle of Jewels.' She then flew away.

"I was in a panic afterwards, determined to find her. The lord of the birds attempted to help me by asking all the birds if they had heard of the Castle of Jewels. Although they were from all parts of the world, none had heard of this castle. Suddenly, a giant black bird flew in from one of the castle windows and settled among the rest of the birds. When questioned about the Castle of Jewels, the black bird told a tale about how it had once come upon a glittering palace encrusted with precious stones that lay beyond the most distant of all mountains, known as Mount Caf. Perhaps this was the Castle of Jewels.

"The black bird transported me to the land bordering the farthest mountain. On the horizon was a shimmering glow. As I walked toward it, a fierce jinn flew down from the heavens, at first threatening to annihilate me. But then when I told him who I was, he gathered me up and flew me to the castle. There, standing upon a balcony, was Shamseh weeping with joy.

"We stayed in her castle for two blissful years. After this time, I became anxious to travel to my homeland and show my wife to my family. However, when we reached this island and rested by its shores, my beautiful wife decided to bathe in the waters, not knowing that a shark waited for her. She was killed, and I buried her at this site. Now I wait for my own death so I can be buried next to her."

Buluqiya was moved to tears by Janshah's tale, and began longing to return to his own home. He prayed to God to take him home to his mother. As he prostrated himself in prayer, a man with skin the color of green grass suddenly appeared. This was El-Khidr, a man who had drunk from the Waters of Life and become immortal. He told Buluqiya that God had heard his prayers. He instructed Buluqiya to embrace him. As soon as Buluqiya wrapped his arms around El-Khidr, he found himself alone standing on the doorstep of his mother's home.

After Yamlikha, the Queen of Serpents, finished her elaborate tales of Buluqiya and Janshah, Hasib was joyous and praised her storytelling skills and her hospitality. "Now," he said, "like Buluqiya, I too would like to return home."

"I cannot let you go," said Yamlikha. "For if you return to the upper realm, you will betray me by going to the public baths, and in doing so be the cause of my death." Hasib was shocked by her words. "I would never betray you" he said. "I swear I will never go to the public baths again."

Finally, Yamlikha agreed to let Hasib return to the upper realm. Unaware that he had been with the Queen of Serpents for two years, Hasib was greeted with shrieks of joy after he entered the house of his mother and wife since they believed he had been dead all this time. Then, when the woodcutters who had abandoned him and left him to die found out he was alive, they sent him half of the fortune they had made upon the sale of the honey.

Hasib prospered and became an important man in his town. However, one day, while passing the public baths, he was persuaded by the bath attendant to enter. Forgetting the oath he had sworn to the Queen of Serpents, Hasib disrobed, revealing to those in attendance a dark discoloring on his belly with which he had been born. Immediately, he was seized by a score of men who took him to the palace of the Sultan where he met with the Sultan's sorcerer-advisor. The sorcerer told him that it had been prophesized that a man with a discolored belly would appear in the public baths one day, and this man would know the whereabouts of the Queen of Serpents. "The Queen of Serpents has the power to heal the Sultan, who is dying of leprosy," said the sorcerer. "To save the Sultan, you must lead us to her chamber."

At first, Hasib denied that he had ever heard of the Serpent Queen. The sorcerer ordered guards to tie him up, then they whipped and tortured him until he was near death. Finally, he confessed that he knew the dwelling place of the Serpent Queen. With more threats to his life, he agreed to lead the sorcerer and his men to the queen's chamber.

The sorcerer ordered the Sultan's troops to dress in battle gear and follow Hasib. Upon reaching the queen's underground chamber, they invaded her domain and captured her. When Yamlikha saw Hasib among the invaders, she said, "What happened to the covenant you made with me?" Hasib wept until he nearly passed out. Yamlikha, the Queen of Serpents, wept with him. Then she said, "I forgive you, Hasib. My death was foretold long before we met, and no one has the power to undo it."

Hasib was forced to carry the queen back to the Sultan's castle. As he carried her, she whispered to him, "Soon, I will die. Listen to me now. The sorcerer will have my body cut up into three pieces, one for the Sultan, one for you, and one for him to consume. While he is preparing the three broths, watch for him to be distracted, then switch the vials prepared for you and him so he receives the portion meant for you. You must then drink the potion." Hasib swore that he would follow her commands.

After they had reached the castle, Hasib watched in agony as Yamlikha, the Queen of Serpents, was led to the sorcerer's chamber where she was killed and dismembered. After her death, the sorcerer prepared her body by boiling it in three separate pots. When the sorcerer was distracted by a messenger from the Sultan, Hasib switched the broths meant for him and the sorcerer. Then, when the sorcerer returned to the broths, he ordered Hasib to consume the vial that the sorcerer believed he had prepared for Hasib. Hasib raised the vial to his mouth, then hesitated, and watched as the sorcerer drank Hasib's own portion. Immediately after drinking the broth, the sorcerer's body began swelling up. As his body threatened to burst open, the sorcerer fell down dead. Hasib then stared at his own portion of the broth, terrified to drink it. But, remembering his promise to the Queen of Serpents, he lifted the vial to his mouth and drank.

No sooner had he consumed the broth than the fountains of the wisdom of Yamlikha, the Queen of Serpents, welled up in his heart and opened him to all sources of knowledge. As he staggered outside the sorcerer's chamber and raised his eyes to the skies, joy and ecstasy overcame him, for he saw the seven heavens and knew the manner of the revolution of the planets of the solar system, and the scheme of their movements and the fixed stars. He knew all aspects of the sea and the land, and understood the causes of eclipses of the sun and moon. He knew the knowledge of the arts of geometry and cosmology, as well as those of astrology and astronomy and mathematics. Then Hasib looked at the earth and saw all the minerals and vegetables that are there and knew their virtues and properties. In an instant, he became knowledgeable of all aspects of medicine and chemistry and natural magic and the art of making gold and silver.

Hasib was aglow with the wisdom of Yamlikha, the Serpent Queen, as he carried the final vial made from her body to the Sultan. When he reached the Sultan's royal chamber, Hasib fed the vial to him. Over the next few days, the Sultan's leprosy dissipated until he was completely cured. The Sultan

> then praised Hasib's curative powers, gathering around him all of his ministers, viziers, and troops and proclaiming Hasib his new supreme advisor.
>
> And so it was that Hasib, an unambitious know-nothing, unskilled even to read writing, became by the powers of Yamlikha, the Queen of Serpents, proficient in all sciences and versed in all manner of knowledge, so that the fame of his learning was blazed abroad in all the land and he became renowned for profound skill in medicine and astronomy and geometry and astrology and alchemy and natural magic and the kabala and all other arts and sciences. His reputation as a wise man, wiser than his own father, became well known, and he lived a prosperous and blessed life until the end of days.

This fantastic tale of wonder, rich with references to various folkloric motifs (the water of life; the language of animals; swan maidens; the green man) is a beautiful example of the elaborate story structure featured throughout the *Arabian Nights*, with many stories beginning with one tale, then switching to another tale within the first one and telling another story from a different narrator who then has another character tell another tale before returning back to the original story. It vividly illustrates the complex narrative structure that Steven Johnson in the previous chapter compares with the default brain network, reflective of the daydreaming mode of thinking as well as the time-bending characteristics of the unconscious.

Although it appears that the three interwoven stories share little in common from a thematic point of view, all feature the revelation of secret wisdom, told by a supreme wisdom figure, Yamlikha, the serpent queen. Yamlikha is certainly related to the Naga serpent tradition. She not only holds the wisdom of the entire universe, but knows its fate, as well as her own fate which she says has been foretold since the beginning of time, indicating that her own existence spans the origins of the universe. She is, in a sense, a god figure who sacrifices herself for the betterment of humanity; her death and the ingestion of her physical essence—a type of holy communion--results in an amazing expansion of human consciousness. In this regard, Yamlikha resembles the great Mesopotamian creator god Tiamat, depicted as a giant cosmic serpent whose death and dismemberment at the hands of the hero figure Marduk resulted in the regeneration of the entire cosmos.

What is also remarkable about the serpent queen is her dwelling place: within the earth surrounded by masses of writhing serpents. Her environment mirrors that of the inner workings of the human nervous system: she is the embodiment of the central nervous system surrounded by a vast serpentine neural network over which she rules. The information she transmits is the microcosmic wisdom of the unconscious which holds the secrets of the natural world since the unconscious is linked with this outer, macrocosmic system.

Figure 6-4: Bronze sculpting of the Buddha sheltered by Muchalinda, the serpent king, while meditating under the Bodhi Tree and achieving enlightenment. (Creative Commons)

Clusters of serpents such as the ones depicted in this tale are found in other tales and myths featuring the transformation of consciousness. When the Buddha, for example, achieved divine insight while meditating under the Bodhi tree, he did so with assistance from Muchalinda, the multi-headed serpent king (Fig 6-4).[15]

Figure 6-5: The Hindu god Vishnu sits upon the multi-headed serpent Adisesha Ananta and dreams the universe into existence. Also pictured are Brahma, the overseer of Vishnu's universe, and Vishnu's female consort Lakshmi. (Creative Commons)

The Hindu creator god Vishnu dreams the universe into existence while reclining upon a multi-headed serpent called Adisesha Ananta known as "time without beginning or end;"[16] when Vishnu wakes up, the universe is destroyed until Vishnu falls asleep and dreams another one into existence (Fig 6-5).[17] The Hindu god Krishna, surrounded by a cluster of Naga serpents, dances on the head of the giant poisonous serpent Kaliya and tames his wrath (see Fig. 6-2).[18] In the Bulgarian folk tale, "The Language of Beasts," a shepherd rescues a serpent from a forest fire, after which the serpent leads him deep into the forest to a gateway made up of writhing serpents; after passing through the gateway, the shepherd is led to the king of snakes who then rewards the shepherd by giving him the power to understand the languages of all animals.[19] Athena, the Greek's wisdom

[15] Wikimedia Commons.
[16] Anuradha: n.p.
[17] Creative Commons.
[18] Creative Commons.
[19] Lang, ed. (1903) 1967: 55-61.

goddess, adorns her breast plate with an image of the Gorgon Medusa whose hair is made up of snake clusters; although Medusa and the Gorgons usually appear as demons, they are like Yamlikha and the Naga serpents: chthonic god figures in possession of secret wisdom, with Athena herself closely associated with this secret Gorgonian wisdom (See Figs. 6-6 & 6-7).[20]

While delving into the origins of human consciousness, Erich Neumann explored the famous Greek myth featuring the Gorgon Medusa and the hero figure Perseus. In most accounts of the myth, Perseus tries to prove himself as a candidate for king by seeking out the Gorgon Medusa in her secretive Otherworld region in order to cut off her head. Medusa's head is lethal if looked upon since her eyes have the power to turn a person into stone. Perseus receives help in his task from the gods Hermes and Athena. Neumann uses the myth as a way to illustrate the evolution of consciousness, with Perseus' heroic actions illustrating the developing ego and the necessity for the ego to do battle with the unconscious—symbolized by Medusa--in order to resist its overpowering influence upon ego consciousness and self-identity:

> …the hero Perseus…is the winged one, and the gods of the spirit [Hermes and Athena] are his allies in fight with the unconscious. His foe is the uroboric Gorgon [Medusa] dwelling far to the West, in the land of death, flanked by her hideous sisters...denizens of the deep. Perseus defeats the unconscious through the typical act of conscious realization.[21]

Other versions of the myth have Perseus and Medusa as husband and wife; in other words, like so many classic hero figures, Perseus is associated with the shamanic tradition with Medusa as his spirit bride rather than a hideous underworld serpent-demon that he must decapitate to prove his heroism. Perseus' journey to her realm is a shamanic trance journey to obtain secret wisdom from "the land of death," or underworld.[22] Perseus' close association with Hermes and Athena—both wisdom figures—mark him as a hero figure whose deeds reflect shamanic practices that attempt to uncover secrets from otherworldly regions. For example, when Perseus journeys to the realm of the Gorgons, he does so with the use of winged sandals that resemble Hermes' own pair, a reference to the shamanic trance-flight. In this light, Perseus' success in obtaining the head of Medusa could refer to his achievement of obtaining wisdom found only in the Otherworld.

---

[20] Creative Commons.
[21] Neumann: 219.
[22] Kerenyi (1951) 1995: 50.

Figures 6-6 & 6-7: Ancient Greek art featuring (top) a Gorgon figure with snake clusters in her hair; (bottom) the Greek wisdom goddess Athena with the Gorgon's serpentine head adorning her breast plate. (Creative Commons)

Neumann, therefore, is wrong to put too much of an emphasis upon the relationship between Perseus and Medusa as a symbolic war between ego and Self with the evolution of human consciousness at stake. Note that, while Perseus has to borrow a pair of winged sandals to journey to the underworld, Medusa has wings, indicating her god status; she is more of a "winged one" than Perseus who must take on some of her own characteristics in order to make his journey to her otherworldly region.

It is true that Jung also emphasized the dangers of unconscious dynamism and how the ego can be swamped by this dynamic power leading to disorientation and even mental instability. Ultimately, however, it is up to each individual to make a major effort to distinguish between ego identity and the impersonal psyche or Self but to never completely sever ties since the Self is the realm of the wisdom of the Yamlikha, the collective unconscious, the individual's connection with the source of all accumulated wisdom as well as the Otherworld. As the Perseus myth illustrates, a journey to the realm of the Gorgons is fraught with danger; making a successful journey requires understanding the traditions and techniques accumulated over the millennia by shaman ancestors and others who have made similar trance-state journeys.

Certain rock paintings made by shamans illustrate how Medusa and the Gorgons are closely associated with a vital energy likened to the energy transmitted via the brain's neural network. In these images, instead of Gorgon-like snake clusters centered around the head, the energy is depicted as a starburst, sun wheel, or swirling swastika image surrounding the shaman's head. The swastika is a powerful life energy symbol, found in many cultures from thousands of years ago, long before the Nazis turned it into an image of death. In fact, the classic pose of the Gorgon, featured in Figure 6-6, with one arm up, another one down, and one leg up and the other down--is in the shape of swastika, underscoring the Gorgon as a figure of a tremendous vital power. These types of rock art images are related to trance-induced states in which the shaman, with eyes closed, can see these types of swirling images filled with pulsating light called phosphene patterns. Some scientists have compared phosphene patterns with neuronal activity. As one archeologist described this trance-induced state, "...people in this condition are seeing the structure of their own brains."[23]

[23] Lewis-Williams: 127.

Figure 6-8: Rock art painting from the Mojave Desert region of Southern California depicting shamans with phosphene patterns appearing as sun burst and swastika-type sun wheel images surrounding their heads. (Photo by Ron Wolf: flickr photo sharing)

The shaman's head in these images has a strong resemblance to the snake-infested head of the Gorgon (Fig 6-8),[24] indicating a possible link between these type of rock paintings and images featuring clusters of snakes surrounding the heads of wisdom figures: the Buddha, Krishna, Vishnu, Yamlikha, and Gorgons.

Neumann also explores what he calls the first stage of conscious development, which he indicates is symbolized by the image of the uroboros, the tail biting serpent. Neumann calls Medusa a symbol of this primal stage of consciousness. According to Neumann, the uroboros "corresponds to an evolutionary stage which can be 'recollected' in the psychic structure of every human being. It functions as a transpersonal factor that was there as a psychic stage of being before the formation of

[24] Photo by Ron Wolf: flickr photo sharing.

ego."[25] Neumann's comments underscore the idea of the unconscious as the source of all accumulated wisdom—including the potential development of ego consciousness. Neumann calls the uroboros symbol "the archetype of the All One, appearing as…Aion…and also as the Primal Being that says, 'I Am Alpha and Omega.' As the Kneph of [Egyptian] antiquity, it was the Primal Snake, the 'most ancient deity of the prehistoric world.'"[26]

"The Queen of Serpents" vividly emphasizes the dimension of the Primal Serpent as an uroboros, the beginning and the end of all that is and all that is known about this world, and therefore an appropriate symbol of eternal time. The image of the uroboros serpent biting its tail underscores its symbolic significance as a cyclically renewable, inexhaustible source of primal energy powering the material world (Fig. 6-9).[27] Also, as Neumann mentions, the uroboros symbolizes "the most ancient deity of the prehistoric world," a comment that relates directly to the python image found in the Tsodilo Hills of the Kalahari Desert, the oldest-known religious icon.

In addition, Neumann references the concept of Aion in the context of the uroboros. Aion has several intriguing associations, and as Neumann notes, it is linked with the image of the uroboros as an energy system as well as one representing time itself as cyclically self-perpetuating and unending. Aion was considered a god entity, the god of eternal time; in addition to being depicted as a cosmic serpent encircling the entire universe, Aion was also imagined as a giant ocean called Okeanos, eternally flowing around the universe.[28]

Another extremely important aspect of the concept of Aion is its link with the vital life fluid of each individual. As Edward Edinger explained: "Aion was thought of as an inner water and it was thought that after the death of the individual, that inner water was left as a snake; the snake was imagined as the soul of the departed one."[29]

Marie-Louise von Franz echoed Edinger's remarks:

> Aion originally denoted that vital fluid in living beings; and thus their life-span and allotted fate. This fluid continued to exist after death in the form

---

[25] Neumann: 11-12.
[26] Neumann: 10.
[27] Creative Commons.
[28] Von Franz 1978: 5.
[29] Edinger: 16.

of a snake. It was a "generative substance," as was all water on earth….Aion, the god of time, is…clearly an image of the dynamic aspect of existence, of what we might call today a principle of psycho-physical energy. All opposites—change and duration, even good and evil, life and death—are included in this cosmic principle….As in Greece, the snake in Egypt was also connnected with time. It symbolized life and health, and each invididual was protected by a "life-time snake," which was a daemon of time and survival after death.[30]

Figure 6-9: This painting by Guido Cagnacci entitled "Eternity" (1650) features the uroboros as symbol of the cyclical nature of life and time and how the image of the tail-biting serpent represents an inexhaustible and self-perpetuating life source. (Creative Commons)

[30] Von Franz 1978: 6.

These comments about the serpent as a symbol of a vital fluid within each individual that endures physical death has a direct relationship with the earlier comments about serpents born from the backbone marrow of heroes. The symbolism of Aion as both an oceanic energy encompassing and empowering the universe as well as a vital fluid that circulates and enlivens each individual—with both of these fluid energy systems symbolized by snakes—illustrates the link between the inner microcosmic system existing within each of us, and the outer macrocosmic system surrounding us. Although completely nonrational, the serpent symbolism nevertheless is stunning in its ability to capture the numinous vitality of these concepts that speak of an inexhaustible life energy maintaining the life of the universe and enduring after a person's physical death. Perhaps what these correlations between snakes and life energy illustrate is Immanuel Kant's spiritual view of reality.

In keeping with its association with eternal time, Aion was also considered an epoch or enduring cycle of time lorded over by a supreme god figure. The ancient Greeks, for example, spoke of four Aions: one ruled by Chronos, one by Ouranus, one by Zeus, and a future one to be ruled by Dionysus[31] (see Fig 6-10).[32] The end of an Aion marked the end of the world; the destruction of the material world was followed by its reformulation and the beginning of a new Aion.

An aspect of the mystery religion tradition relates to the concept of Aion as an epoch ruled by a deity. Certain comments made about the secretive rites of Eleusis indicate that they were rituals with the intent of preparing participants to die in one Aion in order for them to be resurrected and participate in the reformation of the Earth in a new Aion. As the ancient orator Isocrates commented after he was initiated: "Those who take part [in the rites] possess better hope in regard to the end of life and in regard to the whole Aion."[33] In addition, an apocryphal story about the initiation ceremony featured an uninitiated man stumbling upon someone who had just been initiated; when the uninitiated man asked what was going on, the initiated man replied, "Today, at this hour, the Kore, that is, the virgin, gave birth to the Aion."[34] In this context, Aion refers to the child Brimos/Iacchus—i.e. Dionysus--as the ruler of the new Aion, as well as to the initiates themselves, all of them children of the new Aion after having been exposed to the

---

[31] Kerenyi (1976) 1996: 242.
[32] Creative Commons.
[33] Kerenyi (1960) 1991: 15.
[34] Kerenyi (1960) 1991: 117.

inexhautsible life force of the underworld goddess Kore or Persephone/Brimo in the form of a magnificent subterranean fire.

Figure 6-10: Ancient Roman relief image, circa second century, of the Orphic god Phanes surrounded by zodiac icons and encircled by a giant serpent. Phanes was closely associated with Dionysus[35] who succeeds Zeus as ruler of a new Aion. (Creative Commons)

Finally, Joscelyn Godwin in his book on the mystery religion tradition notes that the Pythagorians, who were associated with the cult of Orpheus, "…held that at the end of a Great Year [i.e. an Aion] all were restored to their primal purity in a Golden Age as the whole of Creation rejoins its source."[36] This quote indicates a periodic rejuvenation of all life, with the universe going through a ritual purification after an Aionic period has passed in order to restore its own vitality: the old world becoming young

[35] Harrison (1903) 1955: 650.
[36] Godwin: 37.

again. Obviously, this belief in the periodic purification and renewal of life at the end of a period of time relates to modern New Year's celebrations with the old year depicted as a worn out old man, and the new year represented by an energetic baby. Mircea Eliade commented on a related idea when he referred to a tradition practiced by certain traditional cultures: when someone becomes ill in one of these societies, a shaman sometimes attempts to restore the person's health by reciting the culture's creation or cosmogonic myth:

> It has been shown that a fairly large number of peoples, ranging from the most primitive to the most civilized (the Mesopotamians, for instance), made solemn recitation of the cosmogonic [i.e. creation] myth as a therapeutic method. We can see easily why: by making the patient symbolically "return to the past," he was rendered contemporary with Creation, he lived again in the initial plentitude of being. One does not *repair* a worn-out organism, it must be *re-made*; the patient needs to be born again; he needs, as it were, to recover the whole energy and potency that a being has at the moment of birth. And such a return to the "beginning" is rendered possible by *the patient's own memory*. The cosmogonic myth is recited before him and for him; it is the sick man who, by recollecting one after another the episodes of the myth, re-lives them, and therefore becomes contemporary with them. The function of memory is not to *conserve* the memory of the primordial myth, but to transport the patient to *where that event is in process of accomplishment*—namely, the dawn of Time....[37]

As Eliade, mentions, this cosmogonic memory of creation is an archetypal pattern inherent within all of us and becomes a part of contemporary time when re-enacted in ritual and/or recited as cosmogonic myth. Eliade's comments therefore apply to the mystery religion tradition since what the participants were performing with their symbolic acts taking place in a mythical underground was a re-enactment of the destruction and rejuvenation of the Earth itself; the great fire that flared up at the culmination of the rites symbolically destroyed and purified the Earth and the participants before they experienced a rebirth.

John Weir Perry put into practice the healing power of the cosmogonic myth when he was a psychiatrist working in San Francisco in the 1960s-1970s specializing in the treatment of young adults suffering from schizophrenic symptoms. What occurs during a schizophrenic break is the destruction of a person's orientation with conscious reality resulting in a chaotic mind state. Perry took a non-Western approach to treating his

[37] Eliade (1957) 1975: 48.

patients; instead of administering strong anti-psychotic drugs to control their symptoms, he allowed his patients to act out, draw, sculpt, and write about their experiences. In the written accounts, Perry began to notice recurring patterns in the narratives. Finally, he realized that what patients were describing were apocalyptic scenarios relating to the patients' own psychological breakdown. Usually, an apocalypse is associated with complete destruction; however, apocalypse is an archetypal motif: destruction is only the first stage of the pattern. It is followed by the reformulation and rejuvenation of the world. As Perry mentions, his patients were not only describing scenes of total destruction but also scenes of resurrection.

Perry was able to break down the narratives into various recurring images and motifs:

A. *Center*: A location is established at a world center or cosmic axis….
B. *Death*: Themes of dismemberment or sacrifice are scattered throughout and make themselves evident in drawings (crucifixion, pounding or chopping up, tortures….). A predominant delusional statement is that of having died and of being in an afterlife state (people look like the living dead; in hell or in heaven; or in prison….).
C. *Return to Beginnings*: A regression is expressed that takes the person back to the beginnings of time and the creation of the cosmos (Garden of Eden, waters of the abyss, early steps of evolution….).
D. *Cosmic Conflict*: There arises a world conflict of cosmic import between forces of good and evil or light and darkness, or order and chaos (…Armageddon…destruction or end of the world, or the Last Judgment…all to gain world supremacy).
E. *Threat of Opposite*: There is a fear of a threat from the opposite sex, a fear of being overcome by it or turned into it….
F. *Apotheosis*: The person experiences an apotheosis as royalty or divinity (as a king or queen, deity or saint, hero or heroine, messiah).
G. *Sacred Marriage*: The person enters upon a sacred marriage of ritual or mythological character (royal marriage...with a God or Goddess….).
H. *New Birth*: A new birth takes place or is expected of a superhuman child or of oneself (ideas of rebirth; Divine Child…or Reconciler of the division of the world).
I. *New Society*: A new order of society is envisioned, of an ideal or sacred quality (…Paradise, Utopia…New Age, a New Heaven and New Earth).
J. *Quadrated World*: A fourfold structure of the world or cosmos is established usually in the form of a quadrated circle….[38]

[38] Perry 1974: 11.

One can see a pattern in these archetypal motifs and images that begins within a center of conflict in which a great war takes place leading to chaos, death, and total annihilation. Opposing forces battle, but then there is also a reconciliation of these forces (the reference to the *hieros gamos* or sacred marriage), the achievement of a divine transformation, rebirth and/or birth of a divine child, and creation of a new world order out of chaos and decimation. Perry further explained the pattern in this manner:

> For it is a world in which there is a center, a cosmic axis running through and connecting the human world with the Sky World and the Underworld. In this center powerful events take place. There, the psychotic individual has died and has found himself in an afterlife state. There, occurs a clash of opposite powers, of light and dark halves of the world....There, he is thrown back to the Creation and the first beginnings, and he repeats the evolution of the world step by step. There, he is raised up into a position of supremacy, of world rulership or spiritual leadership. There, a new birth or rebirth takes place in association with an extraordinary marriage to some divine personage. And, finally, around this center come resolutions of cosmic proportions in the form of a redeemed society....[39]

Although the pattern clearly describes a creation myth with motifs expressing the apocalypse archetype in its entirety—catastrophic destruction occurring at the center of the world (cosmic axis) followed by a sacred union or *hieros gamos* with a god figure resulting in the birth of a divine child or hero figure that leads to a new world order--what is most significant about this archetypal pattern is that it occurs in individuals living in a modern urban society with no real cosmogonic myth. We do have the Biblical tale of creation, as well as the New Testament's Book of Revelation that vividly illustrates the apocalypse archetype, but many fail to embrace these creation stories, with some preferring the modern theory of creation, based upon scientific observations of how the universe first formed—the Big Bang theory. But, the scientific theory presents a linear view of universal creation rather than a cyclical or uroboric view. The Big Bang theory cannot explain what, if anything, existed before the universe came into existence, nor what its ultimate fate will be.

The pattern experienced by Perry's patients, therefore, is a completely spontaneous reaction to a psychological apocalypse. The pattern is not only reflective of a cosmogonic myth and the archetype of the apocalypse, but the references to the establishment of a "center [where] powerful events take place" in an afterlife setting that links "the Sky world and the Underworld"

[39] Perry 1974: 9.

are all key elements of shamanism. An individual in this state is experiencing a trance-like journey to the Otherworld, and in this realm experiences the death and rebirth of the entire cosmos, which is reflective of the death of the individual's chaotic state of mind, followed by its reformulation. In other words, the pattern reflects the healing process--of moving from a state of chaos and disorientation to the establishment of a "new age" or newly restored psychological outlook. The pattern also has motifs relating to the mystery religion tradition, most notably descent into the land of the dead, confrontation with a supreme god figure, *hieros gamos*, birth of a divine child, and rebirth into a new world order. It also follows one of the most universal of all mythological motifs: the myth of the eternal return.

Mircea Eliade wrote extensively about the myth of the eternal return, at one point referring to French scholar Henri-Charles Puech:

> …both the entire cosmic process and the time of our world of generation and decay develop in a circle or according to an indefinite succession of cycles, in the course of which the same reality is made, unmade, and remade, in conformity with an immutable law and determinate alterations…. [Within] each of these *aiones* [Aions]…the same situations recur and have already occurred in the preceding cycles and will occur in subsequent cycles—and so ad infinitum….Cosmic time is repetition, and *anakuklosis*, eternal return.[40]

As Puech indicates, eternal return is cosmic time or eternal time, directly related to archetypal time. This time is ruled by enduring archetypal patterns, both macrocosmic and microcosmic. The enduring patterns must periodically be restored to their full potency; thus the necessity for periodic destruction and rejuvenation. The same patterns occur within individuals suffering from a psychotic break: after their breakdown, the psyche responds by producing within the individual images and motifs expressing the death and rebirth of the cosmos with the patient at the center of this cosmic apocalypse.

Perry ultimately recognized the relationship between the narratives of his patients and the description of the myth of the eternal return as it was presented in Eliade's book of the same name:

> …I had in those years no knowledge of the mythic background behind the imagery in "psychotic" episodes. Only after six years of this work did I learn

[40] Eliade (1949) 2005: 89.

> of the myth and ritual parallels….I was deeply grateful when I found Mircea Eliade's profound study of such motifs in his book *The Myth of the Eternal Return,* in which, at last, I could recognize the myth-and-ritual parallels to what I had been observing….[Eliade, for example] outlined the program of the New Year Festivals of the earliest urban civilizations of the [Mesopotamian] Near East for the renewal of sacral kings and their kingdoms annually. In these rites the main features…are the same as in the visions of the "psychotic" persons….[What] we are told by persons having these visions is that they return to creation in order to start over again from the very first fashioning of the world and to repeat the entire evolutionary development that followed, hand in hand with a review of one's own personal history since birth….In reviewing these practices of healing and self-healing, it has become evident that the psyche reaches for cure by reviewing and reenacting its past, its ultimate past to the beginning of its evolution.[41]

As Perry notes, the healing process involved in certain people who have suffered a schizophrenic break with reality follows a pattern similar to Eliade's description of the healing powers of reciting the cosmogonic myth: the psychic healing activity is a natural process reflective of the process of evolutionary development. When the psyche suffers a breakdown, it must return to its origins and experience a rebirthing process. The process can occur within dream scenarios with apocalyptic motifs. Bringing these scenarios into consciousness and understanding their significance can encourage the psychic healing process.

As Perry also emphasizes, it is the entire evolutionary process that is re-enacted. This idea also relates to the mystery religion tradition since what occurred during the culmination of the Eleusinian rites was the symbolic destruction of the world by the volcanic fire goddess Brimo. Out of this subterranean conflagration emerged new life which, interestingly, reflects certain theories about how life began on Earth: as the result of subterranean, or sub-oceanic volcanic eruptions. *New York Times* science writer William J. Broad explains:

> Powerful jolts [from earthquakes]…that [send] killer waves racing across the [ocean]…are inevitable side effects of the constant recycling of planetary crust, which produces a lush, habitable planet….The advantages began billions of years ago when this crustal recycling made the oceans and atmosphere and formed the continents. Today, it builds mountains, enriches soils, regulates the planet's temperature, concentrates gold and other rare minerals and maintains the sea's chemical balance….Many biologists

[41] Perry 1999: 101-102.

> believe that the process may have even given birth to life itself.... [As] volcanoes spewed vast amounts of water vapor, nitrogen, carbon dioxide and other gases...the earth's first organisms probably arose in the deep sea, along the volcanic gashes.[42]

Broad has essentially described the myth of the eternal return from a scientific perspective: the Earth cyclically destroys and renews itself with earthquakes, tsunamis, and volcanic explosions, and in this apocalyptic process new life emerges. Ancient peoples celebrated this cycle of destruction and rebirth and in doing so replicated a modern theory of the origins of life on Earth. The conclusion is that these archetypal motifs are expressions of universal patterns found in nature, in ritualistic behavior performed by humans since the beginning of our history, and in images and icons featuring big snakes.

As the San creation myth illustrates, humans are descendants from serpentine gods that fashioned the Earth at the beginning of time. This creation myth has much in common with yet another term linked with the image of the uroboric serpent, the concept of Aion, the apocalypse archetype, and the myth of the eternal return: the Aboriginal Australian tradition known as the dreaming world, or dreamtime:

> The Dreaming world was the old time of the Ancestor Beings. They emerged from the earth at the time of creation. Time began in the world the moment these supernatural beings were born out of their own Eternity....The Earth [at the time of creation] was a flat surface, in darkness. A dead, silent world. Unknown forms of life were asleep, below the surface of the land. Then, the supernatural Ancestor Beings broke through the crust of the earth from below with tumultuous force....The supernatural Beings, or Totemic Ancestors...moved across the barren surface of the world....In their journeys, they created the landscape, the mountains, the rivers, the trees, the waterholes....They made the people themselves, who are descendants of the Dreamtime ancestors. They made [all the animals]...and all the good plants....Then, wearied from all their activity, the mythical creatures sank back into the earth and returned to their state of sleep. Sometimes their spirits turned into rocks and trees or a part of the landscape. These became sacred places, to be seen only by initiated men.[43]

The Australian ancestor beings responsible for fashioning the material world and creating all living creatures had a familiar physical appearance:

---

[42] Broad: F1, 4.

[43] "Dreamtime Meaning: The Sacred World:" n.p.

> …the vast serpent sent a shockwave through the earth. Aroused from endless slumber by some mysterious and intimate signal, it flexed its whole length as it struggled towards wakefulness. Thrusting forward…it exploded upwards through what till that moment had been the blank surface of the world….Across the entire Australian continent similar serpents were on the move, gouging out deep ravines and pushing up ridges as they went. The ultimate ancestors of the Australian people, these spirits were giving form to a formless world, grinding out the landscape their descendants would inhabit to this day.[44]

It is astonishing that one of the most ancient belief systems still kept alive by an indigenous culture speaks of the material world being formed out of masses of primal material substances by god powers in the form of giant serpents in a state of consciousness likened to dreaming. Dreamtime, therefore, corresponds to the view of the Otherworld that I have been emphasizing: it is an alternate reality that parallels the unconscious state of dreaming. And, it is a reality from which waking world reality—along with ego consciousness--emerged.

As I have mentioned previously, it remains impossible at this point to understand why the psyche uses certain symbols to illustrate natural and seemingly nonrational processes, but what is most crucial to understand is the wisdom inherent in these symbolic references that rise spontaneously from the unconscious and express a reality beyond conscious means to fully understand it. The uroboros, for example, is a completely nonrational concept mirroring Jung's description of the significance of flying saucers: "There is an old saying that 'God is a circle whose center is everywhere and circumference nowhere.' God in his omniscience, omnipotence, and omnipresence is a totality symbol *par excellence,* something round, complete, and perfect…."

According to Australian mythology, and in keeping with the myth of the eternal return, the concept of Aion, and the apocalypse archetype, great cataclysms have destroyed the world in the past, followed by its recreation. One Australian account of the end of the world speaks of a great flood, as so many other cultures do. A film about the dreamtime tradition featuring a cataclysmic tsunami that threatens to drown the world is *The Last Wave* (1977). Directed by Australian filmmaker Peter Weir and featuring numerous indigenous Australian actors, *The Last Wave* is set in contemporary Sydney and deals with a corporate lawyer David Burton (Richard Chamberlain)

---

[44] Kerrigan: 24.

hired to defend five Aboriginal Australian men accused of causing the death of one of their comrades. The accused men deny their participation in the crime, leading David to believe they are hiding the truth which has to do with their practicing tribal customs and adhering to tribal laws rather than the laws of a contemporary urban society. As he becomes more involved with his clients, David begins to experience terrifying, apocalyptic dreams of the world being flooded by a giant wave. His dreams also feature two of the men accused of manslaughter: Chris (David Gulpilil), and Charlie (Nandjiwarra Amagula). During conversations with them, David's suspicions about their tribal practices are confirmed. Charlie is, in fact, a shaman, who caused the death of their companion by reciting a curse while pointing an animal bone at him, a potent example of the power of belief in totemism and sympathetic magic. Charlie killed the man after the comrade stole sacred tribal objects with the intent of either selling or destroying them. Charlie and Chris also reveal to David an ancient tradition involving David's own ancestors who practiced a type of shamanism and in doing so survived a great flood just as the indigenous Australians did tens of thousands of years ago. Because David has begun having dreams of a great flood in which Chris himself appears, Chris tells David the two of them are linked by their ancestor heritages and will suffer a similar fate if they do not take their dreams seriously.

The legal case against the accused men ends in disaster with their being convicted of manslaughter; however, Chris and Charlie escape by willing themselves back into dreamtime. Before Chris disappears, he leads David to the tribal locale which is underneath the city within Sydney's labyrinthine sewer system. David not only finds relics from Chris' tribe, but when he passes through a door carved out of a rock wall over which is painted the image of a writhing serpent, David finds ancient relics from his own ancestor past (Fig. 6-11).[45] He realizes that the serpent image refers to the totem animal of his ancestors. One of the most impressive relics he discovers is a massive wall painting of a great flood.

When he finally staggers out of the sewer system, David finds himself standing along the Australian shoreline. As he walks into the ocean to wash off the filth he accumulated from his travels through the sewer system, he looks up and gazes in horror as a monstrous wave begins to form.[46]

---

[45] Creative Commons.
[46] Weir, dir.: Ayer Productions.

What makes *The Last Wave* so memorable is director Weir's emphasis upon creating a dreamtime-like atmosphere with the effective use of slow-motion imagery especially during dream sequences, the use of traditional Aboriginal music blended with croaking and chirping sound effects from the natural world, and unrelenting images of pouring rain with drowned bodies floating throughout the urban landscape. The film also emphasizes why a great flood is threatening to drown the world. One of the main reasons is made obvious by the way in which the location of the tribe's sacred community is presented: as part of a modern city's "underworld" sewer system, a potent illustration of how this spiritual belief system has become denigrated over the millennia by the sophisticated technological achievements of modern civilization. When David crawls out of the sewer, he is covered in filth. As he approaches the coastline, he walks through a river of waste that slowly trickles out to the open sea.

Figure 6-11: David (Richard Chamberlain) discovers icons and relics from his ancestor past in *The Last Wave*, 1977. (Creative Commons)

The world is coming to an end because humanity has strayed too far from the archetypal patterns established by the ancestor spirits of dreamtime. A key phrase spoken by the character of Chris emphasizes the importance of maintaining and following archetypal patterns. He tells David: "The law is more important than is man," meaning that tribal laws based upon dreamtime traditions established at the beginning of an Aion must be followed to maintain universal harmony. Because we have failed to maintain harmony with our natural surroundings by polluting the Earth, the Earth, therefore, must be cleansed, purified, and re-established to its pristine condition as it was in the beginning. Obviously, the film's underlying message has more relevance today than ever before.

The film also puts a major emphasis upon paying attention to one's dreams. The dream realm is humanity's connection with dreamtime. When we dream, we have the potential to experience this same eternal reality which must be taken seriously. As the character of Chris wisely states at one point, "A dream is the shadow of something real." This is not merely a line from a fictional film about a sacred tradition; it is a statement of fact about this tradition.

In order to remain in harmony with the cosmos, we must maintain inner harmony. One of the most effective ways to do this is to understand dream language, the language of Yamlikha, the queen of serpents--and goddess of the central nervous system. By mastering this language, we become more aware of the inner wisdom inherent within all of us in order for our inner Aion to flow and circulate in a similar manner as the outer Aion, the former imagined as a serpent rising from the base of the spine to the center of one's forehead, the latter imagined as a giant serpent encircling the universe as a massive ocean of energy flows eternally through its body.

# CONCLUSION

# A PERSONAL JOURNEY TO THE OTHERWORLD

During an interview he gave in 1957, Jung reiterated his belief in the importance of taking fantasy thinking seriously, since fantasies have led to humanity's innovative approach to viewing and reshaping the world:

> When you observe the world, you see…tangible objects. But when you observe yourself within, you see moving images, a world of images, generally known as fantasies. Yet these fantasies are facts…. [Fantasy] is like a form of energy, despite the fact that we can't measure it. It is a manifestation of something that is a reality….So psychic events are realities, and when you observe the stream of images within, you observe an aspect of the world….Because the psyche if you understand it…is a quality of matter, just as our body consists of matter. We discover that this matter has another aspect, namely a psychic aspect….It is just as though you were seeing into another aspect of matter.[1]

Jung's comments correspond to those of philosopher Immanuel Kant, in which Kant considered the Otherworld as the waking world viewed from the perspective of spirit or soul. Humanity has imposed fantasies from the inner reality of psyche onto the material world, giving form to a new view of reality reflective of the realm of fantasy thinking and human consciousness. However, the irony is that the modern world created by the human imagination is considered by some to be a world in which artifice has overpowered the natural world, leaving the human world infused with new forms of matter void of soul.

It is interesting to compare the modern view of humanity's tangible reality with that of the indigenous Australian view. Unlike the modern view of nature with humanity's obsessive desire to control natural forces and reshape parts of the natural landscape, the native Australian attitude toward the natural world is to become part of the landscape and preserve its appearance as it was originally shaped during dreamtime. According to the

---

[1] McGuire and Hull, eds.: 302-303.

native Australians, the world was a blank, formless mass in the beginning of dreamtime, and was ultimately given shape by serpentine creation entities living within formless matter. In this regard, the serpentine ancestor spirits responsible for shaping the world are manifestations of an energy existing within matter itself. Dreamtime, thus, has parallels with Jung's comments about fantasy as a type of energy that also exists in matter. Jung would probably agree with the idea of matter having a type of proto-consciousness, and this consciousness is related to the symbol of the serpent as a living entity endowed with secret wisdom that shapes the material world according to the intimations of this wisdom.

The energetic force—Anima Mundi—is to a certain degree the creative force responsible for humanity's desire to reshape reality to the point where it has now become an artificial reflection of the natural world. Our glittering metropolises have become our celestial sphere, the dazzling city lights blunting a clear view of the star-filled sky above; skyscrapers and other buildings have become our forests and mountains; mansions overlooking green belts are our green mounds; millions of miles of paved roads have become our rivers, while the rivers and oceans of the world have become humanity's garbage dumps. And mana, which once endowed special objects within the natural world with superhuman power, now resides in manufactured pieces of paper sometimes referred to as "moola." The more moola someone has, the more empowered he or she feels, encouraging the development of a moola-personality: obsessed with possessing more moola.

To an alarming degree, humanity's imaginative ability to bring to life fantasies of great technological sophistication has served not only to estrange us from the natural world but to encourage a hostile point of view toward raw nature and our place within it. There is a social science theory called terror management, the idea that civilization is the result of humanity's fear of nature. Or, to be more precise, civilization is the result of humanity's fear of mortal death. We build fortresses and other great constructs of steel and concrete in order to boost up our egos so we feel more secure and protected from hostile forces.[2] We are like the natives of Skull Island living behind a great wall that keeps King Kong at a comfortable distance. Also, the more material goods we accumulate, the more we feel that we are endowed with that vital mana/moola life energy. We have the attitude of the protagonist from "The Voice of Death,"

[2] Weiten: 399-403.

believing that, if we surround ourselves with enough material goods, they will somehow be able to help us resist the call of death.

Obviously, there is something lacking in this world view that encourages innovation and the invention of more unique forms of material objects in preference to maintaining established norms and preserving established environmental landscapes. Although humanity's fantasy thinking has led to incredible achievements in science and technology, in many cases the objects we have created are soulless entities, reflections not of archetypal reality but of ego having usurped the role of the Self. Ego has created a world reflective of itself as a god power but one lacking an immortal aspect. Lacking a complementary relationship with the Self, the realm of soul, leads to a linear rather than a cyclical view of life: we are all headed for the earthly black pit that leads to oblivion.

Mircea Eliade commented on this modern view of death as descent into nothingness:

> Anguish before Nothingness and Death seems to be a specifically modern phenomenon. In all other, non-European [and non-Western] cultures... Death is never felt as an absolute end or as Nothingness: it is regarded rather as a rite of passage to another mode of being: and for that reason always referred to in relation to the symbolisms and rituals of initiation, re-birth and resurrection....Death is the Great Initiation. But in the modern world, Death is emptied of its religious meaning; that is why it is assimilated to Nothingness; and before Nothingness, modern man is paralyzed.[3]

Out of modern man's terror over the fear of death comes terror management theory, the obsessive desire to increase ego self-confidence and self-esteem by indulging in more shopping binges and saving up to buy a bigger house with a bigger fence—or a deeper moat--and a more advanced security system.

As a long-time member of a modern technological society in love with innovation and material goods, I am intimately aware of the appeal of such a society and how truly amazing humanity is in its ability to give birth to incredibly intricate inventions that make life so much more comfortable and endurable. The cost, however, is estrangement from nature and an inability to imagine life enduring physical death. A love for humanity's amazing accomplishments also encourages egocentrism: because of our advanced

[3] Eliade (1957) 1975: 235-236.

reasoning system, humanity must be superior to all other living creatures and therefore knows what's best for them and for the natural world.

As I mentioned while describing the early stages of development, egocentrism is common in children, a consequence of their young egos continuing to identify with the impersonal Self. I also mentioned that certain people have problems growing out of this early developmental stage. I was one of those individuals who had trouble letting go of an egocentric view of life. This was due in large part to my having a serious inferiority complex starting at a very young age and continuing through young adulthood. During these years of development, I had little to no self-confidence. Because I lacked the moola to build a physical wall around myself for protection, I built up inner barriers. I refused to speak my true beliefs for fear of ridicule; that way, I could safely hold on to whatever I thought was important while internally criticizing those with a different attitude.

In Chapter Four, I mentioned that, at a young age, I indulged in a fantasy in which I imagined a TV camera following me around filming my entire life and passing no judgment upon anything I did or said. The fantasy was appealing because it gave me the attitude that I could indulge in any type of activity or express an opinion that nobody else cared for and know that these actions and thoughts were completely accepted by my omnipotent TV companion or Watcher. The TV fantasy gradually changed so that, ultimately, I assumed the role of the TV camera, viewing life from this impersonal, all-seeing eye perspective. Anything my TV camera couldn't see or didn't know about didn't exist. Later, as I approached the late adolescent stage, I developed a variation of the fantasy in which I assumed the attitude of another type of omnipotent entity—the creator and overseer of the material world.

I was encouraged to develop this egocentric attitude by some of the books I was reading at the time, two of which were the first books I had ever read about interpreting dreams. One was *The Meaning of Dreams,* by early pioneering dream researcher Calvin Hall. It was Hall who emphasized how dreams are exclusive dramatic creations of the dreamer who populates these inner dramas with people he or she willingly chooses to appear in the dream in order to illustrate the dreamer's concerns. As Hall explained:

> It should be remembered that the dreamer is the author of his dream and that it is he and he alone who determines who shall be invited into his dream. He invites those people for whom he has mixed feelings of affection and antagonism….These people come into our dreams either because they

> represent a feature of a person with whom we are involved or because they are associated with some past conflict that is reasserting itself in our present life because they symbolize some trait within ourselves.[4]

What struck me as so intriguing about Hall's emphasis upon the dreamer being the author of his or her dreams is the implied control that the dreamer has over dream content. I had never felt in control of the content of my dreams. And yet, as Hall indicated, how could anyone else be responsible for dream content other than the dreamer? Hall's common sense explanation about dream authorship encouraged me to further embrace my inner omnipotent power fantasy: I not only controlled all of reality while awake, but also while I was asleep and dreaming.

The other dream interpretation book I read at this time provided further encouragement for holding on to my egocentric fantasy: Erich Fromm's *The Forgotten Language: An Introduction to the Understanding of Dreams, Fairy Tales, and Myths.* Even though Fromm approached dreams from an archetypal perspective—that dreams express a universal symbolic language also found in fairy tales and myths—he still insisted that the individual was responsible for dream content: "…whatever the role we play in the dream, *we* are the author, it is *our* dream, *we* have invented the plot."[5] Fromm also mentioned an aspect of dream reality that greatly appealed to my egocentric inner fantasy life:

> ...despite all [their] strange qualities, our dreams are real to us while we are dreaming; as real as any experience we have in our waking life….The dream is present, real experience, so much so, indeed that it suggests two questions: What is reality? How do we know that what we dream is unreal and what we experience in our waking life is real? A Chinese poet has expressed this aptly: "I dreamt last night that I was a butterfly, and now I don't know whether I am a man who dreamt he was a butterfly, or a butterfly who dreams now that he is a man."[6]

Fromm's comments about how the author of a dream might be actually mistaking the dream world for the waking world inspired me to invent another dimension to my omnipotent inner fantasy: what if life is a dream, and I am dreaming this dream reality? Although I was not familiar with the Australian concept of dreamtime, nor familiar with the Hindu creation myth featuring Vishnu dreaming the universe into existence, this idea of life as

---

[4] Hall: 30-31.
[5] Fromm: 4.
[6] Fromm: 5.

the dream of an omnipotent big dreamer had a strong emotional appeal to me. It helped explain why I felt that modern civilized society seemed so grandly, incomprehensibly absurd. The world at that time seemed something out of a Franz Kafka story. Kafka was another author whom I read during this time in my life, and Fromm's book included a symbolic interpretation of Kafka's *The Trial*, my favorite book of his. In that story, Kafka presented the modern world as obsessed with incomprehensible and contradictory rules and procedures that ultimately contributed to a view of humanity as inhuman cogs caught up in a life-crushing machine that no one understood its ultimate purpose or knew how to control. Kafka's world view was extremely appealing to an adolescent suffering from a major inferiority complex; I figured even I could do better in dreaming up a world less absurd than the one I currently lived in.

When I was in my early twenties, I started my first full-time job, moved out on my own for the first time into a one bedroom apartment, and began my first serious relationship with a woman, all within a year's time. Although I was proud of my accomplishments, taking on these adult responsibilities created more thoughts of being inadequate. To feel more secure and in control of my life, I clung to my omnipotent big dreamer fantasy. However, in early January 1974 when I was twenty-three years old, an event occurred that brought to an end my egocentric fantasy of the grand dreamer and ruler of the material world.

As a confirmed movie fanatic, I invited my new girlfriend one weekend afternoon to see a film playing exclusively in the Westwood area of Los Angeles. The film had opened a few weeks earlier and had already received incredible publicity for its innovative approach to producing big chills and scares in audiences. At the time, I was working as a full-time clerk in a suburban mall bookstore, and the book on which the film was based was our biggest seller: *The Exorcist.* The book's author, William Peter Blatty, had also produced and written the screenplay for the film. My girlfriend had read the book, but I refused to do so, not wanting to spoil the plot before I saw the movie.

It is hard for many people who saw *The Exorcist* years after it first premiered during the Christmas season of 1973 to fully appreciate the sensation it caused upon its initial release.[7] The film introduced new innovations in visual and sound effects, and also pushed the boundaries

[7] See Kline 2018b: 10-35.

when it came to depictions of horror, graphic sex, and profanity. My experience with the film was actually typical: about halfway through the film—right after the scene where the young, thirteen year-old girl possessed by a demon growled out "Let Jesus fuck you!" while shoving a bloodied crucifix between her legs—I became so overwhelmed with repulsion and horror that I staggered out of the auditorium where I joined about a dozen other attendees in the lobby, all of us on the verge of either passing out or throwing up. This common reaction to the film, occurring wherever it played, was to a very large degree an example of mass hysteria with many viewers later developing a fear of being possessed by the devil. In fact, so many people sought out professional help after having been traumatized by the film that a new term was coined by one of the psychiatrists treating some of the masses of new patients suffering from the film's after effects: *cinematic neurosis*.[8] Unfortunately for me, along with my obsessive thoughts of being possessed by the demon from the film, I also developed a severe case of agoraphobia. I was not only afraid to leave my apartment for fear of running into the devil, I was afraid to eat, watch TV, read a book or newspaper, or go out to see another movie, terrified that I would be infected by evil forces over which I had no control. From the time I woke up until the time I bedded down for the night, I shook with terror and struggled to keep from becoming too nauseous to make it to work; if I did make it, I fought off thoughts of contamination whenever I handled a paperback copy of the book that had inspired the abominable film.

Needless to say, the movie's graphic depiction of demonic possession destroyed my omnipotent big dreamer fantasy. I no longer felt I had any control over any aspect of my life, much less the life of the material world. I was left feeling stripped of all defenses against an evil force that I could not see but knew was there, originating in an "unseen reality" waiting to infect me, just as it had infected that innocent girl in the movie, making her indulge in the most disgusting acts I had ever seen. Would I begin to act in similar ways, performing perversions in front of others while throwing out obscene taunts and insults?

Nearly three months after seeing the film, I was still fighting off thoughts of demonic possession, barely able to leave my apartment, eating next to nothing, and sleeping fitfully through the long nights. Finally, after another exhausting day of dealing with these obsessive thoughts, I collapsed in bed and fell into a deep sleep.

---

[8] Bozzuto: 43-48.

What follows is an abbreviated account of a dream that came to me that night:[9]

> I am standing in a cavernous, barren warehouse. In front of me, carved out of the concrete floor, is a pit full of green slime. Within the pit is a filthy, naked boy screaming and grunting with glee as he wrestles with an inhuman creature. The creature has the head of a bulldog, the body of a reptile, the wings of an eagle, and the talons of a lion. The two cavort together in the slime pit until the creature clamps down on the boy's neck, preventing him from breathing. The creature then submerges the boy under the slime as if to drown him. I'm worried about the boy being killed by the creature and look around for help. I spot a woman dressed in a black jump suit sitting placidly in front of a TV as she stares blankly at the moving images. I yell out to her, "Hey lady, your son needs help." She continues to sit staring at the TV screen. I look back at the demon and the boy and realize that, although the boy is a disgusting-looking kid, more like a feral child than a civilized little boy, I feel sorry for him and want to do something to keep him from being killed by the demon.
>
> Finally, I walk over to the slime pit, take a deep breath, and jump in. I sink down until I am chest deep in the slimy substance, then wade over to where the creature is drowning the boy. When I'm close enough, I hit the creature as hard as I can on the side of the head. The demon roars and drops the boy as he turns and attacks me. We grapple in the slime pit until I am able to hit it hard again on the side of the head. This time the creature rises up out of the pit, unfurls its wings, then flies up to a skylight and crashes through, disappearing into the sky.
>
> I pull the boy out of the pit and give him mouth to mouth resuscitation until he starts coughing up green bile. As I continue to hover over the boy, I hear another crash. When I look up, I see the woman who was watching TV now standing up in front of the set which she has destroyed by having thrown her chair through the screen. She strips off her black jumpsuit and stands naked in front of me, then walks up to me, leans next to my ear, and whispers, "You are a hero."
>
> I pay no attention to her words. Instead, I stare wide-eyed at her naked body so close to mine. As I continue to stare at her, the naked boy stands up and runs off to a door leading out of the warehouse. The woman, realizing I am not paying attention to her, follows after him. I follow the woman out of the warehouse.

---

[9] For the unabridged version, see Kline 2013.

When I exit, I am nearly blinded by a white-hot sun shining down upon a decimated urban landscape. Buildings are crumbling apart leaving piles of concrete spread over the cityscape which is populated by legions of people all dressed in black jumpsuits. As the look-alike people trudge through the remains of their city, they appear oblivious to the destruction around them. Creatures like the one I wrestled with in the slime pit fly overhead, crashing into buildings and sending more debris raining down on the automaton-like citizens. A group of young men spots me and surrounds me, all of them making fun of the way I am dressed since I'm the only one not wearing one of the black jumpsuits. They attack me, then force a helmet over my head and clamp it down so I can't remove it. I begin to walk around aimlessly as I struggle to remove the helmet. There is a video screen on the helmet's visor, and it begins flashing images, all of them pornographic scenes of men and women indulging in various sex acts. I'm mesmerized by the images and forget about where I am or what I'm doing. As I watch the undulating bodies perform in front of me, I can feel myself becoming aroused and having orgasm after orgasm.

Finally, I walk into some barrier and crack the visor. The images stop and I pull off the helmet. I have no idea how much time has passed but I can feel beard stubble on my face, indicating that I have been walking around for some time. As I look around to get my bearings, I realize I am outside of the decimated city standing in an open field. In front of me is a gently sloping hill, and floating above the hill's peak is a giant, disembodied head. The head has cold, dispassionate eyes that scan the barren landscape. Its facial features resemble that of my flesh and blood father. As I stare up at the head, I think, "Where am I? How did I get here?" I then say, "This is a dream. I'm dreaming." But, then another thought comes to me: "This is a dream, but it isn't mine." I look up at the head. "It's his dream, and I'm trapped in it." I say to the head, "Let me out of your dream."

The head stares down at me for a second, looking at me with its cold eyes as if I were an insignificant bug. I feel rage build up inside me. I want to run up the hill so I can get close to the head and scream, "Let me out of your ugly dream!" I take steps up the hill, but then stop when I feel the ground underneath me shake. I take another step and the ground shakes harder. I take a step back and the ground quiets.

As I think of ways to convince the disembodied head to let me out of its dream, I hear yelling coming from the crumbling city. When I investigate, I find a riot of citizens storming a decimated drug store with the proprietor standing on a counter top as he takes money from the people in exchange for vials of a gooey-looking substance. Finally, the proprietor yells, "I'm all sold out for now," and the crowd slinks off. After the people leave, I find cracked vials on the ground with pieces of paper stuck in them. I gather up some of the pieces of paper and find they all have disparaging remarks written on them: “Life is a waste;” “Nothing makes sense;” “The end is near;” “Give up and die.”

I ask the proprietor, “What are these?” “Little notes I put into the demon dung I sell,” he says. Then he points skyward to the winged creatures still circling over the city. “I collect the dung from the creatures and put it into the vials along with my nasty comments, then sell it to these stupid people as a weight reduction product. The people are so stupid, they think eating the dung will make them lose weight, but it’s actually the notes that help do that: they make you so sick of life, you don’t feel like eating anything. There is only one person here who is smart enough to understand the weight reduction power of those nasty notes.” “Who is that?” I ask. “Some woman who walks around naked,” he says. “She comes into the store, buys the vials but then throws away the dung and keeps the notes. She’s a smart one. You can tell just by looking at her since she’s the only one who dresses properly for this type of weather.” The man studies me, then says, “You dress differently too. You must also be a smart one. Why don’t you work for me?”

I look around the store and see that it is disgustingly dirty and falling apart. As I ponder working for the man, suddenly, I hear noise coming from the back area. Out of the store’s basement strides the naked woman from the warehouse who runs through the store and disappears out the front door. I run out and spot her as she enters another large building. When I follow, I find the building is full of machinery, all belching out noxious fumes and leaking smelly substances. I try to follow the woman as she runs across a catwalk in between two pieces of machinery, but I lose my footing and fall off, landing in a pit full of goo. When I pull myself out of the pit, I find that I am out of the building and back in the open field in front of the gently sloping hill. Above me hovers the disembodied head with the dispassionate eyes and facial features of my father.

Rage boils up in me again, and I begin running up the hill determined to yell at the head and demand that it let me out of its disgusting dream. The ground shakes violently underneath me but I continue to run up the hill. The hill’s peak suddenly bursts open and begins spewing out large objects which first appear to be massive boulders but turn out to be material objects: refrigerators, washing machines, air conditioners, beds, bicycles, and other manufactured goods blast out of the hill and roll down its surface. I dodge the avalanche of objects as I continue running up the hill. When I spot a flaming station wagon fly up into the sky and barrel toward me, I jump into one of its cracked windows and find the engine is still on. Knowing the car could explode any second, I get behind the steering wheel and drive the car up the hill, dodging debris as I speed up toward the hill’s peak. Just before I reach the peak, I gun the engine one more time, then jump out the window and watch as the station wagon careens up the hill, flies into the sky and hits the disembodied head right between the eyes before it blows up in its face.

> After the car explodes, the entire hill erupts into a mass of bubbling lava. I sink into this river of liquid fire and scream in agony as I feel my skin burn off my body. Then darkness overwhelms me.
>
> Within the claustrophobic darkness, I can feel the lava begin to cool and then harden around me. I realize that I am going to be buried alive in the earth. I frantically claw my way up, scratching at the smoldering earth around me until my fingers bleed. Finally, I break through the earth's surface. I pull myself up out of the black earth and find that I am covered in a layer of crusty lava and burnt skin. I peel off the layer of burnt skin and dried lava, revealing a new layer of unblemished skin covering my entire naked body. I stand and look around, realizing the gently sloping hill is gone, along with the disembodied head and the decimated city. The earth appears flat, black, and smoldering. Even though the earth has no features, I am invigorated by its blank look.
>
> As I continue to survey my surroundings, I detect movement on the horizon. I strain to see what is moving, then smile as I realize it's the beautiful naked woman from the warehouse. As she walks toward me and I watch her movements, I realize that I am looking at the most beautiful woman I have ever seen. There is a golden hue encircling her body as she strides up to me, leans next to my ear, and whispers, "You are a hero."
>
> This time I hear her words. And I believe her. I begin weeping uncontrollably. She takes me in her arms and comforts me. I cling to her, continuing to weep as she kisses my cheeks, then my mouth. We fall to the ground and begin making love on the black earth. After we finish, we lay together and she smiles at me while glancing down at the smoldering earth. When I follow her eyes, I notice a patch of green vegetation growing underneath us where we made love. She then pulls me up from the ground and takes my hand, leading me in the direction where the decimated city once stood.

The first reaction I had after I awoke from this epic dream was to sit up in bed and say, "Wow, that was just like a movie!" I had no idea what meaning, if any, the dream might have, but what was immediately apparent to me was that the dream content was so elaborate and stunning in its imaginative details and epic scope, it was beyond anything I could have thought up on my own. Because of the dream's magnificent intricacy, I realized Erich Fromm and Calvin Hall were wrong: I was not the author of this dream. The content seemed too well composed, as if it had followed a script with an action-packed plot featuring me as a hero trapped in a decimated city run by an evil overlord, but still able to rescue a kid from a winged demon, fight off bullies along with the wicked overlord, and survive a volcanic eruption to end up winning the admiration and love of a beautiful woman.

I was so excited over the dream's fantasy-adventure storyline that I thought about writing a short story based upon it. I began composing the story not long after having the dream. Writing about the dream helped me deal with the debilitating after-effects of *The Exorcist*, although I continued to suffer from agoraphobia for nearly a year.

After writing the short story, I also eventually wrote a screenplay that incorporated some of the dream's fantastic plot developments. However, writing fictional scenarios based on the dream's content seemed to insult the overall effect the dream had on me. Because of its overwhelmingly emotional impact, I felt there must be something about it that appealed to me other than it being a hero's fantasy-adventure story similar to some of my childhood movie favorites such as *The Thief of Bagdad* (1940), *Journey to the Center of the Earth* (1959), and *The Seventh Voyage of Sinbad* (1958).

There was another film from my youth that came to mind when I thought about the dream: *Invaders from Mars* (1953). For a while, I even believed the movie had somehow influenced the dream's content even though I hadn't seen the movie for years prior to having the dream. There were several reasons why I thought the movie impacted the dream's content. First, the movie featured an army of look-alike aliens from Mars who followed the leadership of a disembodied head. While resting in a large glass jar aboard the Martian ship, the disembodied head commanded the Martian hordes, as well as captured humans, to do its evil deeds, staring at them with dispassionate eyes as it manipulated their thoughts from its glass jar vantage point. There was a significant scene involving the film's young hero character, played by Jimmy Hunt, who sneaks aboard the Martian airship and makes his way to the chamber where the Martian head sits in its jar. Jimmy enters the chamber and pounds his fists against the jar, shouting at the head to stop using its mind-control powers upon the citizens of his community, compelling people like his own mother and father to perform destructive deeds upon a local space technology headquarters. Jimmy's rage against his disembodied head expressed the rage-fueled desire I exhibited toward the disembodied head in the dream.

Second, the Jimmy Hunt character helps save the world from a Martian invasion, but immediately after a climactic scene where Jimmy and his fellow Martian-fighting comrades run for their lives as the Martian ship is destroyed, he wakes up in bed in the middle of the night. At first, he believes he dreamed up the entire invasion, but then watches from his bedroom window as a flying saucer appears and buries itself in a nearby open field just before the film ends. This ending to the film is a variation of the "only a dream" plot gimmick; however, it's given a new twist since the audience is not sure if the boy is once again dreaming about a Martian invasion or whether he just woke up from a dream that foretold the invasion. The dream-within-a-dream motif that confuses dream reality with waking reality corresponds to my dream persona's realization of being trapped in the dream of a disembodied big dreamer.

Third, after the Martians are defeated, their space ship blows up in an explosion so massive, it appears to have destroyed the world, similar to my dream's earth-shattering volcanic explosion. In both cases, the world, along with the hero figures, survives an apocalypse.[10]

As I mentioned, for a while, I felt that, somehow, my fondness for this favorite film from childhood had managed to influence the dream. I believed this because I could not see much of anything within the dream that related to my personal life. I did recognize the scene taking place in the drug store as one that was partially inspired by my working at the bookstore since both stores had basements in the back. Also, the theme of being trapped in the dream of a big dreamer entity seemed to be a comment on my own big dreamer fantasy, even mocking my presumptuous attitude of being a big dreamer myself. Of course, the most obvious reference in the dream to my waking life was the resemblance between the facial features of the disembodied head and those of my flesh and blood father.

Years after having the dream, I shared it with two different therapists on two separate occasions. Both zeroed in on the significance of the disembodied head as a reference to a major father complex from which I must be suffering. I couldn't deny that I had a hostile father complex. From a young age, I knew that my father was cold and impersonal as well as too quick to ridicule any personal beliefs I might share with him. It was because of this untrustworthy attitude I had toward my father that I began to hold all of my most private thoughts within; I feared having them ridiculed by him. Because of this habit, my internal life became more rich and satisfying than my outer life, ultimately leading to my grand big dreamer fantasy with thoughts of the world and everything in it as part of a personal dream I could

[10] Menzies, dir.: National Pictures

manipulate. The father complex is definitely illustrated in the dream; my hostile attitude toward the disembodied head and its cold, calculating eyes mirrored the emotionless relationship I had with my father. However, even though I had no idea what significance the dream might have for me, or whether it had any meaning at all, I knew without a doubt that the disembodied head who looked like my father had nothing to do with the relationship I had with my flesh and blood father. This was the only insight I had about the dream after waking up from it, and it remained the only one for decades.

It was not until I saw *The Exorcist* again after it was released in a new director's cut edition in 2000 that the true meaning of the dream began to emerge. By that time, I had become more familiar with dream interpretation, having discovered Jung and his emphasis upon archetypal elements appearing in dreams especially during times of crisis and trauma. The dream had certainly occurred during a traumatic time in my life, but I still couldn't relate any of its content to my personal life. That is, until I decided to read up on the demon featured in the film before I saw the movie again. I knew that William Peter Blatty had based his demon figure for the novel and film on a Middle Eastern wind god called Pazuzu. The demon only appeared briefly in the film, as a giant statue standing in the Iraqi desert. Because of the brevity of its appearance, I had never been certain about Pazuzu's physical features (see Fig C-1).[11] When I found a book on Middle Eastern mythology and looked up the reference to Pazuzu, I was stunned to find Pazuzu described as a god with the head of a dog, the body of a reptile or scorpion, wings like an eagle, and claws like a lion or predatory bird.[12] The description was uncannily similar to that of the demon I had fought during the dream's opening scenes. I realized for the first time that in the first few moments of my epic dream, I had battled and defeated Pazuzu, the god who had haunted me for decades.

When I first encountered Pazuzu in the movie theater, I ran away in terror. However, in the dream, I stood up to him, grappled with him, and saved the life of a child from his fury. I performed heroic feats in the dream because of him, while in my waking life, I cowered and suffered from psychic disorientation for over a year, also because of him. Obviously, the dream was a compensatory reaction to my breakdown in a movie theater. My dormant heroic inclinations—the hero archetype—were stirred to life

[11] Creative Commons.

[12] Black and Green: 147-148.

within the dream to compensate for my waking world attitude, which was the antithesis of a hero.

Figure C-1: Statue of Pazuzu as it appears in *The Exorcist*, 1973. (Creative Commons)

The hero archetype was not the only archetypal power to stir to life during the dream. There was also the anima, or to be more precise, Anima Mundi, appearing as the beautiful naked woman who also acted as a spirit bride. Her appearance is strikingly similar to the famous drawing of Anima Mundi by Renaissance philosopher Robert Fludd (Fig. 4-5), which I had not seen prior to having the dream. Also, the Self, the god image within, appeared as the floating head, "a totality symbol *par excellence,* something round, complete, and perfect." The floating head as god image explains why I refused to believe it was a symbol of the conflict I had with my real father. It was because of the extreme emotional reaction I had to the floating head that convinced me it was not a representation of my flesh-and-blood father. For me, it was as if I were facing down god who was appearing to me as an ancestor spirit from dreamtime. God appeared to me in this manner to illustrate that, if life is, in fact, a dream, I am not dreaming it. I am a part of a big dreamer's dream of reality. Within this cosmic dream, I have control over my fate if I continue to believe in my heroic inclinations.

When I saw *The Exorcist* again in 2000, I realized another dimension of the film: it had a relationship with the *Homeric Hymn to Demeter*, specifically the first part of the hymn dramatizing the rape of the Kore by Hades. As I previously mentioned, in the hymn, the Kore suffers a rape by Hades upon the Nysian Plain, indicating that the god of Nysa, Dionysus, the Greek's premier god of death and resurrection, is actually her attacker. In the film, another rape scene occurs: Regan (Linda Blair), the twelve year-old girl possessed by Pazuzu, is forced to violate herself with a crucifix while screaming out "Let Jesus fuck you." The crucifix itself is a symbol of Christ's death and resurrection. In both myth and film, therefore, a demon or devil figure (Hades and Pazuzu) associated with a god of death and resurrection (Dionysus and Christ), sexually violates a virgin.[13]

As I became more familiar with Jungian psychology, I also delved more deeply into world mythology and ancient spiritual traditions, leading me to descriptions of the mystery religion tradition far beyond the references to the *Homeric Hymn to Demeter*. As I pursued my studies, I noted more archetypal elements within the epic dream which also seemed relevant to the mystery religion tradition. The most dramatic relationship the two had were references to Aion as a cyclical time epoch, and how it seemed that participants in the secret Eleusinian rites were preparing themselves to die in one Aion in order to be resurrected into a new Aion ruled over by Dionysus. I could see how the actions performed by my dream persona near the end of the dream mirrored the culmination of the Eleusinian mystery rites: ritual death by a fiery volcanic eruption and internment in the earth, followed by resurrection out of the purified earth in the manner of a hero as an autochthonic being or ancestor spirit, born out of the earth during dreamtime at the beginning of an Aion.

In the dream, after I emerge from the blackened earth, I peel off a layer of burnt skin and dried lava, revealing a new, unblemished layer of skin covering my body, an action closely mirroring that of a serpent with the same intent: I am shedding my old sense of self-identity for a renewed image, that of a hero rather than someone suffering from agoraphobia. Not long after pulling myself out of the earth, I engage in a *hieros gamos* rite

[13] Friedkin, dir., and Blatty, screenwriter: Warner Bros.

with the beautiful naked woman or Anima Mundi. The result is rebirth of the earth itself as new vegetation springs up underneath the woman and me, similar to the intent of the *hieros gamos* rites of ancient Mesopotamia in which a king made love with a priestess representing Inanna/Ishtar, their actions promising fertility and abundance throughout the kingdom. In my case, the appearance of new life spreading over the blackened landscape symbolizes the rebirth of my wounded psyche. As the earth rejuvenates itself, so does my psyche, indicating a link between psyche and matter.

In a sense, I experienced—or more accurately, I actively participated in—a cosmogonic myth expressing the eternal return. If one looks at the list of motifs relating to the eternal return from the previous chapter compiled by John Weir Perry to chronicle the visionary experiences of his schizophrenic patients, one can see how closely these motifs match the contents of my epic dream. All except for perhaps the final motif—the fourfold structure of the recreated world—appear in my dream, albeit in a different order:

*Center*: The world center or cosmic axis of my dream is the hill in the open landscape over which the disembodied head floats.

*Cosmic Conflict*: The conflict that takes place in the world center is the one between the disembodied head and my heroic dream persona who has the desire to "gain world supremacy" over the floating head. Another conflict takes place in the slime pit between my dream persona and Pazuzu who could be interpreted as another aspect of the Self which appears as a demonic power but whose intent is always the same: transformation of consciousness to restore psychic homeostasis.

*Death*: From the appearance of the decimated landscape at the beginning of the dream, the dream's setting is the land of the dead inhabited by zombie-like automaton humans. Throughout the dream, I am continually threatened with death and ultimately experience a death and type of shamanic dismemberment when I am buried in molten lava and feel my skin burn off my body. Also, the Earth itself goes through a death and purification in the scene where the sloping hill erupts and spews out material objects before completely blowing up.

*New Birth*: After my entombment in the volcanic earth, I claw my way out to the earth's surface, peel off my burnt skin like a serpent, and experience an autochthonic rebirth.

*Apotheosis*: Soon after I emerge from the earth, the beautiful naked woman pronounces me a hero and I finally accept her title.

*Sacred Marriage*: I make love with the beautiful naked woman, the equivalent of a goddess figure—Anima Mundi. In addition, like the bugonia motif and the idea of serpents born from the backbone marrow of heroes, my dream reveals the concept of *hieros gamos* or sacred marriage to be purely archetypal in origin rather than anything consciously created as a fertility rite to ensure procreative abundance within a society. The Mesopotamian *hieros gamos* rite, therefore, is an example of sympathetic magic, which once again brings into question the origins of the multitude of examples of sympathetic magic referred to by James Frazer and others: there is a good chance that the origins of these nonrational cause-effect relationships are in many cases archetypal, expressions of Otherworld reality.

*Threat of Opposite*: The so-called threat to one's sexual identity that Perry refers to is actually the achievement of the state of androgyny: uniting with the beautiful naked woman triggers an infusion of contrasexual energies that results in an ecstatic experiential blending of inherent masculine and feminine creation powers, a type of self-contained *hieros gamos*.

*Return to Beginnings*, and *New Society*: After the *hieros gamos*, a primitive form of vegetative life springs from the volcanic earth—another example of new birth—signifying the rebirth of the Earth, as well as the birth of a new mental landscape and revitalized world view.[14]

After I recognized these archetypal motifs within the dream, I also began picking up on additional references to my personal life. For example, I mentioned previously that the drug store scene has relevance to the bookstore job I had during the time the dream occurred. In addition to this reference to my bookstore job, the strips of paper I pick up smeared with Pazuzu dung represent pages from *The Exorcist* novel which was selling in astonishing numbers during the riotous Christmas holiday season of 1973. Also, when the drug store proprietor tells me that it's not eating the Pazuzu dung that causes weight reduction but the despairing messages because "they make you so sick of life, you don't feel like eating anything," he is commenting on the despairing effects the film based on the book had on me:

[14] Kline 2013: 150-152.

I too became too sick to eat and lost nearly ten pounds during this time. (Apparently, the “Demon Dung Diet” works!)

The dream’s most profound personal references occur in the opening scenes which illustrate the psychological conflict from which I was suffering: I needed to rescue my overwhelmed ego from the influence of *The Exorcist* by confronting the demon from the film. The feral-like naked boy is a representation of the state of my psyche, overwhelmed by the demon’s influence to the point of drowning in panic and hopelessness. The beautiful woman as she appears in the early scenes—hypnotized by animated TV images--represents my soul essence: paralyzed with the fear of death after becoming obsessively fixated upon the brutal images from the film to the point of complete incapacitation. My heroic act of confronting Pazuzu and rescuing the feral boy from his influence broke the death-spell this demon had over my soul. I became the embodiment of the hero archetype which triggered the release of other archetypal powers, symbolized by the beautiful woman stripping off her black jumpsuit to reveal herself as Anima Mundi.

After wrestling with the dream for decades, gradually understanding its numerous archetypal references with relevance to shamanic beliefs, the myth of the eternal return, the concept of Aion, and the mystery religion tradition, I am convinced that the dream is an example of a personal journey to the Otherworld. The emotional factor alone convinces me of this conclusion: the dream remains the most vividly visceral experience I have ever had while in the REM dreaming state. I was completely immersed within another reality during which I felt as if I had lived in this reality for days, even weeks, when only perhaps hours had passed. Despite the dream’s inherent illogic, what I experienced felt vividly, unmistakably real. For example, in the scene where I fell into the river of lava and my skin burned off my body, I could actually feel an agonizingly intense burning sensation overwhelm me at that moment, followed by pure panic over the thought of being entombed in the smoldering earth. Also, as I mentioned previously, the dream had such a strong thematic structure, as if it had been personally scripted for me—which is a statement of fact--I can never take credit for contributing to the dream’s content. It was designed exclusively for me by the Self to effect psychic healing after my traumatic *Exorcist* experience. Even in scenes where I felt I had some control over my actions—for example, in the scene where I drive the station wagon into the face of the big dreamer entity—I am embodying the hero archetype and therefore my actions are archetypal rather than personal.

During my long investigation into the dream in which I delved for years into various mythological and spiritual traditions, I finally realized the dream was not only an example of a personal journey to the Otherworld, it was an initiation into the mystery religion tradition. Throughout this presentation, I have referred to what I believe to be major actions and experiences of the mystery rite initiates: ritual descent into the underworld; confrontation with a mighty fire symbolizing the life force of a god; *hieros gamos* with this god power; ritual death followed by resurrection from the purified earth into a new Aion. My dream contains all of these events, with an emphasis upon purification and renewal of both my dream persona and the earth through volcanic fire, underscoring the link between psyche and matter as well as the healing process that can occur when experiencing a cosmogonic myth.

Jung's comments about how "the whole symbolism of initiation rises up, clear and unmistakable, in the unconscious," corresponds to comments made by the ancients themselves who recognized the possibility of being initiated into the mystery rite tradition by dreaming the initiation process. Jane Harrison, for example, mentions a hypothetical legal case, proposed by the ancient Greek scholar Sopater, in which a man claimed to have dreamed about being initiated into the Eleusinian Mysteries. The man told his dream to someone who had gone through the initiation and asked him if it corresponded to the Eleusinian mystery rites. When the initiated man affirmed the accuracy of the dream's content with the secret rites, the following hypothetical legal question arose: had the initiated man broken the law of secrecy regarding revealing the rites to someone who had not gone through the initiation, an act punishable by imprisonment, banishment, or even death? Jane Harrison commented:

> Is the friend guilty of impiety, i.e. has he revealed the "things done" to one uninitiated? No, argues the initiated man, for the dreamer was really initiated by the [gods] themselves; only one thing was lacking to [the dreamer], he had not heard the voice of the hierophant [the chief priest of the rites] so as to understand clearly the sense of the symbols uttered by him.[15]

The primary gods of Eleusis were Demeter and Persephone; in my case the god power was the Self, appearing as an ancestor spirit in the form of a floating head resembling my father. Just as Demeter in her role of "Queen

---

[15] Harrison (1903) 1955: 570.

Bee" had done with her devoted follower Melissa, the Self in the persona of an ancestor spirit personally conducted my initiation.

Needless to say, the effect the dream had on me was monumental and long-lasting. I have never been able to forget the details due to their emotionally charged impact and overall strangeness. As I mentioned, when I first awoke from the dream, I had no idea if it held any relevance to my waking life. Even though it took me decades to understand the dream's healing intent, it did ultimately have a healing effect on me. When I realized twenty-six years later that I had fought and defeated Pazuzu during the dream's opening scenes, it was as if I had achieved a long-overdue victory over a festering evil force.

As I also mentioned, because the dream expresses a personal cosmogonic myth, I feel a sense of groundedness every time I review it. I also feel a strong affinity with the natural world, especially when I think about the scene where I make love with the beautiful naked woman, the primal soul of the material world. I cannot begin to describe what it felt like to make love with such a goddess figure, but I can say that my relationship with this spirit bride has remained vital and potent ever since. I have dreamed several times of this figure, most notably in the concluding scenes of the personal dream featured in Chapter Two which featured my wife transformed into a naked, golden-haired nymph cavorting next to a fragrant pool. At that moment, she became the most beautiful naked woman and our lovemaking beside the pool a *hieros gamos* rite with the same intent as the one from the epic dream: rejuvenation of one's inherent life energies, and affirmation of life continuing after physical death.

I have been referring to my significant dream as an epic. Jung called these types of dreams--dominated by archetypal motifs--"big dreams." He distinguished them from non-REM dreams that lack archetypal references and deal primarily with everyday concerns and situations. As he explained:

> The "big" or "meaningful" dreams…occur mostly during the critical phases of life, in early youth, puberty, at the onset of middle age…and within sight of death. Their interpretation often involves considerable difficulties, because the material which the dreamer is able to contribute [to their significance] is too meagre. For these archetypal products are no longer concerned with personal experiences but with general [i.e. impersonal] ideas…. [Big dreams] employ numerous mythological motifs that characterize the life of the hero, of that greater man who is semi-divine in nature. Here we find the dangerous adventures and ordeals such as occur in initiations. We meet dragons, helpful animals, and demons; also the Wise

> Old Man, the animal-man…the hidden treasure…all things which in no way touch the banalities of the everyday. The reason for this is that they have to do with the realization of a part of the personality which has not yet come into existence but is still in the process of becoming.[16]

My epic dream closely matches the description of Jung's big dream: "dangerous adventures and ordeals" of a hero figure with an initiatory intent transcending the "banalities of the everyday." In addition, the "process of becoming" Jung refers to is the process of individuation. Big dreams have a similar intent as dreams linked to synchronistic experiences: their intent is to help the person understand his or her path in life, or fate, and provide clues that will keep the person on this path to achieve his or her singular destiny. This is why, as Jung indicates, big dreams appear during key developmental stages: to aid in the transition from one significant stage to the next. They also appear during times of trauma to re-stabilize the wounded psyche. Using archetypal symbols infused with numinous power is the psyche's way to restore psychic homeostasis.

By now, I hope it has become obvious that my big dream was a major influence upon the content of this presentation. The chapter topics all correspond in various ways to the dream content:

*Chapter One*: The dream profoundly impacted my appreciation of the fantasy dimension of the human psyche, its autonomous ability to conjure up scenarios far beyond my conscious abilities and infuse these fantasy scenarios with insightful wisdom from the collective unconscious. It took years of investigation to understand the dream due to the overwhelming infusion of archetypal references throughout the dream scenario; in fact, the dream has so many archetypal references, it could serve as a primer to the language of the unconscious—and, therefore, the language of the Otherworld.

*Chapter Two*: The dream was a vivid illustration of how trauma and the fear of death can trigger a significant dream with the intent of healing through the use of archetypal imagery. The dream was designed to provide healing by immersing me into a dream Otherworld as a hero figure participating in a cosmogonic myth, taking me back to the beginning of creation to re-invigorate my traumatized psyche.

*Chapter Three*: The dream was driven by the animistic spirit which was clearly embodied by the beautiful naked woman. She acted as my soul guide

[16] Jung (1945) 1969: 290-293.

through the dream landscape, infecting me with her life energy which first aroused me lustfully but eventually stirred up a passionate unconditional love for her after I had gone through torturous ordeals that acted to prepare me for the achievement of full hero status and the performance of the *hieros gamos* rite. Also, as I mentioned in this chapter's discussion of horror films and how these demonic dramas have the potential to serve as modern initiatory rites for adolescents and young adults, I believe the effect *The Exorcist* had on me was a type of initiation into the stage of young adulthood, a stage I struggled to embrace by refusing to let go of my egocentric adolescent fantasy of being a big dreamer myself. Watching the film destroyed this adolescent fantasy and my adolescent stage along with it. In other words, *The Exorcist* served as the first stage of my initiation into the mystery rite tradition, with the dream serving as the culmination of the initiatory experience.

*Chapter Four*: The dream's early scenes dramatized a vivid waking world/Otherworld overlap with the viewing of *The Exorcist* as a major influence upon this section. After viewing the film, I experienced the sense that the demon from the film could possess me in a manner that mirrored the actions of the young possessed Regan character in the film; the result was terror over the thought of being manipulated by an evil force that had invaded my waking life. While the Pazuzu demon from the film created panic and dread in my conscious life, in the dream, I rescued my traumatized self—in the form of a naked feral boy—from its overpowering influence, illustrating the dream's main intent: to arouse my heroic inclinations in order to effect a dynamic change on my waking conception of myself, the antithesis of a hero.

*Chapter Five*: Time and space bent radically during the dream as I wandered in the dreamscape for what felt like days. Also the destruction and recreation of the Earth occurred during the dream, expressing billions of years of time—an Aion.

*Chapter Six*: Dreamtime was represented in the scene where I emerged out of the Earth after the volcanic eruption and found it a flat, blank surface; I then began to reinfuse the Earth with life by performing a holy union with the physical embodiment of the source of life: the beautiful naked woman. In this regard, I was a traditional hero figure or ancestor spirit born at the beginning of a new Aion in order to help revitalize and shape the Earth.

In addition, I believe the dream contained a prophetic reference to the development of a technological device that can be carried around for viewing streaming entertainments. In the dream, the device was a helmet that projected pornographic images; in our current world, such devices are called smartphones and can be used for similar purposes. Both the helmet and smartphone encourage distraction from one's physical environment, leading to an estranged attitude toward one's natural surroundings. Since the invention and rabid popularity of the smartphone, I have looked upon the devices with suspicion: could their design have been influenced by a Pazuzu-like demon as part of a sinister plot to reduce modern society to rubble while legions of us are immersed in streaming *Behind the Green Door*? Not long ago while I was teaching a class, a student pulled out his phone and began streaming porn. I thought I was reliving the "porn helmet" scene from my dream and made the mistake of emotionally overreacting in front of him and the entire class by treating him more like a hostile black-clad zombie rather than an irresponsible student. The incident underscored how the effects of the dream remain deeply embedded in my psyche as an emotionally volatile lived experience.

As my dream illustrates, despite all technological advancements and the prominent view of reality that encourages a belief in life ending in oblivion, the Otherworld remains a vibrant alternate reality that speaks of a type of life enduring death. It speaks of a realm where life itself originated and to which all life will return. Because it is a place where the endurable force of life burns for eternity, it is a realm that encourages a reverence for all life forms enlivened by this eternal power.

We are immersed in the Otherworld all of the time. The collective unconscious, inherent within all of humanity, is each individual's personal link with this other reality. Although it might take a big dream or a numinous encounter on a deserted road with a black dog, glowing white rabbit, or a hitchhiking girl dressed in a white prom dress to experience a complete immersion within the Otherworld, the potential is there: you don't have to be a shaman to make a journey to the Otherworld. Having a piece of the Otherworld within also means there is a responsibility to understand the language of this realm, the language of archetypes. However, even if one becomes familiar with this unique symbolic language, it might remain difficult to speak of an Otherworld experience with someone who has not had a similar type of experience because they are singular experiences meant to benefit the individual. They are reminders of our connection with something beyond explanation, something so alien to regular waking life that it calls into question all rational means to validate it, which seems to be the point of such experiences.

To paraphrase—and quote—Ellie Arroway from *Contact*:

I had an experience of the Otherworld. One that changed me forever and helped to more fully define who I am while giving me a glimpse of the origins of existence. I can't prove it happened because it occurred to me in a dream. But, by exploring dimensions of what I went through and comparing them to other similar accounts, I have attempted to illustrate the universality and profound importance of such experiences despite their resistance to being confirmed as legitimate. Because everything that that I know as a human being, everything that I am, tells me: the Otherworld is real.

Figure C-2: A glimpse of the Otherworld.[17] (Creative Commons)

[17] Creative Commons.

# BIBLIOGRAPHY


Adams, Russel B., series ed. *Hauntings*. Mysteries of the Unknown. Alexandria, VA: Time-Life Books, 1989.

Anuradha. "Vishnu Sustains the Universe," *All About Hinduism,* March 8, 2013, http://www.allabouthinduism.info/2013/03/08/vishnu-the-protector/.

Ascher, Rodney, dir. *The Nightmare*. United States: Zipper Bros. Films, 2015.

Baxter, John. *Baxter's Concise Encyclopedia of Modern Sex*. New York, NY: HarperCollins, 2009.

Black, Jeremy, and Anthony Green. "Pazuzu," in *Gods, Demons, and Symbols of Ancient Mesopotamia*, 147-148. Austin, TX: University of Texas Press, 2000.

Borroff, Marie, trans. *Sir Gawain and the Green Knight: A New Verse Translation.* New York, NY: W.W. Norton, 1967.

Bozzuto, James, C. "Cinematic Neurosis Following 'The Exorcist,'" *Journal of Nervous and Mental Disease* 161, no. 1 (1975), 43-48, http://dx.doi.org/10.1097/0000507000-00005.

Briggs, Katharine M., ed. *Folktales of Britain: Legends, Vol. 1.* London: United Kingdom: Folio Society, (1971) 2011.

Broad, William J. "Deadly Yet Necessary, Quakes Renew the Planet," *New York Times*, January 11, 2005, F1,4.

Brownlow, David, and David Gill, dirs. *The Pioneers*. Hollywood: A Celebration of American Silent Film. London, United Kingdom: Thames Television, 1980.

Brunvand, Jan Harold. *The Vanishing Hitchhiker: American Urban Legends and their Meanings*. New York, NY: W.W. Norton, 1981.

Cameron, James, dir. and co-screenwriter. *Terminator 2: Judgment Day.* United States: Carolco/TriStar, 1991.

Cameron, James, dir. and screenwriter. *Avatar*. Los Angeles, CA: Twentieth Century Fox, 2009.

Campbell, Joseph. *The Flight of the Wild Gander.* Novato, CA: New World Library, (1951) 2002.

Campbell, Joseph, ed. "The Queen of the Serpents," in *The Portable Arabian Nights,* 406-422. New York, NY: Viking (1952) 1962.

Chivers, C.J. "The Doomsday Scam," *New York Times Magazine*, November 19, 2015, n.p., https://www.nytimes.com/2015/11/22/magazine/the-doomsday-scam.html.

Chowdhury, Debajyoti. "Why is a Snake Used to Represent the Kundalini?" *Quora*, January 19, 2018, https:// www.quora.com/Why-is-a-snake-used-to-represent-the-Kundalini.

Cole, Joanna, ed. *Best-Loved Folktales of the World*. New York, NY: Anchor Books, 1983.

Cole, Susan Guettel. *Theoi Megaloi: The Cult of the Great Gods at Samothrace.* Leiden, The Netherlands: E.J. Brill, 1984.

Coville, Charles, dir. *What Are Dreams?* United States: PBS/Nova, 2009.

Dalton, Briony. "The Shamanic View of Christmas." *Uplift.com*, December 24, 2016, https://upliftconnect.com/the-shamanic-view-of-christmas/.

Davanger, Svend. "The Brain's Default Mode Network—What Does It Mean To Us?" *The Meditation Blog,* March 9, 2015, http://www.themeditationblog.com'the-brains-default-mode-network-what-does-it-mean-to-us/.

Davies, Owen. "The Nightmare Experience, Sleep Paralysis, and Witchcraft Accusations," *Folklore* 114, no. 2 (2003), 181-203.

Debelius, Maggie. *The Spirit World*. The American Indian. Alexandria, VA: Time-Life Books, 1992.

De Guzman, Andrew O. "The Nightmare Continues," *Marianas Variety,* June 6, 2011, http://www.mvariety.com/ cnmi/cnmi-news/local/37463-the-nightmare-continues.php.

Delano, Marfe Ferguson, and Margery A. duMond. *Dreams and Dreaming.* Mysteries of the Unknown. Alexandria, VA: Time-Life Books, 1990.

Derisz, Ricky. "Donnie Darko's Ending Explained," *Looper.com*, https://www.looper.com/117919/donnie-darkos-ending-explained/.

Dixit, Jay. "Dreams: Night School," *Psychology Today*, November 1, 2007, https://www.psychologytoday.com/us/articles/200711/dreams-night-school.

Douglas, Mary, ed. *The Illustrated Golden Bough*. New York, NY: Doubleday, 1978.

"Dreamtime Meaning: The Sacred World," *Aboriginal Art and Culture,* http://www.aboriginalart.com.au/culture/ dreamtime2.html.

Edel, Uli, dir. *Pay the Ghost*. United States: Voltage Productions, 2015.

Edinger, Edward F. *The Aion Lectures: Exploring the Self in C.G. Jung's* Aion. Toronto, Canada: Inner City Books, 1996.

Ehrenreich, Barbara. *Living with a Wild God: A Nonbeliever's Search for the Truth About Everything*. New York, NY: Hachette Book Group, 2014.

Eliade, Mircea. *The Myth of the Eternal Return.* Princeton, NJ: Princeton University Press (1949) 2005.

Eliade, Mircea. *Shamanism: Archaic Techniques of Ecstasy.* Princeton, NJ: Princeton University Press, (1951) 2004.

Eliade, Mircea. *Myths, Dreams, and Mysteries.* New York, NY: Harper Torchbooks, (1957) 1975.

Eliade, Mircea. *Rites and Symbols of Initiation*. Putnam, CT: Spring Publications, (1958) 2005.

Evans, Hilary. *From Other Worlds: Aliens, Abductions, and UFOs.* London, United Kingdom: Carlton Books, 1998.

Fell, Sam, and Chris Butler, dirs. *ParaNorman*. Hillsboro, OR: Laika, 2012.

Fisher, Martini. "Gods, Goddesses, and…Rabbits? The Surprising Ancient Myths of the Moon," *Ancient Origins*, March 1, 2014, https://www.ancient-origins.net/myths-legends/gods-goddesses-and-rabbits-surprising-ancient-myths-moon-007635.

Foley, Helene P., ed. *The Homeric Hymn to Demeter*. Princeton, NJ: Princeton University Press, 1994.

Frazer, James G. *The Golden Bough: The Roots of Religion and Folklore* (Unabridged First Edition Two Volumes in One). New York, NY: Avenel, (1890) 1981.

Frazer, James G. *The Golden Bough: A Study in Magic and Religion*, Robert Fraser, ed. London, United Kingdom: Folio Society, (1890) 2018.

Freud, Sigmund. *Beyond the Pleasure Principle*. New York, NY: W.W. Norton (1920) 1989.

Friedkin, William, dir., and William Peter Blatty, screenwriter. *The Exorcist.* Burbank, CA: Warner Bros., 1973.

Fromm, Erich. *The Forgotten Language: An Introduction to the Understanding of Dreams, Fairytales, and Myths.* New York, NY: Grove Press, (1951) 1957.

Gaddis, Jason, and Stephanie Marohn. "The Shamanic View of Mental Illness," *JaysonGaddis* (blog), November 19, 2010, https://jaysongaddis.com/the-shamanic-view-of-mental-illness/.

Gardner, John, and John Maier, eds. and trans. *Gilgamesh: Translated from the Sin-leqi-unninni Version.* New York, NY: Vintage/Random House, 1985.

Gazzaniga, Michael, Todd Heatherton, and Diane Halpern. *Psychological Science*, 5th ed. New York, NY: W.W. Norton, 2015.

George, Andrew. *The Epic of Gilgamesh: A New Translation*. New York, NY: Penguin Books, 2000.

Gilliam, Terry, dir. *12 Monkeys*. Universal City, CA: Universal Pictures, 1995.

Godwin, Joscelyn. *Mystery Religions in the Ancient World*. New York, NY: Harper & Row, 1981.

Greenhouse, Herbert. "Premonitions: A Leap Into the Future," *All About Heaven*, 1971, https://allaboutheaven.org/ observations/air-marshal-sir-victor-goddard-the-night-my-number-came-up-024904/221.

Griffith, D.W., dir. *Intolerance*. United States: Triangle Films, 1916.

Haley, E.N. "A Visit to the Spirit Land; Or, The Strange Experience of a Woman from Kona, Hawaii, in *Hawaiian Folk Tales*, Thomas G. Thrum, ed., 58-62. Chicago, IL: A.C. McClurg & Co., 1907, http://www.sacred-texts.com/neu/celt/ tsm/tsm12.htm.

Halifax, Joan. *Shaman: The Wounded Healer*. New York, NY: Thames and Hudson, (1982) 1988.

Hall, Calvin S. *The Meaning of Dreams*. New York, NY: McGraw-Hill, (1953) 1966.

Harding, M. Esther. *Woman's Mysteries: Ancient and Modern*. New York, NY: Harper, (1971) 1976.

Harrison, Jane Ellen. *Prolegomena to the Study of Greek Religion*. New York, NY: Meridian Books, (1903) 1955.

Harrison, Jane Ellen. *Themis: A Study of the Social Origins of Greek Religion*. Cleveland, OH: Meridian Books, (1912) 1962.

Harrison, Jane Ellen. *Epilegomena: A Brief Summary of the Origins of Greek Religion*. Edmonds, WA: Alexandrian Press, (1921) 2001.

Hillman, James. *Pan and the Nightmare*. Woodstock, CT: Spring Publications (1972) 2000.

Hillman, James. *The Dream and the Underworld*. New York, NY: Harper & Row, 1979.

Hillman, James, and Michael Ventura. *We've Had a Hundred Years of Psychotherapy and the World's Getting Worse*. New York, NY: Harper Collins, 1993.

Hobson, J. Allan. *13 Dreams that Freud Never Had*. New York, NY: Pi Press, 2005.

Hobson, J. Allan, E.F. Pace-Schott, and Robert Stickgold. "Dreaming and the Brain: Toward a Cognitive Neuroscience of Conscious States. *Behavioral and Brain Science* 23 (2000), 793-842.

Hooper, Tobe, dir. *The Texas Chainsaw Massacre*. United States: Vortex/Bryanston Distributing Co., 1974.

Irving, Washington. *Rip Van Winkle*. United States: Elegant EBooks, https://www.ibiblio.org/ebooks/Irving/Winkle/Irving_Winkle.pdf., (1819).

Jaffe, Aniela. *An Archetypal Approach to Death, Dreams, and Ghosts.* Schweiz, Germany: Daimon Publishers (1958) 1995.

James, William. *The Varieties of Religious Experience*. New York, NY: Penguin Books, (1902) 1982.

Johnson, Steven. "The Human Brain is a Time Traveler," *New York Times Magazine*, November 15, 2018, n.p., https://www.nytimes.com/interactive/2018/11/15/magazine/tech-design-ai-prediction.html.

Jung, C.G. *Psychology of the Unconscious: A Study of the Transformations and Symbolisms of the Libido.* Princeton, NJ: Princeton University Press, (1912) 2001.

Jung, C.G. "The Psychological Foundations of Belief in Spirits," in *The Structure and Dynamics of the Psyche*, 2nd ed., *Collected Works, Volume 8,* 301-318. Princeton, NJ: Princeton University Press, (1920) 1969.

Jung, C.G. "The Relations Between the Ego and the Unconscious," in *Two Essays on Analytical Psychology*, *Collected Works, Volume 7,* 123-241. Princeton, NJ: Princeton University Press, (1928) 1972.

Jung, C.G. "Basic Postulates of Analytical Psychology," in *The Structure and Dynamics of the Psyche,* 2nd ed., *Collected Works, Volume 8*, 338-357. Princeton, NJ: Princeton University Press, (1931) 1969.

Jung, C.G. "Concerning Archetypes and the Anima Concept," in *The Archetypes and the Collective Unconscious,* 2nd ed., *Collected Works, Volume 9, Part 1*, 54-72. Princeton, NJ: Princeton University Press, (1936), 1980.

Jung, C.G. "On the Nature of Dreams," in *The Structure and Dynamics of the Psyche,* 2nd ed., *Collected Works, Vol. 8*, 281-297. Princeton, NJ: Princeton University Press (1945) 1969.

Jung, C.G. "On the Nature of the Psyche," in *The Structure and Dynamics of the Psyche*, 2nd ed., *Collected Works, Vol. 8,* 159-234. Princeton, NJ: Princeton University Press, (1946) 1969.

Jung, C.G. "General Aspects of Dream Psychology," in *The Structure and Dynamics of the Psyche,* 2nd ed., *Collected Works, Volume 8,* 237-280. Princeton, NJ: Princeton University Press, (1948) 1969.

Jung, C.G. *Symbols of Transformation*, 2nd ed., *Collected Works, Volume 5*. Princeton, NJ: Princeton University Press, (1952) 1967.

Jung, C.G. "Synchronicity: An Acausal Connecting Principle," in *The Structure and Dynamics of the Psyche,* 2nd ed., *Collected Works, Volume 8,* 417-531. Princeton, NJ: Princeton University Press, (1951, 1952) 1969.

Jung, C.G. "Flying Saucers: A Modern Myth of Things Seen," in *Civilization in Transition*, 2nd ed., *Collected Works, Volume 10,* 307-433. Princeton, NJ: Princeton University Press, (1958) 1970.

Jung, C.G. *Man and His Symbols*. New York, NY: Doubleday, 1964.

Keaton, Buster, dir. *Sherlock, Jr*. United States: Metro Pictures, 1924.

Kelly, Richard, dir. *Donnie Darko*. United States: Flower Films, 2001.

Kerenyi, Carl. *The Gods of the Greeks*. New York, NY: Thames and Hudson, (1951) 1995.

Kerenyi, Carl. *The Heroes of the Greeks*. New York, NY: Thames and Hudson, (1959) 1997.

Kerenyi, Carl. *Eleusis: Archetypal Image of Mother and Daughter.* Princeton, NJ: Princeton University Press, (1960) 1991.

Kerenyi, Carl. *Dionysos: Archetypal Image of Indestructible Life.* Princeton, NJ: Princeton University Press, (1976) 1996.

Kerrigan, Michael. "A Timeless Land," in *Journeys Through Dreamtime: Oceanian Myth,* Myth and Mankind, Tony Allan, ed., 24-25. Amsterdam, The Netherlands: Time-Life Books.

Kline, Jim. *The Complete Films of Buster Keaton*. New York, NY: Citadel Press, 1993.

Kline, Jim. "My Father's Nightmare: A Psychological Commentary on a Big Dream." PhD diss., Saybrook University, San Francisco, CA. ProQuest Dissertations Publishing, 2013.

Kline, Jim. "The Oldest Story, The Oldest Fear, The Oldest Fool: The Religious Dimension of the Epic of Gilgamesh," *Jung Journal* 10, no. 2 (2016), 24-36, http://dx.doi.org/10/1080/ 19342039.2016.1157411.

Kline, Jim. "Beelieve: How a Dream About Bees Reveals the Origins of the Religious Experience," *Psychological Perspectives* 61, no. 2 (2018a), 194-205, https://doig.org/ 10.1080/00332925.2018.1461502.

Kline, Jim. "Fleeing From and Fighting With *The Exorcist*," *Jung Journal* 12, no. 2 (2018b), 10-25, https://doig.org 10.1080/19342039.2018.1442103.

Koltuv, Barbara Black. *The Book of Lilith*. York Beach, ME: Nicolas-Hays, 1986.

Kovacs, Maureen Gallery, ed. and trans. *The Epic of Gilgamesh.* Stanford, CA: Stanford University Press, 1989.

Kramer, Samuel Noah. "Sumerian History, Culture, and Literature," in *Inanna: Queen of Heaven and Earth*," Diane Wolkstein and Samuel Noah Kramer, eds. and trans. New York, NY: Harper and Row, 1983.

Lang, Andrew, ed. "The Voice of Death," in *The Red Fairy Book,* 182-185. New York, NY: Dover, (1890) 1966.

Lang, Andrew, ed. "In the Land of Souls," in *The Yellow Fairy Book,* 152-154. New York, NY: Dover, (1894) 1966.

Lang, Andrew, ed. "The Language of Beasts," in *The Crimson Fairy Book,* 55-61. New York, NY: Dover, (1903) 1967.

Lang, Andrew, ed. "The King Who Would See Paradise," in *The Orange Fairy Book,* 24-28. New York, NY: Dover, (1906) 1968.

Lester, Richard, dir. *Petulia.* Burbank, CA: Warner Bros., 1968.

Lewis-Williams, David. *The Mind in the Cave*. London, United Kingdom: Thames and Hudson, 2002.

Lyne, Adrian, dir., and Bruce Joel Rubin, screenwriter. *Jacob's Ladder.* United States: Carolco/Tristar Pictures, 1990.

Lyons, Malcolm C., and Ursula Lyons, trans. "Hasib Karim al-Din and the Snake Queen," in *The Arabian Nights: Tales of 1001 Nights,* 363-453. New York, NY: Penguin Classics, 2010.

MacDonald, L. "Celtic Folklore: The People of the Mounds," *Mark Jacob's Evolution Philosophy,* 1993, https://jacobsm.com/deoxy/deoxy.org/h_mounds.htm.

McGuire, William, and R.F.C. Hull, eds. C.G. *Jung Speaking: Interviews and Encounters.* Princeton, NJ: Princeton University Press, 1977.

Mackenzie, Donald Alexander, ed. "A Vision of the Dead," in *Wonder Tales from Scottish Myth and Legend*, 122-125. New York, NY: Frederick A. Stokes, Co, 1917, http://www.sacred-texts.com/neu/celt/tsm/tsm12.htm.

Menzies, William Cameron, dir. *Invaders from Mars*. United States: National Pictures, 1953.

Milne, A.A. *Winnie-the-Pooh*. New York, NY: E.P. Dutton, (1926) 1954.

Monaghan, Padraic. "What Is Going On in Your Brain When You Sleep?" *The Conversation*, April 8, 2015, http://theconversation.com/what-is-going-on-in-your-brain-when-you-sleep-39723.

Moran, William L. "Introduction," in *Gilgamesh: A New Rendering in English Verse*, David Ferry, trans., ix-xi. New York, NY: Farrar, Straus, and Giroux, 1992.

Nelson, Kevin. *The Spiritual Doorway in the Brain*. New York, NY: Plume/Penguin, 2012.

Neumann, Erich. *The Origins and History of Consciousness.* Princeton, NJ: Princeton University Press, (1949) 1970.

Nichols, Jeff, dir. and screenwriter. *Midnight Special*. United States: Faliro House Productions, 2016.

Nolan, Christopher, dir. and screenwriter. *Memento.* United States: Summit Entertainment, 2000.

Nolan, Christopher, dir. and co-screenwriter. *Interstellar*. United States: Legendary Pictures. 2014.

Norman, Leslie, dir. *The Night My Number Came Up*. London, United Kingdom: Ealing Studios, 1955.

Osten-Sacken, Carl Robert. *On the Oxen-Born Bees of the Ancients (Bugonia) and Their Relationship to Eristalis Tenax, a Two-Winged Insect.* Heidelberg, Germany: Hoerning Publishers, 1894.

Otto, Rudolf. *The Idea of the Holy*. New York, NY: Oxford University Press, (1923) 1958.

Overbye, Dennis. "Interstellar: The Cinema of Physicists," *New York Times,* November 17, 2014, n.p., https://www.nytimes.com/2014/11/18/science/interstellar-the-cinema-of-physicists.html.

Payne, John, trans. "The Queen of the Serpents," in *The Book of the Thousand Nights and One Night, Volume 2,* 1054-1114. Ann Arbor, MI: Borders Classics, (1882) 2007.

Perry, John Weir. *The Far Side of Madness*. Englewood Cliffs, NJ: Prentice-Hall, 1974.

Perry, John Weir. *Trials of the Visionary Mind.* New York, NY: State University of New York Press, 1999.

Petrie, Daniel, dir. *Resurrection.* Universal City, CA: Universal Pictures, 1980.

Piaget, Jean. *The Child's Conception of the World*. London, United Kingdom: Redwood Press, (1929) 1971.

Powell, Corey S. "Is the Universe Conscious?" *NBC News*, June 6, 2017, https://www.nbcnews.com/mach/science/universe-conscious-ncna772956.

Rago, Rozette. "They've Seen Things," *New York Times*, August 14, 2018, n.p., https://www.nytimes.com/2018/08/14 us/theyve-seen-things.html.

Ransome, Hilda M. *The Sacred Bee: In Ancient Times and Folklore.* New York: Dover, (1937) 2004.

Routledge, Clay. "Don't Believe in God? Maybe You'll Try UFOs," *New York Times*, July 23, 2017, https://www.nytimes.com/2017/07/21/opinion/sunday/dont-believe-in-god-maybe-youll-try-ufos.html.

Safire, William. "Behind the Green Door," *New York Times Magazine,* August 1, 2004, https://www.nytimes.com/2004/08/01/magazine/the-way-we-live-8-1-04-on-language-behind-the-green-door.html.

Sandars, N.K., ed. and trans. *The Epic of Gilgamesh: An English Version with an Introduction.* New York, NY: Penguin, (1960) 1972.

Santrock, John W. *Human Adjustment*. New York, NY: McGraw-Hill, 2005.

Shamdasani, Sonu. *Jung and the Making of Modern Psychology*. New York, NY: Cambridge University Press, 2003.

Shubin, Neil. "January is the Cruelest Month," *New York Times*, January 25, 2013, SR8.

Shyamalan, M. Night, dir. and screenwriter. *The Sixth Sense*. Burbank, CA: Hollywood Pictures, 1999.

Smith, Jonathan Z. "When the Bough Breaks," *History of Religion* 12, no. 4 (May 1973), 342-371, http://www.jstor.org/stable/ 1062126.

Tatar, Maria, ed. *The Classic Fairy Tales*. New York, NY: W.W. Norton, 1999.

Unnikrishnan, Kesavan. "Malaysian Minister Blames Naked Tourists for Earthquake," *Digital Journal*, June 7, 2015, http://www.digitaljournal.com/news/world/malaysian-minister-blames-naked-foreign-tourists-for-earthquake/article/435153.

Vallee, Jacques. *Passport to Magonia: On UFOs, Folklore, and Parallel Worlds*. Chicago, IL: Contemporary Books, (1969) 1993.

Vasavong, Aphonetip. "You Can Count on Miracles," in *Successful College Writing*, 5th ed., Kathleen T. McWhorter, ed., 221-222. Boston, MA: Bedford/St. Martins Press 2010.

Vogel, J. P. *Indian Serpent-Lore: The Nagas in Hindu Legend and Art.* London, United Kingdom: Arthur Probsthain, 1926, https://ia801603.us.archive.org/23/items/in.ernet.dli.2015.107348/2015.107348.Indian-Serpent-Lore-Or-The-Nagas-In-Hindu-Legend-And-Art.pdf.

Vogt, Yngve. "World's Oldest Ritual Discovered: Worshipped the Python 70,000 Years Ago," *Apollon*, University of Oslo, 2008, https://apollon.uio.no/english/articles/2006/python- english.html.

Von Franz, Marie-Louise. *The Interpretation of Fairy Tales.* Boston, MA: Shambhala, (1970) 1996.

Von Franz, Marie-Louise. *Shadow and Evil in Fairy Tales.* Boston, MA: Shambhala, (1974) 1995.

Von Franz, Marie-Louise. *Time: Rhythm and Repose*. New York, NY: Thames and Hudson, 1978.

Walker, Barbara. "Brimstone," in *The Woman's Encyclopedia of Myths and Secrets*, 118. New York, NY: Harper & Row, 1983.

Wasson, R. Gordon, Carl A.P. Ruck, and Albert Hoffmann. *The Road to Eleusis: Unveiling the Secret of the Mysteries*. New York: Harcourt, Brace, Jovanovich, 1978.

Weir, Peter, dir. *The Last Wave*. Sydney, Australia: Ayer Productions, 1977.

Weiten, Wayne. *Psychology: Themes and Variations*, 8th ed. Belmont, CA: Wadsworth, 2008.

Wells, H.G. *The Door in the Wall and Other Stories*. University Park, PA: Penn State Electronic Classics (1911) 2004, http://worldlibrary.net/eBooks/WPLBN0000662412-The-Door-in-the-Wall-and-Other-Stories-by-Wells-H-G-.aspx?

Weston, Jesse. *From Ritual to Romance*. New York, NY: Dover, (1920) 1997.

Wilkins-Freeman, Mary E. *The Green Door*. New York, NY: Moffat, Yard, & Co., (1910) 1917.

Yolen, Jane, ed. *Favorite Folktales from Around the World.* New York, NY: Pantheon, 1986.

Zemeckis, Robert. *Back to the Future*. Universal City, CA: Universal Studios, 1985.

Zemeckis, Robert, dir. *Contact.* Burbank, CA: Warner Bros. Pictures, 1997.

# Index